M000188455

BROWN BOOKSTORE

K$15.25

The European Security Order Recast

To Pierre Hassner,
who thought deeply about all of this
before it was fashionable

The European Security Order Recast
Scenarios for the Post-Cold War Era

Barry Buzan
Morten Kelstrup
Pierre Lemaitre
Elzbieta Tromer
Ole Wæver

Pinter Publishers
London and New York

© The Centre for Peace and Conflict Research, University of
Copenhagen 1990

First published in Great Britain in 1990 by
Pinter Publishers, 25 Floral Street, London WC2E 9DS
Reprinted 1991

All rights reserved. No part of this publication may be
reproduced, stored in a retrieval system, or transmitted by any
other means without the prior permission of the copyright holder.
Please direct all enquiries to the publishers.

British Library Cataloguing in Publication Data
A CIP catalogue record for this book is available from the
British Library
ISBN 0 86187 142 1 hardback
ISBN 0 86187 143 X paperback

For enquiries in North America please contact PO Box 197,
Irvington, NY 10533

**A CIP Catalog Record for this book is available
from the Library of Congress**

Printed by SRP Ltd, Exeter

Contents

List of Abbreviations

BRD	Bundesrepublik Deutschland (West Germany)
CMEA	Council for Mutual Economic Assistance
CDU	Christian Democratic Union
CFE	Conventional Forces in Europe (Vienna negotiations on)
COCOM	Western Coordinating Committee on Trade with Communist Nations
CSCE	Conference on Security and Cooperation in Europe
CSU	Christian Social Union (Germany)
DDR	Deutsche Demokratische Republik (East Germany)
EC	European Community
EDC	European Defence Community
EEC	European Economic Community
EFTA	European Free Trade Association
EMS	European Monetary System
EPC	European Political Cooperation
EURATOM	European Atomic Energy Community
FDP	Free Democratic Party (Germany)
FRG	Federal Republic of Germany (West Germany)
GATT	General Agreement on Tariffs and Trade
GDR	German Democratic Republic (East Germany)
GNP	Gross National Product
INF	Intermediate-range Nuclear Forces
MLF	Multilateral Force
NATO	North Atlantic Treaty Organization
OECD	Organization for Economic Cooperation and Development
PDS	Party of Democratic Socialism (East Germany)
PS	Parti Socialiste, Socialist Party (France)
RPR	Rassemblement pour la République, Gaullist Party (France)
SBZ	Soviet Occupied Zone (East Germany)

SNF	Short-range Nuclear Forces
SPD	Social Democratic Party (Germany)
START	Strategic Arms Reduction Talks
UN	United Nations
WEU	Western European Union

Foreword

This book is aimed at the audience of 'informed public opinion': all those who are hooked on the lively debate in the press, aware that the events unfolding at the moment are of historic importance, excited by the fact of living in such times and curious to deepen their understanding of what is going on. It was conceived in 1988 as a project by the group on non-military aspects of European security at the Centre for Peace and Conflict Research, Copenhagen. The idea was to take a long look at the security consequences for Europe of the winding down of the Cold War that was even then becoming apparent. Like many other research projects, this one was caught up in the rapid changes of 1989. The events in Eastern Europe and the consequent process of German unification faced us with the choice of waiting until the dust had settled or plunging ahead and trying to make sense of the process while it was still in full flood. We opted for the latter course partly out of the sheer excitement of doing so, but mostly because we felt that the analytical method we had developed still gave us a firm perspective from which to view the tide of events.

We have tried to combine historical and structural analysis to set the current events into a long-term frame of reference and to provide a systematic set of speculations based on a small number of quite simple variables. The book is academic in the sense that it draws upon a number of theoretical ideas current in the field of International Relations. But we have tried to keep jargon to a minimum and to provide clear summaries of the key ideas and the relevant history.

We would like to thank Frances Pinter for sharing our enthusiasm for this project, for taking the risk of publishing it under highly uncertain conditions and for arranging an unusually rapid process of publication. We would also like to thank the Centre for Peace and Conflict Research in Copenhagen and particularly its director Håkan Wiberg. The Centre sponsored this project, gave it logistical support, published some early drafts as Working Papers and generally provided a congenial and stimulating environment in which the work could proceed. Svend Aage Christensen at the Danish Commission for Security and Disarmament gave us crucial help in transferring files from one format to another. Without his help this whole collaboration would have been vastly more difficult.

The book is a consensus document that is genuinely co-authored by the five of us. In order to make the best use of our varied expertise, the division of labour was as follows: Barry Buzan took primary drafting responsibility for Chapters 1-4, 8 and 9, and parts of 10 and 11; Morten Kelstrup for half of Chapters 6 and 7; Pierre Lemaitre for half of Chapters 5 (5.1 and 5.2) and 10; Elzbieta Tromer for the first draft of Chapter 11 and half of Chapter 5 (5.3 and 5.4); and Ole Wæver for half of Chapters 6, 7 and 10, and parts of 4 and 11. Each of these drafts underwent several rounds of criticism and comment, and everyone had an opportunity to make 'hands on' revisions to the drafts of others. Barry Buzan was responsible for the final harmonization of style. The discussions were an enjoyable learning experience, and a sufficient degree of consensus emerged naturally from them as to make it inappropriate for any one of us to either claim or reject any particular part of the book.

In one sense this book represents a theoretical position: it can be seen as an attempt to use major elements of Neorealist theory. Not all of us are advocates of this theory, and we have different opinions on the need for modifications to it. But we all agree on its importance in the analysis of international relations. Thus the book should not be taken as a collective statement in support of Neorealism. Rather, it reflects a collective agreement to treat this theory as a useful organizing device for this particular project.

BB, MK, PL, ET, and OW
Copenhagen
May 1990

Chapter 1
Introduction

It is no longer controversial to assert that the Cold War is over. Major changes are under way in the whole political and security arrangement of Europe, both East and West. As a result, the familiar rigidities of a strict division that have dominated the continent since the end of the Second World War are dissolving before our eyes, with massive implications for security across a broad spectrum of issues. The post-war era is ending, and the outlines of a new international order are emerging. Changes on this scale have traditionally been accompanied by wars among the great powers. The transformation now unfolding is remarkable, indeed unique, in that it does not result from and shows no sign of triggering such wars. On the contrary, the process of transformation itself is causing a massive drop in military tension.

These changes result from the complex interplay of two large factors, one long-term and the other short-term. The long-term factor is an underlying shift in the distribution of power within the international system. One side of this shift is the relative weakening of the United States and even more so the Soviet Union. The other is the slowly increasing power and cohesion of the European Community as a political actor on the world stage and the rise towards great power status of Japan, China and, more remotely, India. The short-term factor is the extraordinary change of both perspective and policy in the Soviet Union under Gorbachev. The reform process in the Soviet Union amounts to abandonment of many of the major political, economic and military positions that necessitated and sustained the East–West confrontation on both sides. It does not matter whether these changes in the Soviet Union are a result of its declining power, or a cause of it. The consequence is to change radically the security position of Europe, which previously lay at the heart of the Cold War order.

Europeans are losing the security that they gained from both the familiarity and the rigidity of the Cold War. In return, they stand to gain the security benefits of greater freedom, flexibility and interaction, and to lose the burden of living within a highly structured confrontation. But along with these benefits will come a host of security problems. Some of these, such as German unification and instability in the Balkans, are revivals from earlier history. Others will arise from the outcome of untested new arrangements. It is impossible to make exact predictions of the course of events in such exciting times, but neither is one condemned to grope blindly.

The purpose of this book is twofold. Firstly, it is aimed at understanding a historical process by viewing it in structural terms. This combination serves three objectives:

(1) it simplifies a vast mass of historical material in such a way as to clarify the logic of historical explanations of current events;
(2) structural ideas provide benchmarks against which the pace and direction of the current changes can be assessed; and
(3) structural fixtures enable some broad elements of behaviour to be explained and therefore some anticipation to be made of the consequences of change.

The second purpose is to clarify images of possible futures. In so doing we aim to distinguish between more and less probable scenarios, and thereby to highlight not only the possibilities for fruitful action, but also the lines of action that are so remote from the main trends as to be unrealistic. This second purpose is not a traditional exercise in Utopian modelling. We do not seek to define a preferred ideal-type in abstraction from its surrounding realities. If structural analysis has any merit, it is that it makes possible the identification of some broad trends and the major possibilities for change inherent in them. In these terms, what we are seeing is the breakdown of an international order dominated by two great powers and the emergence of a new order in which there are five or more power centres. The direction of change is thus clear.

Knowing the direction of change gives one some ability to anticipate consequences. Anticipation is the key word rather than prediction. Structural theory does not pretend to explain every-thing. Its main use is in explaining the consequences of power-political arrangements within the international system and there-fore also the consequences of changes in those arrangements. It does not try to explain the causes of change arising within states, and it must itself be set into the context of other global factors such as interdependence. This latter will be done in the next chapter. We do not have the theoretical tools to attempt prediction. But knowing the structural direction of change does enable us to anticipate systematically. It narrows the field of action and identifies the broad outlines of the historical framework within which it is possible (or fruitless) to pursue preferred outcomes. Such anticipation is important. Unless prescription is informed by a firm grasp of the main trends and possibilities, it is in continuous danger of slipping into the political bankruptcy of pure Utopianism. But where it can be linked into the main trends, it may have real force to shape the unfolding of events. This is the essential principle of realist-idealism as an intellectual and political approach (Herz, 1981; Buzan, 1984a).

This chapter introduces the concepts, methods and perspectives that shape the argument in the book. The next section reviews the idea of security and sets it into a European context. The following one outlines the structural ideas through which we try to impose some shape and direction on what otherwise can only be seen as a fast-moving, unpredictable and sometimes quite breath-taking sequence of events. The final section gives an overview of the whole content of the book.

1.1. Military and Non-Military Dimensions of European Security

In the context of the international system, security is about the ability of states and societies to maintain the independence of their life and their identity. The dynamics (by dynamics we mean the whole pattern of interplay among and within contending forces) of security arise from the interplay of the threats and vulnerabilities that affect these goals. The bottom line is survival, but security also reasonably includes a substantial range of concerns about the conditions of existence. Quite where this range of concerns ceases to merit the urgency of the 'security' label and becomes part of the everyday uncertainties of life is one of the difficulties of the concept. Security is primarily about the fate of human groups, for it is these that determine the conditions for the personal security of individual human beings. In the contemporary international system, the main unit of security is thus the sovereign territorial state. The ideal type is the nation-state, where ethnic and cultural boundaries line up with political and territorial ones, as in Japan and Denmark. But nations and states do not fit neatly together in many places, a problem particularly evident in such countries as the Soviet Union, Yugoslavia, South Africa, Ethiopia and Sri Lanka. Because of this mismatch, nations are also an important unit in security analysis. Since the structure of the international system is anarchic (which

in International Relations means simply without central government and carries no implication of chaos), the natural focus of
security concern is the units: the states and nations. Thus
'national security' is the central issue, usually referring to the
state, but also applicable to ethno-cultural sub-state groups such
as the Armenians and Azeris existing within or between states.
Since some military, economic and ecological threats affect the
conditions of survival on the entire planet, there is also an
important sense in which security applies to the collectivity of
humankind as a whole, which we will refer to as international
society.

The security of human collectivities is affected by factors in five
major sectors: military, political, economic, societal and environmental. *Military security* concerns the two-level interplay of the
armed offensive and defensive capabilities of states and states'
perceptions of each other's intentions. *Political security* concerns the
organizational stability of states, systems of government and the
ideologies that give them legitimacy. *Economic security* concerns
access to the resources, finance and markets necessary to sustain
acceptable levels of welfare and state power. *Societal security*
concerns the sustainability, within acceptable conditions for
evolution, of traditional patterns of language, culture and
religious and national identity and custom. *Environmental security*
concerns the maintenance of the local and the planetary biosphere
as the essential support system on which all other human enterprises depend. It is well understood that these five sectors do not
operate in isolation from each other. Each defines a focal point and
a way of ordering priorities, but all are woven together in a strong
web of linkages.

Of these five sectors, it is traditionally the military one that
attracts the most attention. This is partly because an expensive
and highly visible sector of state behaviour is generated by the
need to respond to the possibility of armed threat, attack or
invasion. Mostly, however, it is because military means can
quickly and decisively dominate outcomes in all the other sectors.
A state and its society can be, in their own terms, secure in the
political, economic, societal and environmental dimensions, and
yet all of these accomplishments can be undone by military failure.
The fate of countries like the Netherlands in 1940, or of the
Chinese empire during the nineteenth century, illustrates this
long-standing primacy of military power over the other
dimensions of security. It is this quality that explains the traditional dominance of military factors in the broad range of thinking
about national and international security. The very nature of
military action will ensure that it always occupies a special place in
security thinking. But given the increasing constraints on the

resort to force as a rational instrument of policy in relations among developed states, its traditional primacy may well be challenged. Other contenders for leading source of insecurity are the ever more penetrative economic threats arising from debt, interest rates and trade restriction, the societal threat of unwanted mass migration and the rise of planetary environmental problems such as global warming.

The aim of this book is not to dispute the ultimate primacy of military factors, but to set them into the much broader context of security in contemporary Europe. European history makes it impossible to deny the centrality of military security. Europe has given birth to two world wars in this century, and the continent still contains the largest concentration of armed force ever assembled. Until very recently, its political life was delineated by the boundary where the forward defence spheres of the two superpowers met, and was overshadowed by the complex and long-standing alliance structures that grew up to support and sustain the military standoff. There is still considerable inertia in some of these arrangements.

Long-established institutions and hostilities have many self-perpetuating qualities. During the four decades of the Cold War, sustained institutionalization usually made yesterday's arrangements, practices and budgets the best guide to tomorrow's. Reciprocal military rivalry and suspicion in a context of high levels of standing force, created very strong pressures on both sides not to abandon the existing arrangements. In order to sustain them, each made continuous and routine force adjustments in response both to new technological opportunities and to developments and deployments by the other side. The interaction of the balancing (i.e. deterrence maintenance) and modernization processes created a kind of permanent, semi-institutionalized, arms race (Buzan, 1987b, Part 2).

At the same time, however, this deeply rooted set of military structures and processes generated a powerful tension between fear of military defeat or subordination on the one hand, and fear of overall destruction in the process of war, whether won or lost, on the other. The apparent fixity of military rivalry, driven by fear of defeat, was in fact challenged by the mutual interest in survival driven by a common fear of war. In Europe this tension was and is greatly amplified by the historical memory of two great bloodlettings and by the obvious destructive potentials of modern military means within Europe's confined and crowded domain. The security debate in Europe during the first half of the 1980s was marked by a growing recognition of the political force of this shared fear of war.

An additional reason for looking beyond the military dimension is that, although it does have ultimate primacy, it is not the principal cause of insecurity. That military factors are not, by themselves, determining forces is illustrated by the way in which armed states can avoid the arms rivalry that arises from mutual fear of attack, if their relationships are secure in the other dimensions. Britain did not find it necessary to respond to the rise of the United States' Navy during the late nineteenth century. Sweden and Finland have made their self-defence mutually supportive because of the political harmony of their neutrality. France and Britain do not fear military attack from each other's nuclear arsenals. Conversely, it was the rise of fascism which made German power a threat to the other European states and the European system (Jahn *et al.*, 1987, p. 16–17). When the reciprocal interactions of an arms rivalry do get established, they are almost always *partly* autonomous: i.e. self-driving within the military sector. As in the Anglo-German naval race before the First World War, and the post-1945 military rivalry between NATO and the Warsaw Pact, raw arms levels on one side become a major referent for acquisitions and deployments on the other.

But the insecurities of the military dimension seldom, if ever, arise without being driven by more fundamental insecurities in the other sectors. In the case of Europe, the military confrontation was called into being by a host of non-military insecurities. The clash of incompatible ideologies provided a framework in which many kinds of political, economic and societal insecurities were linked together. In a few places, most notably Germany, the traditional European issue of uncertain state territorial boundaries remained important, posing a threat to the identity, and even existence, of East Germany. Much more widespread, was the ideological and governmental insecurity that arose from the adjacency of communist and capitalist systems. The basic construction of government and society on either side of the Cold War lines in Europe stood as a permanent challenge to the legitimacy of the other side. The organizing philosophy and political practice of Marxist-Leninist states, particularly in their Stalinist variant, and democratic pluralist states are in such profound contrast as inevitably to make each feel threatened by, and vulnerable to, the other. In such conditions, it can become nearly impossible for principled opposition within either system to escape identification with the rival system. In Western Europe, the fear was that rivals in the East would exploit the openness of democracy by backing parties that would destroy pluralism if they once obtained power. In Eastern Europe, many governments depended for their tenure on Soviet ideological legitimation and military backing, and were therefore inherently insecure in relation both to their own societies and to the democratic West.

These basic incompatibilities extended into the economic and societal sectors. In the *economic sector*, the imposition of Cold War boundaries not only cut off long-standing trade and financial links between Eastern and Western Europe, but also created another arena of rivalry to multiply the political insecurities. The Cold War was in large part about a socio-economic challenge as to which system could most efficiently produce and distribute material welfare. Khrushchev's much quoted line 'we will bury you' was a reference to Soviet production aspirations, not to its capacity for nuclear destruction. This politicization of economic performance drove a rivalry, which in turn amplifed the fears and obstructions that the two economic systems placed in each other's way.

For the capitalists, the communist system denied access to markets and resources. In so doing, it identified itself with the militaristic protectionism characteristic of the fascist regimes of the 1930s, posing a threat to both prosperity (and therefore domestic political stability) and peace. By enclosing their economies, the communist states threatened the liberal capitalist project of constructing a global market economy as a means of promoting not only peace and prosperity, but also pluralist democracy. Any success for communism restricted the potential of the capitalist project.

For the communists, capitalism was hostile by definition and also threatened a project for global peace and prosperity. Marxist-Leninist ideology emphasized this opposition and, until revised by Khrushchev, officially expected it to result in war. Capitalist practice was self-evidently contradictory to the maintenance of communist government. The operation of capitalism could not but penetrate state and society creating both conceptual and administrative challenges to the commanding control of the communist party. This politicization of economics on both sides made significant economic interaction between them extremely problematic. Each feared that dealing with the other would worsen its own position in the overall political and strategic rivalry. The West, having a technological edge, instituted formal arrangements through COCOM to restrict Soviet access to militarily significant technology. The relationship between the two sides was a zero-sum game: the gains of one were the losses of the other, and vice versa.

In the *societal sector*, the basic tension was between the overarching cosmopolitan ideologies that shaped politics on both sides and the cultural identities of the indigenous national societies in Europe. In the East, homogenizing communism sought to override local religious as well as national and cultural identities. Because of the strength of the churches in Poland and Ukraine, these two provide the best examples of communist efforts to suppress an independent local religion. Local national identities were suppressed in Hungary, Yugoslavia, East Germany and many of the republics within the Soviet Union. In the West, France perhaps best exemplified the widespread national level of resistance to the equally homogenizing effects of liberal capitalism in terms of universal product brands, financial systems, cultural styles, music and language. In the East, societal insecurities linked partly to the Soviet-dominated political and military structures and partly to the weakness of indigenous state structures. In the West, the picture was, and is, more complex and less fraught, because the homogenizing ideology was not almost solely, as in the East, an imposition of the dominant superpower, but also stemmed powerfully from the locally rooted forces that are constructing the European Community. In between the two systems lay the German problem, where a powerful national identity was riven into two states lying uncomfortably on oppo-site sides of the political divide.

The *environmental sector* is a recent arrival on the European security agenda. Except indirectly, in relation to fears of the consequences of further war in Europe, environmental consider-ations played no role in the construction of the post-war order. But since the 1970s, awareness of collective environmental fate has joined the consciousness of economic interdependence that began to develop after the First World War. A series of dramatic events, including the radiation cloud from the Chernobyl reactor, river pollution, dying trees, disintegrating historic buildings and poisoned sea life, has made the European states aware of their vulnerability in this fundamental sector. These essentially local happenings are reinforced in effect by simultaneous global concerns about the greenhouse effect, with its dramatic potential consequences for sea levels and agriculture, and the deterioration of the ozone layer.

As this line of enquiry makes clear, any broadly-based analysis of security in Europe must take into account not only the military, but also the non-military dimensions of the situation. In the European case, there are two compelling reasons for giving particular emphasis to the non-military dimensions. The first is that during the Cold War military issues in Europe came to dominate the day-to-day security agenda in a way that was out of proportion, even with their very real importance. The combined fear of war and defeat fuelled a preoccupation with the military balance that made the security problem look more military than political. This imbalance had several sources, including the politi-cally emotional exploitation of military issues by a wide range of political forces (peace, green, establishment, military-industrial complex, hard left, hard right), often in competition with each other for public and elite opinion. The desire to avoid having to think about thorny issues like the German problem, the future of Atlantic relations and the political security responsibilities of an evolving European Community also played their part.

The second reason for emphasizing non-military dimensions is that the military confrontation was originally initiated by the political, economic and societal insecurities that underlay it. Indeed, the apparent permanence of the whole package of ideological confrontation for four decades after the onset of the Cold War in itself contributed to the undue prominence of military matters. *Détente* brought some easing of the confrontation, and even some settlements of particular boundary and political recognition issues. But the underlying political, economic and societal insecurites changed little in character and came to be seen as static. Trade loosened, but was still contained by COCOM restraints. The two Germanies accepted each other's existence, but while this lowered some sources of tension, it further institutionalized the ideological division of the continent. The crushing of the Prague Spring and the subsequent articulation of the Brezhnev Doctrine made clear the stark difference between limited accommodations between the two blocs and any overall resolution of their mutual insecurity. *Détente* meant rivalry with lower risks of war, not an end to rivalry. By contrast, military insecurity was continuously redefined by the ceaseless flow of new technologies, strategies and deployments. Tactical and theatre nuclear weapons, strategic parity, flexible response, neutron bombs, intermediate-range nuclear forces, forward naval strategies, conventional force imbalances, chemical weapon imbalances, closing technology gaps and a host of other substantial changes, all kept military issues in the public eye.

In the late 1980s, however, quite massive changes in the non-military factors began to break down the fixtures of the Cold War, in the process beginning to redefine the conditions of European security across all sectors. By 1986, the second round of the Cold War had turned into the second round of *détente*, and by the end of 1989, the Cold War was over. In the East, Gorbachev's twin revolutions of *glasnost* and *perestroika* seemed to open up real possibilities of defining economic and political relations in other than zero-sum game terms. In 1989 they led to the dissolving of communist power in most of Eastern Europe, and in 1990 even the Soviet Union began to abandon the communist monopoly of power. Those on the hard right who had argued that arms racing could push the Soviet economy to collapse were proved correct on this point, though totally wrong in their other argument that communist systems had to be opposed with force because once in power they were unremovable and unreformable. In the West, the

European Community regained both political and economic momentum with its 1992 project, and West Germany, the country with the biggest stake in a lessening of confrontation, became more influential. At the global level both superpowers weakened in will and capability to sustain their global rivalry, thereby allowing the European states, particularly those in Eastern Europe, more room to assert their own identities. As a consequence, the international system as a whole moved increasingly swiftly away from the extreme bipolar power structure of the Cold War era and towards the more complex, fluid and multi-centred power structure of the twenty-first century.

These changes require a reconsideration of the whole pattern of security in Europe. New linkages between the military and non-military aspects of security are already apparent. Economic pressures for lower military spending are a potent force in both superpowers and their allies. Reassessment of the threat from the West underpinned Gorbachev's extraordinary turnaround of Soviet foreign and domestic policy. Declining perceptions of socio-political threat from the Soviet Union in Western Europe are beginning to reshape attitudes towards both the Atlantic Alliance and the most appropriate configuration and strategy for Western military forces. Between Eastern and Western Europe perceptions of hostility requiring military preparation have virtually collapsed, and economic relations are opening up apace. It is mainly uncertainty about the outcome of the turbulent internal dynamics of the Soviet Union that sustains a sense of military prudence. The resurfacing of indigenous societal and political forces in Eastern Europe and the Soviet Union has outpaced military adjustments, resulting in huge military deployments that become daily more inappropriate to the new realities of international relations. Understanding the patterns of continuity and change in the non-military dimensions of security is thus important not only because these patterns affect the viability and fundamental ratio-nale of the military structures, but also because the new patterns will define the purposes and many of the conditions for alternative military arrangements.

1.2. Analytical Issues and Methods

Pursuing a security analysis on this scale requires a trade-off that favours scope over detail. A purely historical account is impossible when events are still in motion, and especially so when they are moving as fast as during 1989–90. In such circumstances one has no way of distinguishing between events that are merely histori-cal and those that are historic. But since the subject matter of the

European case is historical, it is difficult to escape the detail without gutting the whole enterprise. The solution to this dilemma attempted here will be to make a synthesis of historical and systemic analysis. Ideas about system structure will be used as the framework within which to locate a broadly thematic historical analysis. Such an approach has the advantage of setting the present events into an overall framework, thereby clarifying their direction, significance and prospects. It does not, however, constitute a historical analysis in the normal sense. A historical analysis requires that explanations and evaluations be sought in the sequence of events and can only be done once the events have passed and the records of them have become available. A structural analysis presupposes that the distribution of power in the international system is in and of itself a centrally important variable. The history that we tell here and the anticipatory scenarios that we draw are based on this assumption. For the cost of narrowing our historical perspective, we gain the possibility of dealing with present and future events.

The main concepts used in this analysis are drawn from the Neorealist tradition, which takes as its starting point the pervasive and durable effects of anarchic political structure (i.e. no central government) on relations among states (Waltz, 1979; Buzan, 1991b). An anarchic structure imposes competitive conditions of existence on the states within the system. To say this is not to say that relations between states are inevitably, or even probably, conflictual under anarchy. Conflict is simply possible and in some circumstances likely. Competition, however, is pervasive and takes political, economic and societal forms as well as military ones. Anarchic political structure favours the emergence of capitalist economies. Where capitalism and anarchy coexist, the pressure for technological innovation to become a central element of international competitiveness, both economic and military, is large. It is thus possible to make a connection between Neorealist theory, which focuses on the politically fragmenting quality of anarchy, and interdependence theory, which focuses on the network of economic and other relations that tends to tie the system together. Neorealist theory has to be modified by interdependence theory if the great dialectic between political fragmentation and economic integration is to be understood (Buzan, 1991a, ch. 6, and 1991b; Kelstrup, 1990a).

In Neorealist theory, the 'shoving and shaping' influence of competition under anarchy tends to produce units that are functionally similar (Waltz, 1979, pp. 127–8). As the current relationships between Eastern and Western Europe illustrate, successful states have a demonstration effect on those seeking to emulate their success. Those that fail to adapt to the ways of the most successful states lose power in the system and expose their domestic politics to what von Laue nicely labels 'invidious comparison' with those more effectively organized (von Laue, 1987). If differential rates of success grow very large, as they did in the eighteenth and even more so the nineteenth centuries, then the processes of 'shoving and shaping' become more forceful. The strong simply take over the weak, reconstructing them in their own image, as the European states did to most of what is now referred to as the Third World (Bull and Watson, 1984, Parts I and II). As well as encouraging (though never reaching) functional homogeneity among states, anarchic structure also generates balance of power behaviour. In seeking to preserve their own sovereignty and security, states will tend to align themselves in such a way as to prevent threats from any one expansionist centre of power from dominating the system. In doing so, they preserve the structure of anarchy itself, which is consequently exceptionally durable.

It is within the idea of the balance of power that two concepts central to the present study reside: the distribution of power and regional security complexes. *The distribution of power* refers simply to the fact that, historically, power is always very unevenly distributed in the international system. In particular, the number of great powers is always measurable in single figures. Great powers dominate life in the anarchy because they control the bulk of the capability necessary for action in the system. The number of great powers, usually between two and seven, defines the degree of polarity in the system (i.e. unipolar, bipolar, tripolar . . . multipolar). Variation in the degree of polarity, especially when the numbers are low, makes a big difference to the overall character of relations in the system. The number of great powers in the post-war system was so low (two) as to give rise to the term 'superpower'. The theory thus predicts that any change will have big consequences. For this reason, even the process of change away from bipolarity, once palpably under way, is sufficient to change the behaviour and perception of the actors in the system. In the Neorealist scheme, changes in polarity count as changes in the structure of the international system. One theme in this study will be that a process of structural change towards a larger number of great powers is fundamentally altering the political conditions of European security as we approach the end of the twentieth century.

Polarity is about the number of great powers in the international system and should not be confused with *polarization* which concerns the pattern of fear and hostility among those powers. A polarized system is one in which the great powers are divided against themselves, as was the case before the First World War and after the Second. The international system always has polarity, but it is not always polarized. As of 1989, the degree of polarity was increasing, but the degree of polarization was in sharp decline as the Cold War faded.

There are arguments about how to identify 'poles' of power, but it is not our intention to make this study a test case for a particular interpretation (James and Brecher, 1988). Emphasis will be placed on the process of transition and its direction, neither of which is controversial, rather than on determining precise points of departure from and arrival at specific numbers, which is. From this perspective, changes in relative capability, such as the rising economic power of Japan, and changes in political organization, such as the slow cohering of Western Europe, carry substantial weight as part of the process of change. Indeed, the question of whether Europe can cohere sufficiently to count as a pole of power is central to much of the analysis that follows. Looked at in terms of politico-military power, the system is still arguably bipolar, though even using this criteria some would agree with Bull that China qualifies as a third pole (Bull, 1977, pp. 200–5). But using a more finely differentiated lens, one can already see manifest multipolarity in the economic and political sectors, in terms of both capability and independent centres of decision (Buzan, 1991b). As the fading superpowers wind down their Cold War arsenals, they will facilitate the transition to multipolarity in the military sector by increasing the relative military strength of Europe, China and even Japan and India.

The second concept, *regional security complexes*, is about distinctive patterns of security relations within regions. The basic definition of a security complex is a set of states whose major security perceptions and concerns are so interlinked that their national security problems cannot reasonably be analysed apart from one another. The idea derives from the interplay between, on the one hand, the anarchic structure and its balance of power consequences, and on the other the pressures of local geographical proximity. Simple physical adjacency tends to generate more security interaction among neighbours than among states located in different areas. Adjacency is potent for security because many threats carry more easily over short distances than over long ones. Security complexes embody durable patterns of amity and enmity occurring within geographical patterns of security interdependence (Buzan and Rizvi, 1986, ch. 1; Buzan, 1991a, ch. 5).

The impact of geographical proximity on security interaction is strongest and most obvious in the military, political, societal and environmental sectors. Military power and environmental damage are much more easily projected over short distances than over long ones. Thus Pakistan is more concerned about the capabilities of the Indian Air Force than is Japan, and Canada is more concerned about American emissions of sulphur dioxide than is Britain. Political and societal threats ànd tensions also operate more easily over short distances. Ethnic and religious groups often straddle adjacent state boundaries in politically significant ways. Being adjacent to an antagonistic ideology is usually discomforting. The conditioning of security perceptions by historical memory also operates more strongly with adjacency, as illustrated by relationships between Greeks and Turks, Vietnamese and Chinese, and Arabs and Persians. The general rule that adjacency increases security interaction is much less consistent in the economic sector. For many Third World countries, even ones with substantial economies such as India, economic interaction with neighbours is relatively insignificant. What counts is a far-flung network of trade and finance, in which distance plays little role. There is evidence that proximity plays a role among advanced capitalist states, as indicated by the moves towards common markets in Western Europe and North America, but the function of geography in economic security is much more uneven than for the other sectors.

All the states in the system are to some extent enmeshed in a global web of security interdependence. But because insecurity is often associated with proximity, this interdependence is far from uniform. Anarchy plus geographical diversity yields a pattern of regionally based clusters, within which security interdependence is markedly more intense between the states inside such complexes, than it is between states inside the complex and those outside it. South Asia provides a clear example, where the wars and rivalries of the subcontinent constitute a distinctive pattern that is little affected by events in the Gulf or in Southeast Asia (Buzan and Rizvi, 1986). The analysis in this book hinges on the idea that Europe can be seen as a security complex: a group of states whose securities are sufficiently interdependent to make them a type of sub-system within the overall pattern of international security.

Many variables affect the basic premise that security interdependence tends to be regionally focused. One such intervening variable is power. At one end of the power spectrum, superpowers such as the United States have such wide-ranging interests, and such massive capabilities, that they can conduct their rivalries over the whole planet. Superpowers, by definition, largely transcend the logic of geography in their security relationships. At the other end are states whose limited capabilities confine their interests and activities to their near neighbours, as in Southeast Asia or Southern Africa. Possession of great power thus tends to override the regional imperative, small power to reinforce it. The great powers form a kind of global security complex amongst themselves, taking the whole planet as their region, and it is for this reason that Neorealist theory focuses on them. Lesser states will usually find themselves locked into a regional security complex with their neighbours. The particular character of a local security complex will often be affected by historical factors such as long-standing enmities (Greeks and Turks, Arabs and Persians, Khmers and Vietnamese), or the common cultural embrace of a civilizational area (Arabs, Europeans, South Asians, Northeast Asians, Latin Americans).

Local security complexes are defined by indigenous patterns of security relations, but this does not mean that they are immune from the system-dominating influence of the great powers. The idea of the distribution of power (the number of great powers in the system) links to that of security complexes through the mechanism of *penetration*. Penetration occurs when outside powers make security alignments with states within a regional security complex. An indigenous regional rivalry such as that between India and Pakistan provides opportunites for the great powers to penetrate the region. Balance of power logic works naturally to encourage the local rivals to call in outside help, and by this mechanism the local patterns of rivalry become linked to the global ones. South Asia again gives a clear example, with Pakistan linked to the United States and China, and India linked to the Soviet Union. Such linkage between the local and global security patterns is a natural feature of life in an anarchic system. One of the purposes of the security complex concept is to combat the tendency to overstress the role of the great powers and to ensure that the indigenous local factors are given their proper weight in analyses of regional security.

Although regional security normally involves a mixture of local and global patterns, there are occasions when great power interests dominate a region so heavily that the local pattern of security relations virtually ceases to operate. This condition is called *overlay*. It usually results in the long-term stationing of great power armed forces in the local region, and in the alignment of the local states according to the patterns of great power rivalry. Overlay can occur across a whole spectrum of degrees of local support for the intrusion of an outside power. In theory, it could occur with total local support (i.e. against a hated common enemy) or against total local opposition (i.e. in the face of colonizing imperialism by a great power), though such extremes are rare in practice. More likely is overlay either with the consent of the dominant local governing elites, as in Western Europe after the Second World War, or with the support of local minority factions, such as the communist parties in Eastern Europe. The period of European colonization in Asia, Africa and the Americas gives a mixed picture of the overlay process, with some cases of substantial elite support for the penetrating power (India) and some cases of sustained opposition (Afghanistan). For overlay to occur without substantial local support requires a massive superiority of power in favour of the overlayer, like that enjoyed by the Europeans in their conquest of technologically and organizationally less developed societies in the Americas, Africa and Australasia.

The concept of overlay plays a major role in the analysis of European security in this book. Chapter 3 sketches the history of the European security complex, and one central theme of subsequent chapters will be to assess how the breakup of the Cold War order affects it. The traditional European security complex collapsed after the Second World War and was overlaid by the two superpowers. That overlay has lasted for more than forty years and is now rapidly breaking up. The European complex has not operated independently since the period of world wars, and the question is what local patterns lie dormant under the imposed rigidities of the superpower rivalry? Overlay is an intensely political process, and it is highly unlikely that four decades of it has had no effect on Europe. Colonial overlay, for example, reconstructed the political organization of five continents on the model of the European territorial state. On this basis, there is little reason to expect a resumption of business as usual in Europe on the pre-1945 pattern. What kind of metamorphosis has occurred within the cocoon of overlay, and how will those changes evolve as overlay recedes?

1.3. Overview

With these ideas and purposes in mind, the rest of the book is structured as follows. Part I sets the issue of European security into the context of the international system. Chapter 2 considers the global patterns of power, interdependence and society within which Europe is embedded. Chapter 3 sketches the history of the European security complex up to the present day. Chapter 4 discusses the increasingly difficult and important question of what the term 'Europe' refers to, how it relates to the nature of national identification, and how it fits into the major post-war patterns of East–West, West–West, and North–South relations.

Part II examines the break up of the post-war order in three different centres. Chapter 5 looks at the process of reform and revolution in the fast disintegrating 'East'. Chapter 6 focuses on the German problem, which lay at the heart of both the European security complex before 1945 and the overlay of Europe during the Cold War, and which is central to the outcome of the present changes. Chapter 7 takes up the changes in the West, particularly the consolidation of the European Community and the tensions that process creates both within Europe and between Europe and North America.

Part III contains three scenarios for the future of European security. Chapter 8 sets the framework for these scenarios by looking at the major centres of power involved — the United States, 'Europe' and the Soviet Union — in terms of three key variables: the relative power, the degree of amity and enmity, and the degree of economic interdependence among them. Different possibilities of combination in these variables serve as the foundations for the scenarios. This chapter also looks at the possibility that some kind of buffer zone in East-Central Europe will be a feature in most European futures. Chapter 9 examines the possibilities for a return to Cold War and finds that a reconstruction of anything like the 1945–89 pattern is highly unlikely. Chapter 10 investigates the possibility that a coherent European actor will emerge as the dominant entity on the continent. Such a development would eventually obliterate the European security complex by transforming its structure away from anarchy and towards some more coherent political form. At the same time, it would change the distribution of power at the global level by creating a new pole of power in the international system. Once Europe had integrated sufficiently to transform its anarchic structure, it could not avoid becoming one of the major power centres in a more multi-centred international system. Chapter 11 takes up the possibility that Cold War will be replaced by a fragmented Europe, rehabilitating many of the patterns of the pre-1945 European security complex. The Epilogue offers some reflections on events up to late July 1990 in relation to the anticipations in the scenario chapters.

PART I – THE SYSTEMIC CONTEXT OF EUROPEAN SECURITY

Chapter 2

Global Patterns

Three patterns set the global context for European security: one to do with the distribution of power, the second to do with the rising density of the interaction networks that tie the international system together and the third to do with the character of international society. The distribution of power is important for two reasons: it reflects the fundamental anarchic structure of international politics that defines Europe's place in the international system; and it bears heavily on the fate of the European security complex after overlay. Density and international society are important because of the way in which they modify the security problems posed by the competitive, balance-of-power consequences of anarchy (Buzan, 1991a, chs. 4, 6).

2.1. The Distribution of Power

The twentieth century has seen some remarkable changes in the distribution of power. The number of great powers, or 'poles' in the system has fluctuated dramatically. The First World War eliminated Austria-Hungary and the Ottoman Empire as great powers. Up to the Second World War, the system was firmly multipolar, being dominated by seven great powers (Britain, France, Germany, Italy, Japan, the Soviet Union and the United States). The pattern of defeat, occupation and exhaustion resulting from that war knocked the four European powers and Japan out of the top rank, marking a dramatic shift from a historically common multipolar structure to a historically rare bipolar one. The United States and the Soviet Union rose to the new rank of 'superpower', and moved quickly to stamp the pattern of their rivalry on the rest of the international system. In doing so, they pushed to the top of the international agenda an ideological conflict between capitalism and communism that had been brewing for nearly a century. This fusion of a bipolar power structure and a zero-sum ideological rivalry not surprisingly produced a singularly intense polarization of world politics. The bipolar system resulted directly from the war in that the two superpowers were the principal victors, and also in that their rapid elevation to superpower status depended as much on the collapse of other power centres as on the inherent strength of the two countries themselves. This latter point was particularly true for the Soviet Union. The pattern of relations that it imposed can thus fairly be termed the post-war order.

To the extent that the power structure of the post-war order rested on the collapse of the older centres of power, the order itself was inherently vulnerable to the process of post-war recovery. The collapse of the old power centres as a result of the war was dramatic, but not deep or permanent. The basic societal and political qualities that made them centres of industry, finance and power remained, even though war damage had destroyed or depleted many of their industrial, military and financial assets. As their recovery progressed, the relative power of the United States and the Soviet Union could only decline from the artificially induced heights of the immediate post-war years.

In addition to the recovery of older power centres in Europe and the Far East, the post-war order has also been challenged by the rise of new power centres. The principal agency here has been decolonization, encouraged by both superpowers, in which the largely European- and Japanese-dominated empires were converted into territorial state structures on the European model. This process tripled the number of states in the international system and offered opportunity for independent new centres of power to arise. The development of these new power centres has naturally been slower than the recovery of the crushed pre-war great powers. Whereas the old great powers had only to reconstruct the physical fabric of their industrial and financial strength, the new arrivals had the much more daunting task of first constructing the social and political foundations for an industrial economy. The difference between reconstruction and development is so large that it would not be inaccurate to see them as wholly different types of problem. As yet, only a few have achieved conspicuous success with development, mostly from the ranks of those with long-standing civilizational traditions that could in some measure be blended with the requirements of both industrialization and the territorial state. Of these, only China, India and Brazil also have the legacy of size necessary to make a bid for great power ranking under contemporary conditions. These few, however, have already registered their challenge to the post-war power structure, not least by their shared passion for acquiring independent arms industries and the full spectrum of nuclear technology.

As a consequence of these two lines of development, there can be no doubt that the extreme bipolar structure of the post-war decades is weakening steadily, and in some sectors dramatically, towards a multipolar one. For those centres of power temporarily knocked out by the war, recovery has long been complete in the economic sector. As living memory of the war fades away, there is good reason to think that political recovery is now moving into its final stages (Buzan, 1988). The rise of new centres of power is, of course, an open-ended process that will not peak and fade from significance. As discussed in Chapter 1, there is room for argument about the precise degree to which the system has already become multipolar. Though important, these debates are peripheral to the present study. What is important is that the broad direction of change towards multipolarity is clear. The question for this study is how does European security fit into this process?

2.2. Density

The second pattern that is vital to any assessment of Europe's position in the global system is the rising density of the interaction networks that tie the system together. In raw physical terms, rising density is driven by a combination of increasing population with increasing technological, organizational and financial capabilities and incentives for action. Given the sustained pace of an apparently open-ended technological revolution, density could be expected to increase even if the human population became static in numbers. Because of the age/fertility structure of the population, this event is still several decades distant at the earliest. Density, then, is about more people doing more things. It means that people's activities are more likely to impinge on the conditions of other people's existence, both intentionally (advertising, propaganda) and unintentionally (traffic accidents, noise), and positively (trade, culture) as well as negatively (pollution, recession). Density is defined by interaction and breeds interdependence. As it rises, it increases the need for specifically political interaction to deal with its consequences. This political action may be cooperation or it may be conflict.

In concrete terms, rising density is measurable across all of the sectors of security. Military capabilities have reached levels where it is possible for the major powers both to involve the whole planet in conflict, and to inflict levels of destruction that could well eliminate the human species. In the political sphere, ideas now circulate globally, many issues are discussed in global or semi-global forums as a matter of routine, a wide variety of regimes help to facilitate cooperative behaviour, and the model of the industrial democracies has emerged as a kind of universal Holy Grail of development, albeit by very different routes (von Laue, 1987). Economically, the world is increasingly tied into a global market of production, trade and finance, whose circulation system is an ever more efficient transportation network by land, sea and air, and whose nervous system is a world-wide web of electronic communication and data processing facilities. Societally, the system of states is still deeply parochial, but elements of a global society are emergent in such things as the nearly universal acceptance of a political order based on mutually recognizing sovereign states, the use of English as a common language and at the global individual level in the spread of common materialist values (Bull, 1977, pp. 315–7; Buzan, 1991a, ch. 4). Environmentally, the collective impact of human activity is producing effects of regional and global scale, in the process creating both common fates and a need for collective action. Should global warming produce a significant (i.e. over one metre) rise in sea level, as seems far from impossible, the environmental sector may well confront humankind with its first truly systemic challenge some time in the next century.

The major theoretical question arising from density, is how its increase affects the general character of international relations within an anarchic structure? This question defines the central concerns of the liberal (and more recently neoliberal) view of the international system (Nye, 1988). Answers to it point in the direction of behaviour increasingly governed by a system of shared norms and institutionalized regimes. The principal political impact of rising density is to increase the levels of interdependence among states across a broad spectrum. In the military sphere, states depend for their survival on the restraint of their rivals, nowhere more so than in the context of mutual nuclear deterrence. In the economic sphere, they depend for their prosperity and development on complex patterns of access to external markets, resources and credit. In the environmental sphere, they increasingly depend on each other to adopt restraint towards ecologically damaging activities. Interdependence makes relationships costly to disrupt. It also gives states an expanded repertoire of instruments with which they can influence each other's behaviour. Interdependence is unlikely to reduce conflict and may increase it by giving states a broader agenda of issues over which their interests and circumstances will differ. But where interdependence is strong, it should reduce incentives to resort to armed force. Such a resort is costly not only in itself but also in its consequences. In addition, armed force is unlikely to be a well-tuned instrument for many interdependence issues.(Nye and Keohane, 1977, ch. 2).

This line of reasoning points towards the conclusion that rising density will, other things being equal, tend to lower the salience of military security and raise the salience of non-military aspects of security on the foreign policy agenda. The natural pressure of rising density is away from the traditional anarchic imperative of 'look after yourself!', and towards the more economic imperative: 'specialize!'(Waltz, 1979, p.107). This logic is apparent in the current diffusion away from advanced industrial countries of basic industries, such as steel and shipbuilding, and in the international stratification of production for major goods such as computers, aircraft, cars, and even armaments (Neuman, 1984). The evolution of the European Community provides a fascinating case study of the contending logics of anarchy and interdependence at play. On issues ranging from defence to currencies, the states within the EC are clearly torn between their tradition-driven, self-regarding, anarchic imperative of 'look after yourself', and the contemporary interdependence imperatives to specialize and harmonize. European security has to be located within the complex dialectic of conditions that the tension and interplay between these logics defines.

The dividing logic of anarchy and the binding logic of interdependence are both powerfully at work in the contemporary international system. Nowhere more than in Europe is the complex dialectic between these contradictory forces to be found. Western Europe originated the sovereignty/anarchy political structure that now dominates the entire international system. It is also one of the highest density regions in the system. It is therefore not surprising that Western Europe is now the place where the dialectic between anarchy and interdependence has reached its most advanced state of development. The density that played such a role in the original 'European miracle' of intense development still operates. But, under the much more advanced conditions of late twentieth-century interdependence and the much weaker power position of the individual European states in the international system, density is pushing Western Europe away from a strict system of sovereign states and towards a *sui generis* integrated structure of some sort. The final shape and scope of this European structure is yet to be determined and is under massive cross pressure from the events in Eastern Europe and the Soviet Union. The nature of the outcome is one of the main variables that will shape the future of European security.

2.3. International Society

The condition of international society is an important element of international security. Bull and Watson define international society as:

a group of states (or, more generally, a group of independent political communities) which not merely form a system, in the sense that the behaviour of each is a necessary factor in the calculations of the others, but also have established by dialogue and consent common rules and institutions for the conduct of their relations, and recognize their common interest in maintaining these arrangements.

To the extent that an international society exists, it not only makes it easier for states to accept each other's political legitimacy, but also facilitates civilized (i.e. non-violent) interaction among them. Anarchical society, in other words, is capable of generating order only if the units within it can adopt norms against which their own and others' behaviour can be communicated, regulated and judged. This is especially so when the density of the system is high enough that the units cannot ignore each other's presence and activity. Hedley Bull worried that the common norms underlying international society had been seriously weakened by the expansion of a culturally cohesive European system into an incoherent multi-civilizational global one (Bull, 1977, pp. 38–40, 257–60, 315–7). It can be argued that Bull's portrait was an excessively gloomy one and that even to the extent that he was right at the time of writing, his analysis is now dated (Buzan, 1991a, ch. 4).

The core idea in international society is a society made up of states (Wight, 1977; and 1986, pp.105–11) rather than a global society of individuals. To what extent homogeneity of national societies is a necessary condition for the existence of a society among states is a problematic question. The assumption that such homogeneity was necessary might explain some of the misleading gloom from Bull and others. Cultural diversity could increase within the international system but only be detrimental to international society if it hindered formation of the shared norms and procedures necessary for civil relations among states. Some degree of basic cultural affinity is widely assumed to be necessary for an international society to develop (Wight, 1977, pp.33ff.), but this does not preclude substantial diversity. Different types of societies will tend to foster, as well as depend on, different legitimizing principles for the international order (Kissinger, 1957, 1966; Aron, 1966). This was clearly the case in the nineteenth century when dynastic empires and national, liberal democracies tried to devise a 'fair' system for securing European stability and change. The fact that they succeeded in establishing the Concert of Europe demonstrates that even competitive national differences do not preclude international society. Some norms converged sufficiently to sustain a significant international regime, while others remained competitive.

Before the French revolution the link between domestic and international society was less important because diplomacy and foreign policy was conducted in a closed world of internationalized elites. Democratization and the rise of public opinion meant a fundamental challenge in international affairs. Diplomats became nationalized (Morgenthau, 1978; Craig and George, 1983), and the constituency of international society was consequently extended to the whole population. This created a tougher task for diplomacy in developing a sufficiently shared international code for smoothing relations among diverse and powerful national societies.

During the Cold War, differences between the superpowers were so deep and so extensive that they precluded agreement on 'fair' rules of the game in terms of norms for change and stabilization of the international status quo (Jahn, 1981; Wæver, 1989c). Changes in national societal orders, especially revolutionary ones, will generally be of high significance for the state of international society. But as argued above, the Cold War polarization was extreme and unusual. There is no reason to think that under normal circumstances, diplomacy cannot successfully mediate the differences among national societies sufficiently to establish an effective international society of states.

Indeed, there are several reasons for thinking that international society is in fairly good shape by the standards of most of this century and that the trends are improving ones. Most basic is the near universal acceptance of the territorial state as the fundamental unit of political legitimacy. Except for Islam, all of the universalizing political ideologies have been firmly nationalized. As the Gulf War demonstrated, even Islam is heading in that direction. Mutual recognition of sovereignty is the system norm, and the number of serious boundary disputes — perhaps the major source of international insecurity in an anarchic system — is declining as the now universal state system settles down.

In Western Europe the territorial state is increasingly contested as the sole unit containing political legitimacy. But the process of integration in the EC does not question the principle of territorially-based political units. It just complicates the picture by creating a dual track: on some occasions a kind of super-state exists when it is internationally recognized by others as a legitimate political actor; on other occasions its constituent states are the international actors. The precise nature and possible outcomes of this process will be one of the themes investigated in this book.

In theory, the state system can be a stable depository for the natural diversity of human culture. Provided that there is general agreement on boundaries and widespread norms and institutions for cooperation, the system of sovereign states is well designed to handle the legitimization of relations among diverse social and political cultures. Indeed, given the range and intensity of that diversity as an undeniably dominant historical reality, a system of sovereign states may be the only way of constructing a stable international political order for many decades to come. In such a system, peace can be conceived in terms of 'non-violent conflict culture' (Jahn et al., 1987, p.55). In this conception, peace does not require harmony. Disagreement and conflict are assumed to be part of the human political condition both within and between states, but war is ruled out as a legitimate instrument of policy except for the purpose of defence against a military attack. If international society is strong enough to support legitimate mechanisms for change, then anarchy can be a framework within which international disputes and conflicts can be both carried on or settled without large-scale violence.

In addition to the basic consensus on the state system, three other norms are emerging as major elements of international society. The first is the consensus amongst the major powers that wars between them are no longer a desirable or fruitful way of settling differences. In some of the great powers, most notably the major sufferers of the last war in Europe and Japan, this norm is quite deeply embedded in their societies. In others, it is more a function of nuclear deterrence and the fear that victory and defeat will be indistinguishable. This norm has emerged with exceptional strength in some regions, notably North America, the Soviet Union and Western Europe, and for rather different reasons among the ASEAN states (Buzan, 1988, pp. 12–13). Within, and sometimes between, some of these regions, security communities (groups of states in which the states neither fear, nor prepare for, the use of force among themselves) make a profound modification to the security characteristics of anarchy. Indeed, one of the pivotal characteristics of the emerging multipolar system is the fact that the three major capitalist centres of power are linked together in a massive and commanding security community. By standing back-to-back in this way, they give themselves an enormous advantage in the overall competitive environment of the international system.

The second norm concerns the desirability of market-based economies both within and between states. When Bull wrote in

1977 the international system was so deeply divided on this question as to make it the major cause of threats of war involving superpower rivalry. But during the late 1980s market economies have moved decisively into a position of intellectual and practical dominance over centrally planned ones, and this has taken much of the heat out of the Cold War. As the twenty-first century approaches, the international community, or at least the group of major powers at its apex, is beginning to look less ideologically divided than at any time since 1917. As this new norm consolidates, it will weaken, and perhaps even eliminate, the zero-sum ideological divide that was such a powerful driver of fear and hostility during the Cold War era.

The third norm arises from increasing concern over ecological issues. Because of the nature of the issues, this concern carries with it a strong global consciousness. Changes in the planetary atmosphere and biosphere affect everyone in a way that distributes burdens and concerns much more evenly than is the case with the longer-running issue of overpopulation. This is an exceptionally useful counterweight to the deeply ingrained societal parochialness that almost everywhere still dominates the human condition. Ecological, or 'green', consciousness is by no means universal. But its rise has been dramatic, and it looks well set to be ever more widely promoted as the issues on its agenda begin to impact on people everywhere in their daily lives.

This positive evaluation of international society is further supported by the fact that the type of differentiations now current among national societies generally take forms compatible with the basic principles of the international society that grew from the Western world. The collapse of communism has removed one challenge to this norm. Also important is the decline in the presence of the Third World as a counter-Western actor based on 'guilt power'. In some ways this was a more fundamental challenge to the moral hegemony of a Western-inspired international society than was the East–West conflict. The Southern challenge sometimes questioned the legitimacy of the diplomatic code and the whole mode of conducting international politics in a state system. On other occasions the state system was embraced strongly by the South, most notably in the UN and its agencies. In this area the changes happening at the end of the 1980s could be as decisive as those in East–West relations. All the major evaluations written in the mid-1980s tended to see Western international society as increasingly challenged and incapable of organizing 'a non-Western World' (Bull and Watson, 1984; Brown, 1988; Rengger, 1989). But it now seems that the category 'West' is gaining a globally accepted positive standing which restructures the value systems in international relations. International diplomacy is thus strengthened by its ability to operate on the basis of a less contested set of norms; a more full-blown international society.

Given Europe's pivotal position in the old superpower rivalry, this strengthening trend in international society is a major asset for European security. For Europe, the apparent convergence on market-based economies removes a central element of the Cold War, and thus reinforces the norm of war avoidance. Green consciousness potentially provides a powerful common norm in the high density environment of Europe, though at present this is much better developed in the Western than in the Eastern half of the continent. Ironically, it is the state norm that poses the most serious issues in the continent that both gave it birth and transported it to the rest of the international system. In some very important ways, the territorial state as the basic unit of political legitimacy in the system is under severe assault from the development of the European Community. We may be looking at a repetition of earlier political aggregation processes such as those in Germany, Italy and the United States, where the end product was simply a larger state. But the probability seems higher that the European process is unique, and that it will result in something less than a new state, but considerably more than just a common market and a security community. How this entity will fit into the international system is a major question both for the states that are merging into it and for the other major powers.

Chapter 3

The European Security Complex

Within the three global patterns of polarity, density and international society lie the more regionally based patterns of security complexes. The European security complex has occupied a central position in the history of the international system for most of the last five centuries. Up until 1945, the European complex was defined by the close interlinkages of its amities, enmities and balance of power. As Watson notes, the dynamics of interaction in Europe had developed sufficiently to form a single security system in the continent during the seventeenth century (Bull and Watson, 1984, p. 64). Although discernible sub-systems existed within it, such as that amongst the Nordic states and in the Balkans, the complex as a whole was united by a great power dynamic that periodically generated system-wide wars. Poland's security might not be related directly to Portugal's, but both were caught up in a wider European pattern. Through the process of colonization this security complex eventually dominated the pattern of security for the entire international system.

With overlay from 1945 to 1989, the European security complex virtually ceased to exist as an entity defined by its own interactions. It became instead the nut in the nutcracker of a global rivalry dominated by the two superpowers. During this period, the case for seeing Europe as a security entity rests on the common position of all the European states under overlay. All were threatened by Soviet power, and all were threatened by the danger of war inherent in the superpower rivalry (Buzan in Wæver, *et al.*, 1989, ch. 1). Since 1989 a new metamorphosis has begun, the final shape of which still hangs in the balance. It is not yet clear whether some form of the Cold War order will continue, or whether some new version of the pre-1945 dynamics will emerge or whether the European complex will be transformed into a single pole of power by the processes of integration.

The evolution and transformation of the European complex has been dramatic in its shifts and changes, and intricate in its history. There is room here only to sketch its broad outlines. The purpose of the sketch is to locate the main themes of European security, put them into the context of the international system and relate them to the present changes. One key theme relates to the issue of Europe's historic centrality in the global system. The analysis below points very strongly to the conclusion that Europe's centrality is at last about to wane. Over the next few decades, Europe will almost certainly become just another region in a truly global multipolar international system. This loss of centrality marks a profound change in the conditions of European security and a major opportunity, indeed necessity, for new thinking and new policies.

3.1. Pre-1945: The European Complex and Its Breakdown

For more than four hundred years before the Second World War, the extremely vigorous internal dynamics of the European security complex dominated, and in many respects defined, the international system. The invention and consolidation of the sovereign state in Europe unleashed human energies in the social, economic, political and military spheres in a wholly unprecedented fashion. It was the interaction created by the outpouring of these energies that fashioned an international system out of what had previously been a collection of relatively insulated human centres. The intense military and economic competition of life in the European anarchy produced a set of great powers whose surplus energies and expanding capabilities enabled them to pursue their rivalries not only within Europe, but increasingly on a global scale (McNeill, 1963, Part III; Bull and Watson, 1984, Parts I and II). By the early years of the twentieth century, the European powers controlled most of the planet, much of it directly in the form of colonies and most of the rest through the mechanisms of informal empire. Only two non-European powers had managed to establish themselves: the United States, which was a direct offshoot of European colonization, and Japan, which was the only non-European society to emulate European ways quickly and effectively enough so that it could join European imperialism, rather than be absorbed by it.

The most singular feature of the European security complex during this period was the packing of so many great powers into such a confined geographical domain. Never were there fewer than five great powers in Europe, and at different times Russia, Britain, France, Spain, Italy, Holland, Portugal, Sweden, Austria-Hungary, Germany and the Ottoman Empire all enjoyed great power status. The dynamics of security relations in such a dense, high-powered security complex focused on control over territory and maintaining or overthrowing the balance of power within the complex. Territory was closely associated with power, and innumerable wars were fought over who controlled what. The normal condition of the complex was that no one power had sufficient strength to subdue all of the others, but this did not stop a regular succession of bids to do so. At different times, Spain, France and Germany all attempted, and all failed, to match the unifying success of the Roman empire.

The making and resisting of bids to dominate Europe thus has a long and central role in European security. In the modern period (post-1648), only the Ottomans attempted such a bid from outside the system, and they also failed. The outward thrust of European power took some of the pressure off the local security complex by allowing the European states to expand without immediately threatening the core interests of neighbouring powers. But such outward expansion also increased the strength of the successful imperialists, thus feeding back into the central insecurities involved in the European balance of power. The conflicts attending the periodic bids for dominance were part of the process by which the European powers became so disproportionately strong in relation to the rest of the world. In order to attempt to break, or hold, the balance of power in the anarchic 'hothouse' of Europe, the European states had quickly to adapt to advances anywhere that increased the power of rivals (von Laue, 1987, ch. 2).

But these conflicts also had a destructive side, both within and outside Europe. In the end, it was the effect of the two German bids for dominance that destroyed both the global ascendency of Europe and the autonomous character of the European complex. During the mid-nineteenth century, the rise of German power in the context of the industrial revolution created a real danger that one power would finally be able to overawe the European balance. The threat was differently based, but equally potent to, that posed a century earlier by revolutionary and Napoleonic France. It was also clear to many of those who contemplated the issue, including many Germans, that not too far behind the German ascendency lay a gathering potential for a Russian bid. If the huge manpower and other resources of Russia could be mobilized and multiplied by industrialization, then Russia would become by far the biggest power on the continent. And by the late nineteenth century industrialization was already making its mark on Russia. By the early years of the twentieth century, the viability of the European balance was thus in serious doubt. The German problem was coming to a head, a Russian problem was looming in the wings, and preparations for what was to be the last great military contest for control of Europe were already well under way.

The story of what future generations might come to see as Europe's last civil war between 1914 and 1945 is too well known to require detailed elaboration here. Suffice it to say that the German bid came extremely close to success. In both rounds, the intervention of the United States was decisive in the defeat of Germany. In the First World War, this intervention seemed to sustain the central role of Europe in the international system, particularly so because of the subsequent retreat of the United States into isolationism. But this illusion was brief and quickly shattered by the Second World War. In reality, the rescue of the old world by the new was both the herald of, and the vehicle for, Europe's transition from being a dominant to a subordinate security complex. The American intervention signalled not only the rise of extra-European powers to a world role and the ending of Europe's global primacy, but also Europe's loss of control and autonomy over the dynamics of its own security relations. One great consequence of the two world wars was thus to break forever the long period of confluence between the European security complex and the global pattern of security. Before 1914 the balance of power in Europe was effectively the world balance, with Japan and the United States playing relatively peripheral and regional roles, albeit ones rapidly increasing in importance. After 1945, the world balance of power was truly system-wide in scope.

A second consequence of the two wars was the collapse of the Western European powers and Japan as great powers. Destruction, defeat, depletion and occupation all played a part in this unprecedented thinning out of the ranks of the great powers. Fully industrialized total war had turned out to be a much bigger, more devasting and more costly enterprise than almost anyone had imagined. The collapse of so many great powers itself generated two other major effects: decolonization and the elevation of the Soviet Union to superpower status. Rather by chance, the two powers that emerged strong from the conflagration of 1914–45 were both anti-colonial. Their motives were partly ideological and partly influenced by the fact that the withdrawal of European control would create opportunities for them. The five powers that collapsed included all of the major holders of overseas empires. The process of decolonization began almost immediately after the war, and was virtually complete within two decades. Western European and Japanese control over much of Asia and Africa was replaced by a host of newly independent and mostly very weak states. As discussed above, decolonization unleashed one of the forces working against the long-term sustainability of the bipolar system.

The collapse of Western European and Japanese power greatly assisted the elevation of the Soviet Union by the simple act of surrounding it with power vacuums where before there had been major centres of power. China also benefited in the same way, as well as by its release from colonial pressures. In Europe, the failure of the German bid for dominance simply replaced the security problem posed by the Germans with an even bigger one posed by the Soviet Union. As a result of the war, the Soviet Union was in possession of most of Eastern Europe, and its military and political power loomed large over the exhaustion and wreckage in Western Europe.

But the rise of Soviet power, as well as giving the Soviet Union a dominant position in Europe, also took it out of Europe and on to the world stage. There have always been doubts about whether Russia was part of Europe or whether it was a separate civilizational entity (Bull and Watson, 1984, ch. 4; McNeill, 1963, pp. 604–11; Toynbee, 1957, vol. 2, pp. 170–73). In some ways Russia's relationship to Europe is like that of the United States (an offshoot), in other ways it is like that of Japan (a defensive adaptation). These doubts have been equally strong in Russia and in the rest of Europe. They arise not only from cultural issues but also from its geographical position and growing role in Asia. The experience of the Russian revolution adds to more traditional reasons for thinking of the Soviet Union as a civilizational entity distinct from Europe. Although the ideology of the revolution was distinctly European in origin, its application created a society and government sharply divergent from the European political mainstream. So long as Europe dominated the world power structure, then Russia was *de facto* part of it. But as Europe slid into subordination, the Soviet Union became a truly world power, a superpower, for which Europe was only one, albeit very important, frontier. In rapid succession therefore, the collapse of Western European and Japanese power, the onset of Soviet–American rivalry and the signing of the Sino–Soviet alliance, decisively changed the position of the Soviet Union, making it, like the United States, an extra-European power.

A third key consequence of the two rounds of the European civil war was to drive home forcefully the lessons of density and interdependence. On the political front, war bred revolutions, subjecting Europe to a three-way ideological tension among communism, fascism and democracy. As in the time of the French Revolution state boundaries proved highly permeable to ideology in the closely packed, and intellectually interlinked environment of Europe. On the military front, the process of war consumed and destroyed resources of all kinds on such a massive scale as to confront Europeans with an intense dilemma between fear of war and fear of defeat. Even after the First World War, the question of whether the price of defence was higher than the cost of defeat was firmly on the public agenda, expressing itself in sustained popular peace movements and a widespread revulsion against war (Buzan, 1973). From 1919 onwards, the possibility that another war would destroy European civilization began heavily to condition perceptions of security and defence. The European states had become too small in relation to the destructive capacity of their military power to make all-out war a rational means of settling disputes.

On the economic front, the reality of interdependence was made manifest not only by the huge disruption caused by the wars, but also by the inability of the victors to punish the losers without damaging their own economies seriously in the process. Germany could not be saddled with huge reparations, or stripped of its industry, without spiking the engine of prosperity on which all of the other European states depended.

For all of these reasons, the period of internecine warfare between 1914 and 1945 brought about the collapse of the European security complex. The dynamics of European security no longer ran independently and no longer dominated the pattern of security relations in the international system as a whole. Europe was still central in the question of global security, but now only as the principal object of larger rivalries, and not, as before, the centre of world power. The pre-1945 European security complex depended on the continuance of the huge disproportion in power that first propelled Europe into global dominance. The rise of outside powers, hastened by the European civil war, destroyed those conditions forever. In this sense, the pre-1945 idea of a European security complex with an independent and world-dominating dynamic can never be resurrected, though a European regional security complex in its own right is not out of the question in the post-1989 world.

3.2. Overlay and the Post-War Era

In fact, the question of restoring even an independent European security dynamic, let alone a globally dominant one, was quickly swept aside as the new bipolar power structure made itself felt after 1945. From 1947 to 1989 the European security complex was defined primarily by the common fate of its overlay by the superpowers. By the late 1940s, the Western Europeans were appealing to the United States for a third time to rescue them from a threat of continental empire, this time posed by the Soviet Union. The Soviets had taken their military position at the 1945 ceasefire line as an opportunity to reconstruct in their own image the governments of the five states plus East Germany under their occupation. Combined with a local communist-led civil war in Greece and direct Soviet probes against Iran and Turkey, these developments and the British and American responses to them led to the well-known series of events that established the main line of superpower confrontation down the middle of Europe. The Truman Doctrine, Marshall Aid, currency reform in West Germany, the Berlin Crisis, the founding of COMECON, the founding of NATO, the failure of the EDC, the recruitment of West Germany into NATO and the establishment of the Warsaw Pact rapidly drew nearly all of Europe into rival superpower blocs. The Americans, who were initially reluctant to commit themselves, quickly adjusted to the imperatives of bipolarity. Like the Soviet Union, the United States had interpreted the Second World War as justifying a need for a forward defence policy in the post-war era. The Soviets had not hesitated to establish their own glacis in Eastern Europe, and the United States did not take long to blend the NATO commitment into its own security desire for forward defence.

This process was reinforced by a parallel one in the Far East, where American-occupied Japan soon faced a newly successful communist government in China. The Sino–Soviet alliance and the war in Korea rapidly consolidated a 'bamboo curtain' to match the 'iron curtain' that had descended across central Europe. In both of these regions the process of overlay was firmly consolidated by the early 1950s, the Korean war in particular giving a system-wide stimulus to the militarization of superpower confrontation. Overlay meant the replacement, or sometimes the reinforcement, of the previous local patterns of antagonism and alignment by those stemming from the superpower rivalry. This realignment was always done with the support of local elites (which in Japan and Eastern Europe mostly owed their office to the overlaying power) and was not therefore an imposed event wholly against local views. What it did mean, however, was a surrender of the autonomy of local security relations and a willingness to subordinate security policy to the imperatives of the superpower confrontation.

Overlay cut a deep divide through both Europe and Northeast Asia. On either side of its boundaries military alignment swung almost totally into Cold War patterns. With the exception of China, overlay also meant the direct stationing of superpower military forces in the region. In some places this was voluntarily accepted by the local states, as in Western Europe, whereas in others, it arose from post-war occupation regimes, as in Eastern Europe, Germany and Japan. A considerable degree of political homogeneity was imposed, sometimes in line with local majority forces, as in Western Europe, and sometimes against them, as in most of Eastern Europe. Economic systems also divided, with distinct and largely self-contained patterns of finance, production, technology and trade developing within the two blocs. In Germany, Korea and China, the partitioning effect of overlay relentlessly split nations into opposing states, though again with the collaboration of divided local elites.

Western Europe mostly accepted overlay with relief, for it solved many pressing problems all at once. American aid greatly accelerated Western Europe's recovery from the economic effects of the war. American military support stood off the Russian problem, so providing military security. In combination, American military and economic support also bolstered the domestic political position of the parties of the right and centre-left, against challenges from Moscow-orientated communist parties, many of which had quite strong support because of their leading role in the struggle against fascism. Overlay also solved the German problem, partly by breaking Germany into two opposing states, and partly by subordinating the still-large West German state to a long-term American presence. Whether these arrangements, plus the shift of hegemonic threat to the Soviet Union, had permanently solved the German problem, remained a matter for debate. One lesson of the two world wars was that Germany could recover quickly and might attempt a third bid for dominance. Another was that Germany's window of opportunity to construct a regional empire, like Japan's, had passed forever. In the light of Soviet and American power, the German problem for the post-war era was now primarily one for the Germans themselves, of how to adapt to their politically divided condition.

The pattern of overlay dominated, and indeed defined, the security structure of the post-war era. With the exception of the Sino–Soviet relationship, which disintegrated within a decade of its inception, overlay held firm for more than four decades. The military dependence of Western Europe, Eastern Europe and Japan on their respective superpower allies constituted something of a mirror image, the big difference being that only in Eastern Europe did the stability of the subordinate political regimes also continue to depend on the superpower military presence. Economic linkage within both sides was strong, though in the West it evolved from dependence into interdependence and competition. By the 1980s clear signs were emerging that the overall economic performance of the West was much stronger than that in the East. Political homogeneity was also strong, though again in the West, unlike in the East, this became internally stable in nearly all of the individual countries. For Europe, the four decades of overlay meant a virtually total suspension of the indigenous security dynamics that culminated in the First and Second World Wars.

Instead, Europe was locked into the cocoon imposed by the rigid superpower rivalry. It was subordinate rather than dominant, and dependent rather than independent. Only a few exceptions such as the open rivalry between Greece and Turkey, and the prickly and independent posture of France, offered a living reminder of pre-1945 dynamics.

The image of a cocoon is appropriate, because within the wrappings of overlay a profound metamorphosis was going on within Europe. There were some amusing ironies in this process, for it was the European states and Japan that had earlier imposed overlay on most of the Third World in the form of colonization. Decolonization liberated the Third World at the same time as the Europeans and the Japanese themselves underwent a kind of overlay at the hands of the superpowers. The metamorphosis within colonial overlay produced a political system of territorial states on the European model. Within Western Europe, overlay provided a long period of calm and stability during which the lessons of the war informed the slow and painful creation of a new political order. These lessons were and still are: (1) that the old European powers are no longer world-class powers; (2) that the dilemma between fear of war and fear of defeat in Europe is so acute that general warfare is now a wholly unacceptable method of settling disputes within Europe; (3) that the economic interdependence among the European states is so great as to require sustained and institutionalized cooperation; and (4) that although the European states are still deeply distinct in societal terms, they do share a common civilization and increasingly a common fate that collectively distinguishes them from the rest of the world, including the Americans and the Russians.

Defining boundaries around European civilization is made extremely difficult by the immense world-wide impact that Europe has had. Both Russia and the United States are in some very central respects part of European civilization, as are Latin America, Australia, South Africa and, more arguably, India and Japan. But inasmuch as a common civilization reflects a common history, time and geography work to differentiate the European core from its numerous offshoots. Common fate — and the more immediate civilizational identities that it stimulates — is therefore an easier way to define the European core. In security terms, Europe's common fate as the nut in the nutcracker of superpower rivalry has been clear for forty years. The prime military threat for nearly all European states (Greece and Turkey excepted) is war between the superpowers, and it is this common threat that inspires the powerful European consensus in favour of war-avoidance. It might, of course, be argued that this consensus is as yet too weak to support a general agreement on defence cooperation. Even

Western Europe is sharply divided on defence policy. But it none the less contrasts powerfully with attitudes in 1914, when most of the major European powers entered the First World War with a kind of social-Darwinist enthusiasm that in Western and Central Europe is now found primarily among football hooligans. This change is one of historic significance for international relations in Europe. In economic, and increasingly in political terms, the European Community is defining a common future for Europe — a future characterized by democratic regimes, market economies and societal pluralism — that is now beginning to extend its reach to include non-members in Northern and Eastern Europe.

A new Western European political order has been, and still is, growing out of these lessons. In part, this order marks a change in European international society away from the unbridled balance of power behaviour of the old era and towards the war-avoidance priority of the new. In Western Europe, and haltingly though increasingly in Europe as a whole, the balance of power system has been replaced by a security community, within which none of the states now expects or prepares for a military attack by any of the others. In Western Europe, this security community has grown up within the common military structure of NATO, but is politically and societally distinct from it. In part, the new order marks a modification to the very structure of anarchy within Europe, by an exceptionally dense layer of overlapping organizations and institutions ranging from the European Community through the Western European Union to the Nordic Council. Some of these organizations, particularly the European Community, have begun to erode the basic sovereignty of the Western European states. How far this process will go is still an open question. These organizations lock the European states into a durable and expanding framework of intense consultation and cooperation. This framework does not in itself override the structure of anarchy, but it does change the balance between the logic of anarchy and the logic of interdependence (discussed in Chapter 2) increasingly in favour of the latter. Partly this change results from the reality of interdependence within Europe, and partly it results from the pressure of international anarchy: the anarchy *around* Europe creating pressure towards the formation of a European actor.

In one sense Europe is thus retaining its central political role in the international system. It is becoming the testbed for two profound and parallel experiments in the development of international relations. The first is whether and how well-established sovereign states can transcend the structure of anarchy by creating a new type of integrated structure. The second is how a set of states construct their relations so as to preserve the

essentials of the sovereignty/anarchy structure, while at the same
time adapting themselves to the heavily institutionalized and
penetrated conditions of high-density interdependence.

3.3. The Breakup of Overlay and the Post-Post-War Era

What are the security consequences of this metamorphosis? How
might the new Europe evolve as overlay disappears? How will it
relate to an international security environment in which its own
change is simply part of a larger transformation? These questions
will be taken up in detail in Part III, but it is useful to set down
now some markers stemming from the history of the European
security complex.

After the events of 1989, there can be no question that overlay
in Europe is breaking up quite rapidly. A whole array of internal
and external forces, some of them in the making for several
decades, have been pushing in that direction. The internal forces
in Western Europe included: (1) the development of a robust
Western European economy; (2) the steady consolidation of Western European political cooperation to the point where substantial
foreign policy and defence cooperation is emerging; (3) growing
public and elite dissatisfaction with the post-war arrangements;
(4) the waning of Western European communist parties; and
(5) the resurgence of West Germany as a strong, independent
political actor. The current spurt of the 1992 project is perhaps a
significant watershed in Europe's reclaiming of an independent
position in the international system. The internal forces in
Eastern Europe leading up to 1989 included: (1) the growing
demoralization, corruption and incompetence of communist
parties; (2) the loss of economic momentum; and (3) the consolidation of civil society against communist rule. During 1989, the
internal balance of forces in Eastern Europe underwent
fundamental change. From late 1989 onwards the process of
German unification bridged Eastern and Western Europe and
dealt a massive blow to overlay by removing its keystone.

The external forces furthering the breakup of overlay included:
(1) the relative decline of the United States in relation to its allies,
with possible Atlantic crises as the Americans tire of supporting
Western European defence dependence; (2) the shift of attitude in
the Soviet Union under Gorbachev and the consequent lowering
of threat perceptions in both Eastern and Western Europe; (3) the
apparent deflation of the ideological aspect of the Cold War, with
the major communist powers effectively conceding the principle
that markets, pluralism and civil society are a sounder basis for
the political economy than central command; and (4) the waning

of the bipolar power rivalry between the United States and the Soviet Union as power diffuses away from the big two.

The certainty that overlay is breaking up does not guarantee a detailed picture of what follows. Nevertheless, four big features are clear, and seem likely to be influential. First is that if the United States and the Soviet Union continue to see themselves as superpowers and if they define their own security in terms of forward defence, then they will retain strong security interests in Europe. The two 'ifs' in this proposition are both vulnerable to the steady weakening of the superpowers within the international system and to the draining of the economic substance out of their ideological confrontation. In particular, there is a big question mark over the superpower status of the Soviet Union as it enters a period of major political, economic and societal reconstruction — and possibly upheaval. But the two superpowers will remain militarily the greatest of the great powers for at least the next decade, and the institutionalized momentum of their mutual insecurity will not dissipate completely for a long time. They may well continue to see themselves as superpowers and thus retain expansive definitions of their own security requirements, for longer than others do, and will therefore continue to see Europe as central to their own security calculations. The key to transforming these perceptions will be when both superpowers begin to perceive Europe itself as more important than the presence or influence of the other in it. The most likely agent of such a transformation in perceptions is the consolidation of the European Community.

The likelihood that the EC will continue to develop as a consolidating core, attracting all of the rest of Europe, including many countries and nations that were until recently shut off by the Iron Curtain, is the second feature. This core seems unlikely to develop into a superstate for a long time, if ever. The emergent European entity will probably be composed of ever denser layers of overlapping organizations and institutions, binding still sovereign, or at least part sovereign, states into a closely woven network of standardization, consultation and cooperation. The effect will be to weaken internal barriers to exchange and movement within the Community. Some states will be more closely integrated into this core than others, since the many-layered effect will allow selective participation. Others will 'integrate' by bringing themselves unilaterally into line with core standards and procedures. Among other things, this core will institutionalize, perpetuate and extend the European security community. The question is whether this process will stall at some relatively low level of integration, leaving Europe still politically fragmented, or whether it will continue sufficiently to create a European pole in the international system.

Third is that as overlay breaks up, Eastern Europe seems likely to emerge as a source of local security problems. There are several reasons for this. After the great wave of mass uprising against the communist regimes during 1989, most Eastern European governments are new, inexperienced, still unstable in relation to their own societies and facing grave economic problems. Few of these countries, except Czechoslovakia, have an enviable tradition of indigenously generated political stability, and the full consequences of the withdrawal of Soviet political control are yet to be seen. The shift away from the certainties of rigid Soviet domination and central planning and towards pluralist politics and market economies, will create considerable hardship and disruption. All Eastern European states face major problems of economic reconstruction if they are to survive and prosper in the competitive environment of international capitalism. The danger is that they will fail to meet these challenges successfully and end up sliding into Latin American style political and economic instability. Even after 1989, they are still to some extent caught between their continued economic linkage to the Soviet Union and the attraction of the Western European core. The modalities of a difficult military disengagement and reconstruction are still to be worked out. On top of this, there are potential disputes within and between Eastern European countries that are coming to the surface as overlay recedes. Tension between Bulgaria and Turkey looks set to grow offering obvious grounds for cooperation between Greece and Bulgaria. Friction between Hungary and Romania has survived the fall of Ceauçescu, and there are potential border troubles between Romania and the Soviet Union over Moldavia. Elsewhere in the Balkans, Yugoslavia could easily be heading towards civil war and/or disintegration. The Polish–German border is still sensitive enough to require major efforts at reassurance for the Poles in the light of German unification.

That points to the fourth feature, which is the revival of the German problem as a feature of European security. The events of 1989, most particularly the dramatic breaching of the Berlin Wall, propelled the two Germanies unstoppably towards some form of unification. By mid-1990, this process was on a fast track, with East Germany effectively being absorbed into the West German economic and political structures. The inevitability of unification arose from the collapse of East Germany and West Germany's unwillingness and constitutional inability to halt the inflow of East Germans. The prospect of a unified Germany raises big political questions at several key points of the current change in Europe. For the European Community it raises the matter of, in one sense, an unexpected new entrant, with the consequence that the overall economic and political weight of Germany as the biggest power in the Community will increase even further.

For the alliance systems, and for the Soviet Union in particular, it creates excruciatingly difficult problems about the future alliance structure in Europe and particularly about how to handle the large troop deployments in East Germany that form the bulk of the Soviet Union's forward military position in Europe. Leaving them in a united Germany would be unacceptable except as a transitional arrangement. Turning the whole of Germany over to NATO could be interpreted as a major defeat for the Soviet Union, perhaps having repercussions in its unsettled domestic politics. A neutral Germany with no foreign troops would disrupt NATO and create fears of the breakup of Western European cohesion. The German question is once again on the European security agenda, but not in its pre-1945 form (fear of German military power) and not in its Cold War form (a problem for Germans). Just as the division of Germany lay at the heart of the division of Europe during the Cold War, so in the post-Cold War era the unification of Germany lay at the heart of the possible outcomes for the future security order in Europe.

Chapter 4
Conclusions: What Is Europe, and What Is Its Place in the International System?

Many aspects of Europe's security are profoundly affected by the character and structure of the international system. But at the same time the stability and character of the international system are deeply affected by what happens in Europe. At no point in this century, or the previous one, has European security been a subject confined to the interests of Europeans. The historical centrality of Europe in global security is illustrated by George Washington's late eighteenth-century advice to the United States that it should steer clear of entanglements in the Old World. To consider Europe's security has therefore been to consider its place in the international system. That rule applies also to the exercise of thinking about the future of European security. But in order to consider Europe's place in the system, one has first to have some understanding of what is meant by 'Europe'. This is not an easy matter. The discussion following will consider what the boundaries of Europe are, how the identity 'Europe' is constructed and what place Europe occupies in the international system.

4.1. What are the Boundaries of Europe?

The argument in Chapter 3 differentiated contemporary Europe from its main cultural offshoots in North America and the Soviet Union. If accepted, this results in a definition of Europe as Poland to Portugal. But the present period of change reopens many questions, of which this is one.

Wæver has argued that in security terms there are four Europes. In ascending order of size they are: one encompassing the European Community (basically Western Europe); one from Poland to Portugal (non-superpower Europe); one from the Atlantic to the Urals ('Gaullist Europe' or Gorbachev's 'Common European House'); and one that stretches effectively from Vancouver to Vladivostock (CSCE Europe) (Wæver 1989a, pp. 287–94;

Jahn *et al.*,1987, pp. 29–31). All of these Europes are in some ways real, but each of them emphasizes different elements of the geographical, cultural, historical and political package that is Europe. Each of them contains a political statement as well as a historico-geographical one. As Wæver puts it, they represent 'competing organizing principles', each with sharply different implications for European security (Wæver 1989b, p. 291).

During the Cold War, EC Europe emphasized the alienation of Eastern Europe by its absorption into the Soviet sphere after 1945. It put both Eastern Europe and the Soviet Union outside Europe. It frequently formed one pillar of the Atlanticist vision embodied in NATO, but also supported a narrower European vision centred on the evolution of the EC into a union tightly enough integrated to count as a great power. Given the dramatic crumbling of the Iron Curtain in the late 1980s, this view looks hopelessly dated. As Eastern Europe became free of the Soviet Union, the potentiality of the EC began to expand beyond Western Europe. Although the core of the EC is, and will for some time remain, Western Europe, the idea of Europe as the EC is beginning to blur into the Europe of Poland to Portugal. As it does so, it creates an image of the European security complex transformed into a single pole of power in the international system.

Europe from Poland to Portugal reasserts a European identity between the superpowers, and therefore has a post-Cold War flavour about it. It puts the differentiation of Europe from both superpowers on as equal terms as possible, in the sense that both lose position as Europe reasserts itself. But given the different nature of their overlay policies, the Soviet Union has more to lose in this Europe in two senses. Firstly, it loses control of an empire, the possession of which was important to its ideological legitimacy, its forward military defence and its whole standing as a superpower. Secondly, if this Europe coheres politically, the Soviet Union acquires a strong independent neighbour right on its border. However, both of these things are happening in an environment of massive change in both ideological and balance of power relations. These changes almost certainly make it inappropriate to judge the impact of a resurgent Europe on the Soviet Union in narrow Cold War terms.

In the Poland to Portugal view, the Soviet Union and the United States are both offshoots of European civilization, but they have left the nest and now have independent identities of their own. The United States is close to Europe in civilizational terms, but remote geographically, whereas the Soviet Union is close geographically, but more remote in civilizational terms. The United States remains strongly related to Europe in society, politics, culture and economic organization, but discernibly different and increasingly with its own history. Between 1917 and the mid-1980s, the Soviet Union moved away from Western Europe in establishing different — and opposed — societal, political and economic forms of organization, in so doing reinforcing the idea that it was not part of Europe. The depth of this difference, combined with geographical proximity, is what fuelled the Cold War. The continuation of this view is that the Soviet Union will remain a distinctive and self-regarding entity, in many ways a product of Europe, but no longer a member of the European security complex. Its geographical reach makes Europe only one of its frontiers, along with Central Asia and the Far East.

The traditional tension in the Soviet Union between Slavophiles and Westernizers seems set to continue. These place the Soviet Union clearly outside Europe, though not quite in the same category as China and other Third World countries still struggling to reconcile their own cultural identity with the need to master the West's societal, political and material accomplishments. In this sense, the Soviet Union can be seen as the least advanced of the colonial powers, but not, like Japan, having fully matched the West at its own game. The Soviet Union's post superpower role is to be a Eurasian great power, engaged on several fronts adjacent to its own borders. It has 'common houses' not only with Europe, but also with Northeast Asia, and with the Middle East. As any but the very wealthiest class of urban dweller in the late twentieth century knows, living in a common house does not necessarily denote occupation by a single family. It does make a measure of consultation, cooperation and accommodation necessary and desirable, but it does not make it advisable to take the locks off the doors. Where cultures clash under conditions of close proximity, tensions, rows and misunderstandings are almost inevitable.

One difficulty with Poland-to-Portugal Europe is the grey area comprised by Turkey and some of the western components of the Soviet Union. The Baltic republics definitely, and perhaps also the Ukraine, Armenia and Georgia, consider themselves European in a way that differentiates them from the Russians. Turkey hangs awkwardly on the periphery of Asia, not clearly part of either Europe or the Middle East, and part of the increasingly potent political divide between 'Christendom' and Islam. On the ground, and in terms of human and societal geography, there is therefore no neat division between Europe and the Soviet Union. Europe from Poland to Portugal in fact merges into the Soviet Union and the Middle East rather than being sharply demarcated from them by clear boundaries. Hidden in this Europe is, therefore, not just a threat to reduce the security sphere of the Soviet Union, but to break up the inner Russian empire.

Although the resurgence of European identities within the Soviet Union was not widely predicted, to the extent that Eastern Europe was seen as the captive of a non-European Soviet Union, the whole idea of Poland-to-Portugal Europe was latent in the Cold War: the awaited liberation of Eastern Europe would reunite a Europe distinct from the Soviet Union. Current developments have fulfilled this wish. Eastern Europe is liberated. But the process that made this possible has both changed and weakened the identity of the Soviet Union in such a way as to begin blurring the boundary between the Europe of Poland to Portugal, and that of Atlantic to the Urals. If the Soviet Union breaks up, and Russia and some of the fragments follow Eastern Europe in adopting Western forms of political economy, will there still be any need to differentiate between Europe and the Soviet Union?

Gaullist or Gorbachev Europe reflects a pre-1945 image of a European security complex including Russia, and stretching from the Atlantic to the Urals. By emphasizing the continuity of geography, it ensures that Europe includes Russia and excludes North America (May, 1984). It only accomplishes this by arbitrarily severing Western Russia from its vast Asian territories, a symbolic and wishful act that seeks to solve the Russian identity problem using the same technique that Alexander applied to the Gordian knot. This Europe asserts a political differentiation from the United States and supports a dominant Soviet position on the continent. It is therefore opposed to Atlanticist views which link Western Europe and the United States. For Western European security it poses the Russian problem. In Russian domestic politics it reflects the views of Westernizers rather than Slavophiles.

CSCE Europe is constructed by seeing Europe in terms of the whole superpower confrontation centred in Europe. Although CSCE itself grew out of attempts to transcend Cold War relationships, this Europe assumes a continuity of the engagement of the United States and the Soviet Union in European security. The CSCE rested on the recognition that the security interdependence of NATO and the Warsaw Pact required a cooperative framework embracing all of the two alliances if relationships were ever to be stabilized on a basis other than the balance of terror. It also satisfied the demand for a non-bloc based organization of sovereign states whose purpose was to look beyond the Cold War bloc structure, while still being compatible in the short to medium term with the management of the Cold War. In practice, the CSCE has been active in the areas of human rights, free movement of persons, arms control and confidence-building measures.

The functional view underlying CSCE Europe can provide a basis for a broader civilizational (rather than geographical) view of Europe encompassing both its Russian and North American offshoots. It emphasizes Poland-to-Portugal Europe's role as the prime forum for American–Soviet rivalry and its consequent centrality in the bipolar pattern of global security following the Second World War. Because its main root is in the Cold War, CSCE Europe is backward looking. But because of its potential to transcend the Cold War it is also forward looking. In this sense, it is like NATO an organization that seems destined to bridge the old and the new eras in Europe. This dual character makes it an important transitional device in the recasting of the European security order. In the process of transition the CSCE is likely to have its character and principles of operation radically changed. To the extent that CSCE becomes a key forum and machinery for a European security regime, it will almost certainly need to move away from the consensus decision-making rules that now govern, and limit, its activities.

Given the weakening position of the Soviet Union, the CSCE view of Europe may have strong attractions for Soviet reformers. Not only does it sustain Soviet superpower status, it also fits the orientation of the reformers, who represent Europeanist opinion in the perennial tug-of-war between Slavophiles and Westernizers. Like Europe from the Atlantic to the Urals, CSCE Europe thus becomes important in the domestic Soviet debate about reform and reaction, though since it also ensures the United States' engagement in Europe it does not carry the advantage so long sought by Soviet diplomacy of splitting NATO. The United States might also be attracted to this Europe, both as a way of forestalling Soviet influence over Europe, and as a way of bolstering its own flagging superpower image.

The simultaneous coexistence of these four Europes makes Europe not so much a place as an issue. This ambiguity complicates any attempt to locate Europe within the international system. If Europe is Poland to Portugal, then it can be located between East and West. If it is Vancouver to Vladivostok then it comprises the whole East–West nexus. If any one Europe looks like becoming dominant, it is Poland to Portugal, but with the addition of the grey areas further east. Europe as 'Poland to Portugal plus . . .' begins to absorb EC Europe and parts of Gaullist Europe. CSCE Europe can be rejected as not a real Europe, but itself a way of addressing Europe-as-Poland-to-Portugal's place in the system. It is not inconceivable that Europe from the Atlantic to the Urals could yet win out, but that would in itself transform the structure of the international system by merging two poles of power into one. In what follows, therefore, we will talk about Europe primarily in terms of Poland to Portugal, with an implicit possibility of 'plus . . .'.

4.2. States, Nations and Identities in Europe

Some of the most important processes dealt with in this book are transformations of political units in terms of their territorial composition and/or the nature of their political organization. This is the case in Germany, Eastern Europe, the Soviet Union and the European Community. In understanding the current changes it is therefore helpful to have some insight into the meaning of *nation* and *state*, and in particular, more specific knowledge about state formation and national identity. In relation to Europe this understanding is necessary for two reasons: (1) the process of Europeanization affects the identity and interaction of states and nations, and (2) the process can itself be seen as a kind of state and identity formation at a European level. In this context the most important question is whether states and nations will remain as closely linked as we have come to expect.

The centrality of the state to the global political order does not necessarily entail an unchanged role for national identity. Because states and nations are often seen as two sides of the same coin, an unfounded assumption about the permanence of national identity is often carried into political analysis. Taking a historical view of state and nation, asking when, how and why they arose in European political life, is one way of getting a more open-minded conception of this issue. How do state and nation link together? On what conditions do these links rest? And under what conditions could the links begin to open up? These questions will be investigated in five steps: first, the central argument about the origins of nations; second, the origin of the state; third, the making of the nation-state under different conditions in different parts of Europe; fourth the impact of these different developments on the fate of democracy; and fifth, the prospects for post-national identities in Europe.

What is Europe? It can be seen as a combination of the nations within Europe plus the formation of an overarching civilizational identity with the label 'European'. The nations are firmly on the agenda all over Europe at present. In Eastern Europe and to some extent Germany they are so because they seem to be reborn. It is widely expected that these 'new' nations will grow more powerful in the years to come. In Western Europe the national factor is crucial because of the way it interacts with the development of the EC. Can a continuation of long-established national sentiments be fused with growing Europeanness in a co-existence of multiple identities? If they are not compatible, will the nations fade and be replaced by a European super-nation, or will they strike back when really hit by European integration? At present 'Europeanness' seems to be increasing, both as a Western European consciousness within the EC, and more broadly in an all-European form extending into Eastern Europe and the Soviet Union. The East Europeans are in a difficult situation. They have no enthusiasm for a separate East or Central Europe: they want to join *the* Europe together with the West. Since they are dependent on the Western will to allow them to join, they are uncertain about their prospects for inclusion in the European institutions being constructed by the West. Paradoxically, this uncertainty occurs when the emotional sense of Europeanness is strongest in the Eastern part of Europe, where the leading slogan is: return to Europe.

It is generally assumed that all this must be a question about *identities*: national versus European. It is, however, a relatively recent idea that states are, or should be, closely related to the identity of their peoples. Anne Knudsen (1989, p.4f., our translation) expresses this very precisely:

Of course, people of this world have always been different. They have spoken differently from those on the other side of the strait, the mountain or the river; they have eaten differently, dressed differently, believed in other gods or saints, sung different songs and told their children different stories when they put them to bed. Until about the time of the French revolution this, however, had nothing to do with politics. The King was completely indifferent to how people spoke, ate or dressed so long as they paid their taxes and their tithe. One could exchange duchies and whole provinces as if they were farms and that was the reason why civil servants in Denmark spoke German and in Russia French without a living soul finding this the least odd. Nor did the early considerations of international law pay attention to cultural or linguistic identitites. Everyone was obliged to obey his — God given — authorities unless these authorities ruled tyrannically, i.e. completely unreasonably and illogically.

After the French revolution, when royal power had lost its divine reference, there was a need for transcendental values to back up state power. This was when national identities appeared on the scene. Nationalism served not only to legitimize the state, but also to provide a new context and identity for individuals otherwise disorientated by the loss of their traditional and local sources of identity (Habermas, 1987, p.165; Nipperdey, 1986, pp.142–5, 150). Once this identity shift occurred, control over popular processes of identification became an important source of power (cf. Carlsnaes, 1986, pp. 140–4, 164f.; Eckstein, 1982).

Of course, national sentiments were present much earlier. In England one could talk of national identity since the fifteenth century (Dyson, 1980, p. 38) or maybe even the fourteenth (Seton-Watson, 1977). But this identity was not bound up with political power. Prior to the mid-eighteenth century sovereign states rested on principles of legitimation different from national identity and not dependent on strong ideas of a nation or a people. Ethnicity as a political force is a recent development: in England unity under one monarch had been achieved some 500 years before nationalism came into play as a political force. The link between power and identity, between legitimacy and cultural soul, is thus historically specific, rather than being a universal political truth that stretches across all time. In modern Europe, forging a link between national identity and political legitimacy became necessary because the development of the state (its organizational and economic expansion, and its political stability) could not have been sustained without a shift from elite to mass-based political foundations. Those states that made the shift quickly gained a decisive competitive advantage over those that did not. In reality (i.e. power terms), there was no choice once the French Revolution had opened the door. One of the decisive, and still open, questions of the day is to what extent the link between national identity and state power remains the essential foundation of political organization.

It is not necessary to present either the history or the theory of European state formation here. Suffice it to recall that in late medieval Europe pressure was building up towards the concentration of political power on the basis of territorial exclusivity. Many things fed into this movement: pressure from emerging capitalism, the increasing density of the European international system and the anarchic logic of competition and power balancing. The result was the creation of centralized states based on absolute monarchy, and territorial exclusivity and continuity (Elias, 1983; Herz, 1957). Thus evolved the modern sovereign state based on territorial exclusivity and centralization of legitimate violence. At the same time the idea emerged that the state was responsible for, or related to, the economy contained within it (Foucault, 1979). Up until that time the concept of economy had retained its original reference to households. Not until modern times do state and society become embedded in the economy (Polanyi,1944).

Several modern states were formed before the Peace of Westphalia in 1648, including England, France, Spain and some in Scandinavia. But it took some time for the nature of this transformation to gain recognition for states and jurists to acknowledge what had happened and to adjust their behaviour and understanding to an international system based on sovereign states (Holzgrefe, 1989). Martin Wight has argued that the state system was born in the early fifteenth century, but full realisation of it was delayed for 200 years. Thus: 'At Westphalia the states-system does not come into existence: it comes of age' (Wight, 1977, p. 152).

At this stage one could not yet talk of nation-states. The nation is essentially a modern phenomenon and does not make much sense when it exists as a purely passive idea, not yet articulated. But when the project of nation-building started, some states had better preconditions for building nation-states than others. Three categories existed. First were those such as France, England and Spain that possessed the immediate pre-conditions for nation-building: they were relatively homo-geneous in language, ethnicity and geography. Even so, this ethnic coherence should not be called a nation before it acquired political self-consciousness. It is misleading to picture France as a nation before the project of nation-building. To do so overlooks the hard work done in homogenizing into Frenchmen people who did not generally think of themselves as French, but instead had local and functional identities. This process is expressed in the famous book title: *Peasants into Frenchmen* (Weber, 1976).

The second group were those such as Germany and Italy, where several political units shared the same ethnic basis: where one ethnic group was covered by several smaller states or duchies. The third group comprised those multi-national empires such as Austria–Hungary and Russia which had no preconditions for forming a nation-state out of the existing political unit. The Habsburgs did remarkably little to attempt nation-building, which meant that their empire rested on a pre-modern form of legitimization (cf. Kissinger, 1957). For both of these groups, the ideas of nation and state existed in tension. Sub-national states faced the pull to dissolve themselves into a larger entity, and multi-nation states faced the threat of dismemberment into their constituent nations.

These different circumstances led to different concepts of the nation. In the second category, where the nation did not have a political correlate, strong ideas were developed about the nation resting in the common language and culture. An early tendency was to see the nation as more important than states (Herder), but eventually the nation-state became the ultimate goal, the culmina-tion of the nation (Fichte, Hegel). The romantic nationalism of the nation-state eventually became influential all over Europe, but it had a much deeper impact in Germany and in Eastern Europe. In the West it was counterbalanced by a less collectivist, more individualist, conception of politics, in which legitimacy rested more with individual consent (social contract) than collective identity (Finkielkraut, 1987). In this more republican approach, the nation-state was primarily characterized by the participation of individuals together forming a collective will.

. Romantic nationalism stressed that all understanding was necessarily limited to a certain culture, and culture was seen as national. This conception of natural cultural communities being necessarily national is often continued in contemporary theory. National cultures certainly are real, but other cultural communities and differences are too. States have mobilized national sentiments at crucial moments, but it is an open question whether this is still necessary, or indeed possible, under contemporary conditions. It is therefore important not to build into political theories unquestioned predispostions about the links between nation and state. Instead, one needs to study the diversity of possible relationships, both in the past, and under present conditions.

These different developments of nations and nationalisms will be pursued further below in the sections on Eastern Europe and Germany (Chapters 5 and 6). But before we return to the main question of this section — the nature of the European identity, and its relationship to current national identities — we need to understand how the fate of democracy was influenced by regional variations in nation-formation.

The ideas of peoples' sovereignty, liberalism, democracy and 'rule by countrymen' developed in most parts of Europe mainly in the nineteenth century. What type of state this idea unfolded in (nation-state, part-nation state, or multi-nation state) made a major difference to its fate. The options are shown in Figure 4.1.

The Germans (as well as the Italians) did not form a nation-state in early European history. When romantic nationalism reached the Germans, in the last century, it did not find an already formed nation-state, and the consequences of this are explored in Chapter 6.

In the case of Eastern Europe the experience was not uniform. Poland is in some ways parallel to Germany (and Italy) with a long-standing national identity unfolding most of the time in a divided nation, and often under foreign rule. In other ways Poland is close to the Western type in actually forming an early state (1320–1795, with some kind of Polish kingdom dating back to 966). National consciousness was formed during the time of division, i.e. with the struggle for national liberation. The Poles were to become an exception among the many nations in Europe in losing their independence. The Polish state lost its independence late, at the end of the eighteenth century, and 'its political subjection coincided with the period of liquidation of the feudal system and the creation of the modern nation and society' (Halicz, 1982, p.10). The link between liberal democratic ideals and national self-determination was strong in most of the Polish move-

Figure 4.1 - State, Nation and Democracy in European Political Evolution

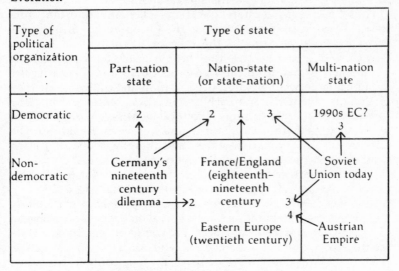

Type of political organization	Type of state		
	Part-nation state	Nation-state (or state-nation)	Multi-nation state
Democratic	2	2 1 3	1990s EC? 3
Non-democratic	Germany's nineteenth century dilemma →2	France/England (eighteenth– nineteenth century 3 4 Eastern Europe (twentieth century)	Soviet Union today Austrian Empire

1 = 'normal' development in the eighteenth–nineteenth century
2 = the three possibilities for Germany (beside staying non-democratic and divided). These will be dealt with in Chapter 6.
3 = present Soviet dilemma
4 = the route taken by most of Eastern Europe in the late eighteenth century and early twentieth century when the empires fall apart.

ment, at least until independent statehood was achieved. The famous slogan 'For Our Freedom and Yours', as well as the active participation of Poles in liberation struggles around the globe, signified a close link between the Polish struggle and the universalist aspect of nationalism (Mastny,1989, p. 14ff.; Seton-Watson, 1977, pp. 120–30).

Most of the rest of East-Central and Southeast Europe reached their present relationship to nationality and statehood along a different track. Their experience was defined by conception inside eighteenth — and early nineteenth — century empires. Their dramatic birth, partly causing and partly caused by the death of these empires, was always being manipulated as a part of great power politics in Europe. As the Austrian and Ottoman empires dissolved, and the Russians sometimes retreated, strong national movements developed. But since these neither grew out of continuous, old nations as in western Europe, nor took the form of joining together parts of a nation, as in Germany and Italy, they often led to competing organizations. These liberation struggles were based in quasi-mythic concepts of the nation, as in the case of Germany, and these concepts provided the ultimate argument for defining the pattern of the successor states.

These seemingly remote questions play an important role today. They do so in part because the European nations are still decisive actors, as seen in the case of Germany and Eastern Europe, and in part because they bear crucially on the process of quasi-state formation in the European Community. What is the relationship between political organization and collective identity in the late twentieth and early twenty-first century? Must the formation of a larger European political identity and organization necessarily take the same form and route as it did for the nineteenth-century nation-states, and thereby necessarily clash head on with the still robust European nation-states?

Jürgen Habermas amongst others has argued that in Western Europe we are on our way to 'post-national state identity' (Habermas, 1987) and that the Germans present a particularly instructive case. Elaborating on the liberal individualist conception of nation (as a social contract), he wants to emphasize state identity as a choice for democracy and for a conscious, active, relationship to one's own history. In this context he wants German unification to be realized not through the back door (paragraph 23 of the constitution, allowing accession by individual Länder) but through a national referendum (paragraph 146) to indicate that there is nothing necessary or objective about unification. It is a choice made by today's Germans and not a historical necessity arising from the existence of a primordial nation (Habermas, 1990). Before 1989, the Germans had gone further than most others in the direction of developing a 'patriotism of the constitution' (Sternberger 1990), and this should be continued in order to stress the universalist dimensions of the democratic, constitutional state.

As will be shown in Chapter 6, this kind of thinking was not influential enough to prevent the reconnection in Germany of cultural identity and political identification. This does not detract from the relevance of the general argument about recognizing other political possibilities than nationalism for constructing collective organizations. In the West, it is increasingly noticed that the modern states are *en route* to becoming multi-ethnic, and much less 'nationally' homogeneous. William McNeill has argued that this tendency indicates that the homogenizing nation-state was actually only an episode in the broader human history of specialization and pluralism (McNeill, 1986). The basis for this denationalization of statehood must be the development in each person of a multitude of identities. In fact we are often organized politically in relation to many of our identities: social, occupational, sexual, ideological, generational, cultural, as well as national.

We do not expect to live in a community where everone shares the same cultural code. Some see this as part of the post-modern condition. It is not necessary to live in a monocultural space, which was the idea behind national culture.

In a multi-cultural society national identity is one among several points of identification, not the basic code to everything else as it is in romantic nationalism. There is admittedly a certain tendency even within the post-modern condition to see cultures as basic, and as relatively closed and impenetrable. Note for example the extensive growth in the study of 'cultures': company cultures, computer culture, subcultures, youth cultures, sexual cultures, and so forth. These are, however, no longer seen as national systems. We are so many other things as well as 'national', and we do not expect political organizations to overlap all the communities we belong to. This diversification of identity points towards an increasing possibility in Western Europe of organizing political units more pragmatically, from practical political and economic considerations, instead of from fixed national ones.

This development can be seen as the second phase in the release that began when traditional, static societies disintegrated, and the resultant emptiness of identities was first filled by the large community of the nation (Aron, 1970, pp.11–14; Walker, 1989). On the other hand there is also a certain fear in Western Europe that the impulses from the reborn nations in the East will lead to a revitalization of nationalism in the West. The question is a philosophical one. Will the disappearance of older absolutes necessarily lead to a continued search for new absolute sources of meaning where the nation will either endure, be contested by new social ideologies, or be overturned by new territorially-based state identities (Europe/EC)? Or, on the contrary, will there be a gradual evolution in the direction of human acceptance of indeterminacy, overlapping identities and absence of teleological meaning? In the latter case it is much more likely that European identities and organizations can take on an increasing role without overturning or provoking the nations.

4.3. Europe's Place in the International System

The question of what place Europe occupies in the international system sets the framework for analysis of the future of European security. Since the Second World War, the structure of the international system has been bipolar, and Europe's position has been that of principal front line in the forward-defence spheres of the superpowers. The East–West rivalry has been the dominant context of European security, dividing the continent into two sharply separate social, political, economic and military systems. As argued above, the makings of this situation began as early as 1917, with the Russian Revolution and the intervention of the United States in the First World War. Within the overarching pattern of the East–West Cold War lay three sub-patterns:

(1) East–East, comprising relations between the Soviet Union and its European allies;
(2) West–West, comprising relations among the Western European states, and between them and the United States; and
(3) the German problem, comprising the frozen, but unresolved, relationship of state and national structures in Germany strung across the Cold War line.

The East–West framework began to collapse during the late 1980s, and as it did so, each of these three sub-patterns began to assume more importance as a determinant of the post-Cold War security order in Europe. Since these sub-patterns now contain the major dynamics of change, the three chapters in Part II will examine each in some depth.

Within the Cold War context East–East relations were framed by the Warsaw Pact, COMECON, and the right claimed by the Soviet Union and exercised on several occasions, to intervene in the domestic politics of its allies in order to protect socialism (the Brezhnev Doctrine). The result was an extremely rigid and lopsided set of relations in which Soviet military forces doubled as imperial garrisons as well as providing forward defence against the West. Up until the mid-1980s, only Stalinist heresies were tolerated, as in Romania (and in Asia, North Korea). All attempts at more liberal versions of socialism were crushed. But from the mid-1980s, the Soviet Union under Mikhail Gorbachev itself unexpectedly began to lead a programme of reform, one consequence of which was to destroy the idea of orthodoxy on which East–East relations had previously rested. This unleashed a flood of changes, the magnitude and character of which would have invited ridicule had they been forecast even as late as 1987. To have said then that within three years West Germany would be offering to pay the Soviet Union to keep its troops in East Germany would have seemed silly rather than visionary.

By mid-1990, Eastern Europe seemed secure in its political and economic detachment from the Soviet Union. Arrangements for Soviet military withdrawal were under way in Hungary and Czechoslovakia, and large reductions were being negotiated for East Germany. The Soviet Union was itself undergoing major societal and political change. By mid-1990, it was clear that the Cold War order in Eastern Europe had collapsed completely. But it was not clear at the time of writing what kind of East–East (or indeed East–West European) relations would succeed the old order. All of the East was moving pell-mell towards the West, but it seemed highly likely that its reception would not be uniform. A few, notably East Germany, would quite quickly make it into the EC. Others, probably including Czechoslovakia, Hungary and Poland, could win associate status. But it was far from clear how the Soviet Union itself would be received, the outcome depending both on the success or failure of the Soviet revolution, and on the success or failure of European integration. East–East as a meaningful category was shrinking rapidly to residual status, perhaps incorporating only some economic links, some assurances about military security and some traditional alliances such as that between Russia and Bulgaria.

West–West relations within the Cold War context began with a heavy economic and military dependence of the Western Europeans on the United States. They evolved steadily towards something approximating economic parity and a lesser, though still considerable, degree of military dependence. This relationship has involved two separate but linked dynamics, one concerning the long process of integration in Europe centred on the EC, and the other concerning the evolution of the relationship between 'Europe' (which was, and in some cases still is, an entity sometimes more supposed than real) and the United States. As Europe strengthened, burden-sharing in the struggle against the Soviet Union became a central issue, as increasingly did differences of opinion about the character and extent of the Soviet threat. Within Europe the issue is, and remains, integration: how much, how fast, how wide, in what sectors, and with what institutions? The 1992 project marked a great leap forward after a longish period of stagnation. Inasmuch as this leap constructed a quite solid image of 'Europe' (Western) in the eyes of those outside the EC, it has been an important input into the breakdown of the East–West framework. That success now faces the EC with hard questions about what sort of entity it wants and needs to become in a post-Cold War international system.

In the West more broadly, Europe, and especially the EC core, has emerged as one of three major centres of finance and industry within the OECD grouping. The older Atlanticist vision placed Europe in a twin-pillar relationship with the United States. The newer, and ever more dominant trilateralist image, has Japan as the third pillar in a global democratic-capitalist triangle. In the Cold War context this three-pillar arrangement has been viewed as a loose alliance system with the United States as the linchpin. But as Soviet power declines and the ideological struggle wanes, it is increasingly relevant to see it not so much as an alliance, but rather as a strong security community. By convening themselves as a group which has no expectation or fear of military attack among its members, the major centres of capitalist power have constructed a new type of great power alignment, and one that could give them a commanding position in the international system for the foreseeable future.

West–West security issues in this context centre on the dialectic between cooperation and competition among the major capitalist powers. Cooperation has been sustained since 1945 partly by the economic hegemony of the United States, partly by the shared capitalist fear of communism in general and its linkage to state power in the Soviet Union in particular, and partly by the logic of increasing interdependence. As the two superpowers, their rivalry and the political potency of communism all decline, the first two of these supports lose their strength. The Leninist prediction is that, other things being equal, rivalry should dominate capitalist relations, and this view has contemporary echoes (Kaldor, 1978). The security question is whether interdependence alone can sustain cooperation in the absence of both hegemony and a common communist/Soviet threat. If it can, then West–West security questions amount to little more than assuring the balance between economic cooperation and competitiveness: not easy, but not a crisis question by security standards. If it cannot, then major transformations towards neo-mercantilist positions have to be considered. Such moves carry very considerable political and military baggage. They could eventually destroy the very idea of a distinctive West–West context, effectively merging it with the East–West one into a new global synthesis of multipolar bloc rivalry (Buzan, 1991a, ch. 6).

At the centre lies the German problem, the skeleton in the closet of Cold War stability. The question of how the German nation relates to a state structure has been around for a long time. For several centuries up to 1870, it was a problem for Germans, resting on the fact that Germany had maintained a highly fragmented, and therefore highly vulnerable, medieval political structure, while most of the rest of the European nations had consolidated themselves into nation-states. From 1870 to 1945 the problem was transformed into one for the whole European balance of power. The successful unification of Germany quickly created a great power that was too big for its neighbours to live with comfortably, but too small to dominate the continent as a superpower. As discussed in Chapter 3, the tension caused by this development generated two world wars which destroyed Europe's long pre-eminence over the international system. From 1945 to 1989, the German problem was again one for Germans, which was how to live with a strong sense of nation, in a system that divided Germany into separate states on either side of a highly militarized ideological confrontation. So long as overlay prevailed, there was no escape from this deeply uncomfortable situation. The Germans had to accept it as the price of their failed attempts in 1914–18 and 1939–45 to dominate Europe by force. Within this situation, East Germany was faced with the particularly difficult problem of how to legitimize itself as a distinct state. The events of 1989 quite literally knocked down the wall between the two Germanies, thereby once again returning the German problem to the European stage. How, and how fast, Germany is to be unified, how it is to relate to the EC, and how NATO is to adjust to a powerful process of integration that has already dissolved both its front line and the alliance system of its erstwhile enemy, are the key questions of round four of the German problem.

These processes of change simultaneously redefine both Europe and the structure of the international system. As the system shifts away from bipolarity towards a more multipolar distribution of power Europe's centrality to the pattern of global security wanes. The fading of the Cold War reduces its ideological and strategic importance to the superpowers, who are anyway becoming too weak to sustain their forward power projections on the post-1945 scale. The meaning is draining out of the whole idea of a Europe positioned between East and West. At a minimum, some new version of the European regional security complex will come into being. At a maximum, Europe will consolidate into a pole of power. It looks increasingly likely that, in some form, Europe will become one of the poles in the new more diffuse international system. If this happens, it will be an entirely new experience. During the last 350 years, European powers have either dominated the system (up to 1941), or been dominated by it (after 1945). In the post-Cold War era, Europe looks set to become just one centre of power among several. Rather than dominating or being dominated by other powers, it will simply create its own space between them. The security dynamics of such a system are hard to predict in detail, but it is unlikely to develop the sustained and highly focused hostility that marked the Cold War. On past record, a multipolar system should have more flexible and varied relational patterns among the great powers. But we have never lived in a multipolar system in which most of the great powers commanded nuclear weapons and in which a genuinely global diffusion of power was in operation. Europe is unlikely to be the centre of attention in such a system. Its security will depend more on its own internal construction than on the rivalries of outside powers, though the dictates of geography and history mean that the United States and the Soviet Union will continue to be the two powers of most concern.

Both the East–West and multipolar frameworks for defining Europe's place in the international system generate a heavily 'Northern' perspective on European security. What about North–South? Until the late nineteenth century, the South was a primary forum for European security. Colonial rivalries played a central role in the overall European balance of power. But with the rise of the German problem, South issues gave way to the sustained crisis of the European 'Civil War'. The ending of that war in collapse, overlay and decolonization kept the South at the margins of European security concerns. Although not negligible, North–South is the least pressing of Europe's security contexts at the moment. The military and political, and to a considerable extent even economic, issues it raises pale into insignificance when compared with those arising in the East–West and multipolar contexts.

As a security problem North–South is likely to manifest itself much more in local form than as a dominant global axis. Across the Mediterranean and in the relationship between the United States and Mexico one can talk about North–South problems that threaten to become local security problems for the North. But at the overall level of global politics 'the South' seems to be in retreat as a challenger. This retreat is simultaneous with, and not unconnected to, that of the East. East–West rivalry opened up political space for the South and gave it leverage on the West. The collapse of the East leaves the West in a virtual monopoly position in terms of legitimate political ideology, and consequently much less vulnerable to the criticism and moral and political manipulation of the South. As a political programme built on guilt power and mass, and expressed for example in the demand for a 'New International Economic Order', the South did make a claim on the West which was from time to time seen as a threat that would sooner or later have to be accommodated. This is now less and less the case. The 'South' as a position and a programme seems to be disintegrating and, like the 'East', conceding victory to the 'West'. An important part of this change is the decreasing strength of *tiersmondisme* in the first world. The Third World critique was, for more than a decade by definition progressive and fashionable in the dominant cultural milieux of the West. But the combination of increasing Europeanism, belief in 'Western' values and models, and rising contempt for the failures and savageries of much of the South's performance, mean that the Third World has lost this position, increasingly sinking into the intellectual, as well as the economic, periphery.

In North–South perspective, Europe is one of the poles within the North, but one with a historical link to the South because of its many connections from colonial days. These connections make

Europe a particular target, though by no means a unique one, for some kinds of threats arising from the Third World, most notably terrorism, migration and demands for both economic aid and restructuring of economic relations. In other respects, Europe shares with the South, as well as with the other parts of the North, a whole set of security problems concerning such planetary issues as disease, environment, trade and debt. Since decolonization, Europe has played a sharply decreased role in the military and political affairs of the Third World. Although France has retained a significant role in Africa and Britain still maintains the Commonwealth, the Europeans have mostly been content to leave such matters to the superpowers. As the superpowers decline, it remains to be seen whether European 'high politics' security perspectives expand back into the Third World in such a way as to make Europeans once again active in these sectors. Such speculation is highly dependent on outcomes in the East–West and West–West contexts, and for that reason will only feature secondarily in this study.

PART II - THE BREAKUP OF THE POST-WAR ORDER

Chapter 5

The East:
Reform, Revolution
or Disintegration?

Until the revolts and radical changes in the late 1980s, post-war Eastern Europe was neither stable nor secure, though it was often seen as both by those observing it from the West. Its instability was demonstrated by the repeated social uprisings, military invasions or threat of them, citizens' attempts to flee the countries, and the governments' expulsion of those involved in activities contrary to state security. It was by definition not secure because of its governments' vulnerability to activities ranging from telling political jokes, through smuggling of bibles and ordinary books, and taking part in lectures at 'flying universities', to secret screenings of forbidden films, or any meeting of more than three people. For more than forty years under the façade of communist uniformity, this region was constantly exposed to political tremors. The reason why these tremors were seldom noticed in the West as signs of instability is to be found more in the West than in the East. At the root of this blindness was the fact that Soviet control in Eastern Europe was a keystone to the Cold War stability and security of Europe as a whole. The stability of the Iron Curtain was the main guarantee of war avoidance between the superpowers.

With the rise of Solidarity in Poland during 1980–1 an avalanche was set loose. Yet for nearly a decade it looked as if this too had been checked by establishment forces, and that only scattered effects would result. But then in the Autumn/Winter of 1989–90 the East European 'refolution' (a term coined by Ash, 1989a, to indicate non-violent reform processes leading to changes in political structure so radical as to be revolutionary), previously limited to Poland and Hungary, spread rapidly to the rest of the Soviet Union's Warsaw Pact allies. Quite suddenly, both the East European ruling elites and the West were presented with radical uprisings which went much further than just demands for political and economic reform.

The history of the East European populations' demand for constitutional reform is long. It reaches back to East Germany in 1953, Poland and Hungary in 1956, Czechoslovakia in 1968 and also Poland in the same year, Poland again in 1970 and 1976, and again in 1980–1. These are just the major uprisings. Minor oppositional movements and their suppression were a continuous background feature. Although the demonstrating workers and intellectuals alike were denounced as hooligans, counter-revolutionaries and suchlike, their demands were relatively modest. They did not ask for the whole system to be changed, just for it to be made more tolerable. Their political slogans were summarized under the headings of 'socialism with a human face' (Czechoslovakia) or 'we are the true socialists' (Solidarnosc). At the economic level they were often labelled as 'market oriented reforms within a socialist economic system' (Brus, 1973, 1975; Tromer, 1989). The current East European changes reach much further. The Poles are heading for a capitalist economic system, while the Czechoslovaks and Hungarians are contemplating wide-ranging political reforms.

The end result of this revolutionary process in Eastern Europe is expected to be more freedom for individuals and more communication across the East–West border. But it will also produce immense internal problems of change, and a period of less predictability in international relations. In some ways it will result in a more unstable region and a less secure Europe (Hassner, 1989). Yet this new and possibly more unstable Europe has to be compared with its predecessor, which was not a stable region, but one kept in stalemate by the overlay of the Cold War. From the point of view of European security it was the political and military machinery that generated the 'stability' of the Cold War that was becoming a threat. This threat arose not only from the dangers of the military confrontation in Europe, but also from other developments, not least the environmental situation. In the long run, it generated growing internal tensions between government and society in both Western and Eastern Europe. Until the autumn of 1989 it could be said that the major changes in East–West relations took place at the societal level, pushing for changes at the system and state level (Hassner, 1989).

During recent years Europe has ceased to be a purely geographical concept. It has come to have social, political and civilizational meaning as well. Having been excluded from this 'Europe' for forty years because their states failed to establish a democratic political system (Vajda, 1988), the populations of Eastern Europe are now rallying around West European democratic and liberal ideas. Thus, despite the unrest that is often interpreted as a danger to the European peace order, in respect of values Western

Europe is in the fortunate position of having become more, not less, secure. The East European reforms contribute to the strength and stability of West European political values, allowing Western Europe to stand in the victorious position of the stronger elder brother. The paradoxical situation is that this security has been achieved not through stability but by means of change. The resultant dilemma is that the increased level of security these changes bring might result in a picture full of turmoil, overthrown power elites, rebellious masses, crumbling military systems and a situation characterized by growing chaos and insecurity.

This chapter deals with what used to be 'the Soviet Union and Eastern Europe'. 'Eastern' then became 'Central' Europe, and further questions were put to both the terms 'union' and 'soviet' in the Soviet Union. The political and economic structures that were laid down forty and seventy years ago are likely to affect these states' direction and speed of development and reconstruction for several years to come. The societal, cultural and political level of development in the individual countries affects the shape and coherence of their process of revolution. It will also determine the internal coherence of these societies and their strength to survive the coming processes of change. This chapter starts by introducing the reader to the political, economic and societal structures of the Soviet-type society. It then shows how these structures worked in the Soviet Union and Eastern Europe, and the effect of this history on the present problems and prospects of economic and political reform. The concluding section tries to stipulate possible Western reactions to current and future reforms and also to their possible negative spin-offs in economic and political crises.

5.1. The Common Features of Soviet-Type Societies

Political parties in Eastern Europe and in the Soviet Union are looking to the West for models to replace the collapsing Soviet-type systems. The processes that are unfolding can be viewed as a transformation of the Soviet-type systems through a process of Westernization. In this transformation four main factors are in play: the legacy of the Stalinist past, the structures and methods of the Soviet-type system, the process of Westernization, and the revival of national-cultural identities. Whether the outcome in the different East European states and the Soviet Union will be reform, revolution or disintegration depends on both the interplay among these factors, and the policies of the West (Z, 1990; Schöpflin, 1990; Staniszkis, 1989b; Stalin, 1954–5).

The Stalinist ideology — the Stalinist model

A common feature of the polities in Eastern Europe is that they
were subjected to an initial transformation according to the mould
developed in the Soviet Union under Stalin. This mould reflected
the logic of Stalinist ideology, itself a development of Leninism
(Stalin, 1954–5; Schöpflin, 1988). According to one definition,
ideology is composed of four elements: 'a philosophy of history, an
analysis of the present stage of man's development in the light of
that philosophy, a projection of that analysis into the future, and
an analysis of the human actions necessary to hasten the inevitable outcome predicted in the projection of events into the
future' (Garstin, 1954, p. 3). This definition certainly fits Stalinism.

The Stalinist conception of history was deterministic. As in
physics, history developed according to specific laws. The development of humanity had passed from primitive communism,
through slave-owning society and feudalism, to capitalism. The
next step would inevitably be a move from capitalism to communism. As capitalism became the prevailing socio-economic form
during the nineteenth century, communism came on the agenda
of history. The move from capitalism to communism would be a
move from a qualitatively and materially inferior social system to
a qualitatively and materially superior one. Capitalism was
doomed to recurrent crises and would bring about still deeper
poverty for the masses. The internal dynamics of the capitalist
states would inevitably lead to war.

Contrary to this, communism would mean material abundance
and equality, the disappearance of problems of nationality and
eternal peace between states. The social force that would bring
this transformation about was the working class, the class
exploited by the capitalist system. By conquering state power, the
working class could establish the dictatorship of the proletariat
and put all the means of production at the disposal of the state.
This would make it possible to develop production and the society
in a conscious and planned way towards the goal of communism.
However, in order to be successful in their enterprise, the
working class needed the leadership of the communist party to
accelerate the inevitable march of history. As humanity was
developing according to specific laws it was considered possible to
establish a science that could discover these laws. The name of
this science was Marxism–Leninism. By mastering Marxism–
Leninism, the communist party had the ability to accelerate the
historical processes and thus to speed up the development from
the bad past to the bright future. The communist project was thus
basically a future project.

Only the party was considered able to master this science. The individual's ability to master the science was considered to be higher in direct proportion to his or her rank in the party. The communists conceived themselves as being the scientists and generals heading the attack on the old, and as being the architects of the new. This theory justified centralizing of power within the party, and the subordination of the polity to the steering and control of the party. From the monopoly on truth the party derived the legitimacy to wield absolute power. The communist world view also gave the party a rather free hand regarding the choice of means permitted to achieve the goal. After all, when the yardstick was the bright future of humankind, the loss of 6–11 million lives during the collectivization in the Soviet Union (Z, 1990, p. 310) could not be considered too much. From the monopoly on truth the communist party also derived the legitimacy to judge what was right and what was wrong, who were enemies and who were friends. Thus, when the 10 million strong independent Polish trade union, Solidarnosc, took to the streets in the 1980s, they were defined as 'hooligans' by the communist press and thereby liable to punishment. This is despite the fact that, according to communist theory, the working class is the leading social force and that the vast majority of the members of Solidarnosc were workers. Being the masters of Marxism–Leninism, only the party had the right to judge its own performance.

With the take-over of state power in Russia by the communist party, the struggle between the two systems, the capitalist and the communist, assumed a new dimension. Previously, the fight was waged within states between contending political forces. Now, the resources of a state could be mobilized for the international struggle, thus linking up the domestic and the international arenas. The global communist objective was to try to change the international balance of power by weakening the capitalist states and strengthening the communist ones. Under Stalin this analysis was fused with great Russian nationalism: the Soviet Union being the first socialist state, the Russian communist party was considered the most advanced and therefore entitled to rule over the communist parties of other states. On this basis, Stalin developed the hierarchical logic of Marxism–Leninism to its logical conclusion. Being the head of the party and therefore the grand master of Marxism–Leninism, he opted for aquiring absolute power. His instruments were his personal secretariat (Rosenfeldt, 1978, 1980) and the secret police. These were used to coerce and liquidate his opponents within the party and the society, and to steer the development of the state.

Control over the party and the instruments of coercion were

regarded as crucial both for control of the state and for defence against inherently aggressive capitalism. Consequently, one of the first steps in imposing the Stalinist model on other states was to gain control of the party, the military and the police. Later came control over all other elements of the state apparatus. All independent non-communist parties and organizations were destroyed. In their place, communist mass organizations were created to serve as transmission belts between the communist party and the masses (Tomaszcewski, 1989, pp. 17–210; Hankiss, 1989, pp.1–7). By establishing command and control over all spheres of society, including the private life of the subjects, it was considered possible to accelerate the advent of the communist future. Considering this very expanded role of the state, it is no wonder that an overgrown state apparatus has been a characteristic feature of Soviet-type societies.

The economy also reflected the emphasis on accelerating the advent of the communist future, which was to be obtained through rapid growth via enforced accumulation. In order to achieve this goal, priority was given to heavy industry (coal, steel, energy generation, heavy metallurgical manufactures and, later, chemicals). Emphasis on heavy industry was also motivated by the desire to boost military capacity, seen as necessary because of the perceived inherently aggressive nature of capitalism. A further reason for this priority was the desire to expand the number of workers in heavy industry, as they were considered to be the social basis for the communist project. Consumption, be it of consumer goods, agricultural products or services, was looked upon as a necessary evil, to be kept as low as possible in order to maximise resources for investment and defence. In order to control the economy, all means of production were nationalized or collectivized. This happened in the Soviet Union between 1917 and 1937, in Eastern Europe between 1944 and 1949. Political control of the economy was to be ensured via a centralized planning apparatus which was to fix investment priorities, prices, wages, and the input and output of all the various production units.

The Soviet-type system

The death of Stalin in 1953 triggered uprisings in East Germany and Poland and disturbances in many places. This was partly due to the stark suppression and Russification of the Stalinist system, and partly due to the fact that the standard of living had deteriorated considerably during Stalin's last years. Stalin's successors, Nikita Khrushchev and, after 1964, Leonid Brezhnev, tried to reform the Stalinist system. The powers of the secret police were curbed, and attempts were made to provide more consumer goods. The stark Russification stopped, and more leeway was given for local communist leaders to use nationalism in order to gain support for the system. But the basic features — the one-party system, the monopoly on information and the ultimate control by the Soviet Union — were never allowed to be questioned. If necessary, the Soviet military was used to quell uprisings, as in Hungary in 1956 and in Czechoslovakia in 1968.

Under these influences, a post-Stalinist political and economic structure emerged everywhere except in Romania. The actual working of these Soviet-type systems was far from the Stalinist ideal of having complete, centralized political control over all spheres of society. The polity that emerged was a strange hybrid of Stalinist and post-Stalinist elements, whose actual functioning contradicted the main tenets of the Stalinist ideology. It is to this hybrid that the terms 'Soviet-type system' and 'Soviet-type economy' apply, designating the contradictory elements of the polities in Eastern Europe and the Soviet Union as they actually existed before the 1989–90 revolutions. These terms are used here instead of terms which only refer to the self-understanding of the communist parties, such as 'socialist people's democracy', 'communist state' or 'centrally-planned economies'.

The use of the term 'Soviet-type system' does not imply that these states were identical. One crucial difference between the Soviet Union and the Eastern European states was that the former was the hegemonic power in relation to the latter. Another was the different mix and weight of the four basic features in each country according to its historical and geographical attributes. The Stalinist legacy, for example, was stronger in the Soviet Union and Romania than in Hungary, and the pull of the West stronger in Poland and Hungary than in Bulgaria. Despite these differences, all of the states in question have some basic features in common, and it is these that the term 'Soviet-type system' refers to. The models of Western social science, though often used by sovietologists, are not sufficient for analysing this type of polity. It is necessary also to interpret the problems and changes in these states on the basis of a conceptual framework developed specifically for the analysis of Soviet-type systems (Z, 1990, p. 296). These can be considered under the following headings: the economy, ecology, the political sphere, the social structure, and the instruments of coercion.

*The economy.*Some of the key parameters of the Stalinist model have survived right to the eve of the current revolution. This is true of the hard imperative of growth via fulfilment and

overfulfilment of the plan (Kornai, 1980, pp. 21–63). Paradoxically, this contributed to the negation in practice of the Stalinist
ideal of having total, centralized political control over the economy. Such control presupposes both absolute transparency (i.e. a
perfect and complete flow of information) between the planning
apparatus and the production units, and the ability of the central
planners to receive and process a vast amount of information.
Neither has ever been the case, and as time passed, it became less
and less so. In practice, the managers had to operate in an
environment of great uncertainty about reliable supplies of
inputs, and responded to constant pressure to overfulfil the plan
by doctoring the figures reported to the planning apparatus
(Winiecki, 1988, p.4). As a result, instead of the economy being
politically controlled from the centre, the Soviet-type economies
have developed distinctive characteristics which set them apart
from both the Stalinist ideal and the market economies. They
have aptly been termed 'economies of shortage' by the Hungarian
economist Janos Kornai (Kornai, 1980, 1986).

In the market economies the basic factor limiting production is
lack of demand. If there is prospect for future sales, credit and
resources are available. Demand for inputs is limited by the
prospects of future sales. In the Soviet-type economies, the basic
limiting factor on production is a shortage of inputs. This is not to
say that raw materials and intermediate goods are not produced in
huge quantities. They are. The shortage exists only in relation to
an almost infinite demand. Firms have an insatiable demand
because the 'soft' budget constraints under which they operate
mean that their losses are covered by the state. Therefore neither
credit limits nor operating inefficiencies limit demand.
Households also contribute to surplus demand despite the fact
that, theoretically, demand from wages should balance supply via
the state planning of wages. Because of constant shortages of
labour, managers are under pressure to increase wages, and they
have been very successful in finding ways of doing it (Winiecki,
1988, pp. 38–69). The resultant shortage of resources and
intermediate goods has generated a chronic tendency to hoard
inputs.

Another characteristic feature of the Soviet-type economies has
been that they suffered from 'two-fold underspecialisation'
(Winiecki, 1988, p. 74–7). Firms attempted to be as self-sufficient
as possible in as many intermediate goods as possible. They did
this in order to avoid bottlenecks arising from unreliable external
sources of inputs. The same drift away from the efficiencies of
specialization within a division of labour occurred at the state
level. Within COMECON, all the states were more or less
producing the full range of industrial goods, no matter what their

natural resource endowment. This double underspecialization has contributed to the extremely inefficient, wasteful and polluting production methods typical of Soviet-type economies.

The Soviet-type economies have not been able to pass from the crude and unsustainable type of growth based on adding more manpower, resources and equipment to existing production facilities (extensive growth), to more sustainable and sophisticated growth based on using existing manpower, resources and production facilities more efficiently (intensive growth). This failure was due to the fact that under central planning it was costless and safe for managers to expand by adding more production facilities, but risky for them to introduce new technology and more effective use of the work-force. The managers and the staff were first of all concerned about the fulfilment of plan targets of the current planning period, as premiums and bonuses were tied to the execution of the plan. Every innovation, technical or managerial, had to be introduced into the already existing production facilities. Even if innovation would eventually result in increased output, the risk associated with introducing it, a risk of too long a period of technology absorption leading to lost production, would cause managers generally to avoid such methods of expansion. Adding new buildings and production facilities did not involve that risk (Winiecki, 1988, pp. 17–21). As argued above, the Soviet-type economies started out by being skewed towards heavy industry for ideological and military reasons. Expansion of existing heavy industries demanded expansion of heavy industry, and consequently they became self-feeding extensive growth-machines. Compared to market economies, the heavy industrial sector has become more and more overgrown in the Soviet-type economies. For the consumers this state of affairs has resulted in a growing gap between the standard of living in the West and in the East, and in decreasing motivation to work.

There have been numerous attempts to change the performance of the system without changing its basic features. One has been to give higher priority to the production of consumer goods at the expense of heavy industry. In general these attempts have failed, even where it has been promoted by the highest political bodies (Smolar, 1978, p.88). This was due to the fact that the existing structure of production was closely intertwined with the interests of the ruling elite, the *nomenklatura*. They were not short of consumer goods, as they had their own system of distribution, and their privileged position was tied to heavy industry, looked upon as the most important sector. Reforms were often decided during periods of acute crisis when public discontent threatened the system. They were stopped when the reforms began to be implemented, often when the acute crisis had passed, either due to suppression or due to promises for change. At this point the reforms had begun to hit part of the *nomenklatura*, and/or it had become clear that the reforms, if they were to be successful, demanded more fundamental changes of the political-economic structures; in both cases triggering more fierce resistance among the ruling elite (Csaba, 1989; Mrela and Zielonka,1987; Kornai, 1986). Another attempt was that made during the 1970s to bridge the gap in productivity between the East and the West by imports of Western technology. This did not work either, as the managers had no motivation to adjust to new technology (Winiecki, 1988, pp. 170–204). The main consequence of these imports was to create a heavy burden of foreign debt. Servicing this debt required further curtailment of consumption during the 1980s.

*Ecology.*Official reports kept secret under the old regimes have shown that the blackest spots on the ecological map of Europe can be found in Eastern Europe and in the Soviet Union (NOAH, 1986), and there are good reasons for regarding them as caused by the operating methods of Soviet-type economies. The Marxist-Leninist attitude towards nature, like the Western, is basically exploitative (Ziegler, 1987, pp. 23–45). However, there are several factors that have made the consequences in the case of Soviet-type economies much worse. Production is heavily skewed towards the most polluting sector, heavy industry. The method of production neglects costs, and so leads to an enormous waste of resources compared to the output of useable goods. Thus, in order to produce £1,000 of GDP (Gross Domestic Product) in 1979–80, in the Soviet Union 1,490 kilos of coal equivalent and 135 kilos of steel were needed, while in West Germany 820 kilos coal equivalent and 38 kilos of steel were needed. (Kennedy, 1988, p. 638). This waste degrades the environment both in terms of direct industrial pollution and in larger than necessary resource extraction. Its products also contribute to pollution both by their poor operating quality (for example Trabant cars) and by the frequent replacement that low quality production necessitates. The centrally administered system has also fostered individual irresponsibility; while in the West, the feeling of social responsibility among the citizens has been the key force in the fight against pollution.

*The political sector.*The ideal of having total political control of all areas of the social system in the hands of a centralized party was never achieved, not even during the high tide of Stalinism. There were always pockets of resistance in the society to playing the role of being a means for the ultimate economic and political goals set by a small minority. After the death of Stalin in 1953, and with the improvement in communication technology, areas outside the control of the party, or areas with diminishing party control, multiplied. These included aspects of private life, some areas of academia (science and social science), the legal system and the arts. In spite of suppression, a civil society emerged, defined as 'the privately controlled or voluntary organized spheres of society' (Keane, 1988a, p. 1; Keane, 1988b). Nevertheless, one-party rule has been a dominant feature of these systems right to the eve of their fall. This inhibited the linking of different areas of resistance, and for a long time prevented any move to put basic changes on the political agenda. The extent to which areas of civil society were linked up in the different states varied. Except for Poland, the areas of civil society remained scattered right up to the eve of the fall of the Soviet-type systems, and consequently one of the legacies of the Soviet-type system is a politically atomized society. (Hankiss, 1990). It is significant that the polls carried out before elections in most of the ex-Soviet-type states have shown a large number of uncommitted voters.

*Social structure.*In Eastern Europe and the Soviet Union, a much larger section of the working class is employed within heavy and extractive industries than in the West (Andorka and Kolosi, 1984; Sørensen, 1990). They are relatively well paid. Furthermore there is a comparatively larger number of employees in the state bureaucratic apparatus. If campaigns of Westernization are pressed home, there will be many candidates for unemployment within both these groups. There is also a rapidly growing number of people living below the official minimum subsistence level. They are mostly pensioners, families with many children and people living in villages. So far they have not constituted a strong political pressure group. But if a social security system and retraining courses are not instituted, they could become not only a moral issue, but also a political problem especially when added to growing numbers of the unemployed. Another problem for the process of Westernization is the general low level of wages for the intelligensia. If this is not dealt with, a large-scale braindrain is likely. Already the problem has manifested itself in several Eastern European states.

At the apex of the social pyramid of the Soviet-type systems was the *nomenklatura*, composed of the upper layers of the party/state apparatus. They were extremely privileged in terms of access to goods and services, but compared to the Western upper class did not have hereditary property rights. In the Soviet-type system, all major means of production were in the hands of the state. However, a revolution of Westernization raises the important question: who are the heirs of the state? Previously, the basis for the privileged status of the *nomenklatura* was their political position. Now, being aware of where developments are heading, part of this strata is trying, often successfully, to move the basis for its high social position to ownership of the means of production and distribution. In doing so, some are cooperating with Western investors and some are opposing them. There are also proposals for giving the property rights to the workers, intellectuals and peasants (Hankiss, 1989, 1990; Lane, 1985, 143–202).

Instruments of coercion. The military, the police and the paramilitary troops have been crucial for the control of Soviet-type systems. The Soviet Union has kept the ultimate control of these instruments, partly by the overwhelming size of the Soviet army, partly through training courses in the Soviet Union for future officers from the military and police forces of the East European states, and partly by very careful Soviet screening of candidates for top posts in the East European states. In the Soviet Union, the military and the police have been under the tight control of the party, except for short periods when control of the party has been disputed (Holloway, 1984, p. 157). The revolution of Westernization will pose a social problem for officers from the previous system. They could also become a threat to the revolution if the transformation process runs into serious difficulties. If a situation with economic chaos and intensive infighting between contending groups emerges in the Soviet Union, the military could be decisive in settling the dispute. A conservative backlash in the Soviet Union could also have serious effects on unconsolidated revolutions in some East European countries. A Soviet Union in the grip of backlash is likely to give at least political support, and maybe more substantial assistance, to political forces positive to the Soviet Union. If pensioned officers in East European states got some hope of regaining their previous privileges and status, and a moral mission to save their country from economic and political chaos, quite a few would probably join the fight against Westernization.

On the eve of their fall, the Soviet-type systems had reached a dead end (Estrup, 1990; *International Herald Tribune*, 16 May 1990; CIA Report, 1990). Their economies were hardly able to sustain themselves. They were characterized by serious sectoral imbalances, and several had huge foreign debts. Financial collapse was threatening because of a massive overhang of forced savings, a chronic shortage of goods, and both open and hidden inflation. Prices had no relation to costs.

As political systems, they had never enjoyed legitimacy in the Western sense of being the choice of the majority. Even for many communists, the Soviet-type systems had lost that legitimacy which the communist parties had derived from their theoretical ability to guide the state towards a higher form of development. Within the communist parties groups emerged demanding radical reform, even Westernization, as it became clear that these states were not on the road to the abundance of the communist Utopia, but on the road to bankruptcy.

This is not to say that the collapsed Soviet-type systems are facing the same development problems as those confronting the African states. If the yardstick is where capitalist states such as Korea and Spain were when they took off to a dynamic, intensive growth, in general, the post-Soviet-type states possess most of the basic elements of an industrial state, though beset with structural problems. Their problem is more akin to reconstruction after a destructive war than to development. Many of the social, technical and educational infrastructures for industrial society exist. The problem is how to reconstruct these assets in such a way as to remove their many distortions and inefficiencies without causing political chaos. They have too much heavy industry, too small a service sector, too much pollution, too much basic research, too little applied research, no appropriate financial institutions, too much bureaucracy, too little capital and too much pent-up demand. The main problem facing the post-Soviet-type systems is that they have been operating for many decades in a highly dysfunctional manner. The challenge for them is how to establish a new *modus operandi*, and they are looking to the West for models. For many East Europeans this is a search for their European past.

Westernization

All of the ex-Soviet-type systems have embarked on 'Westerniza-tion' (a term expanded from von Laue, 1987), which means a process of adopting the core elements of a capitalist state. These elements are: a mix of private and state ownership, the market mechanism, integration into the world market, a democratic, pluralistic political system, participation in global and regional political and economic cooperation, the rule of law, a social security system fitted to a market economy, and the ideology of materialism and individualism, but also caring for the under-privileged.

If Westernization is to be successful, it is necessary to adopt it as a 'package deal'. The market mechanism as the main instrument for allocating resources and investments only becomes politically stable when combined with the other elements: pluralist politics, the rule of law, welfare and so forth. There seems to an inner logic connecting the different elements and making all of them necessary for the system to function. It is one of the conclusions drawn from attempts at introducing some elements of the market economy in Hungary and in the Soviet Union, that these reforms have failed because they were not accompanied by political reform (Csaba, 1989, p. 21; Kornai, 1986, pp. 1732–34) Historically, all the capitalist states that have been successful in Westernization have at some stage achieved an interplay of these different elements. This has been the case of South Korea, Spain and Greece. This is not to say, that all Western states are identical. The polities in the West do not operate according to one logic either: political systems differ. There is the logic of the market mechanism, but there is also the logic of state intervention, which is used to achieve very different goals in, for instance, Scandinavia as compared with the United States or Japan. The fact that there are so many variations of the Western model is due to the necessity to shape the 'package deal' to the particular requirements and desires of the different national-cultural heritages specific to each country, and to political differences. An example of failure to achieve a functional synthesis is the attempt at Westernization of Iran under the Shah (Hankiss, 1990).

The preparation for the revolution of Westernization of the Soviet-type states has been very much assisted by improvements in communication technology, though the possibility for penetration of this influence differed markedly from state to state. The twentieth century has been dominated by masssive flows of information, and by the general public's access to information channels, such as radio, photo-copy machines, personal computers, fascimile machines, telephones and TV stations. Everywhere these information flows penetrated they served both to undermine the central control of communist parties and to bring into question their myth of a superior society.

National-cultural identities

Politically, economically and legally the Stalinist model and the Soviet-type systems are the antithesis of those seen in the West. For them to embark on Westernization is therefore to embark on a revolution. The prospects for this course in the different East European countries and the Soviet Union depend on a complex interplay of the factors outlined. But the historical-cultural background and geographical position of the countries concerned are also important for the outcome. Major aspects of the national culture and identity have been suppressed for a long time in the Soviet-type systems, and the national historical and cultural pasts existing before the Stalinist mould was imposed are now reviving. The character and influence of the national-cultural past differs very much among the ex-Soviet-type states. Some are nation-states, others are multinational constructions. Some have long histories of self-rule, others not. Some look to Orthodox Christian traditions, others to the Roman Church. Because of this diversity, this factor will be dealt with specifically for each country in the sections that follow.

5.2. The Soviet Union

In the case of the Soviet Union, a revolution of Westernization faces extraordinary difficulties. Russia and the Soviet Union have had a history of centuries of domestic absolutism and external expansion. The Soviet Union is a multinational state, and the civil society has been severely suppressed. The attempts at reform pursued so far have brought the economy to the brink of financial collapse. However, there are also some resources specific to the Soviet Union that could be mobilized to facilitate a revolution of Westernization.

Russia

The history of the Russian state has been very different from those in Western Europe. In Western Europe there were mutual obligations between the rulers and the ruled, and the various sections of the society had a relative autonomy in relation to the suzerain. In Russia,

Not even in theory was any leeway left to any stratum under the state ideology that crystallized out of the indissoluble trio of autocracy, orthodoxy (the church) and the people. This trio converged upon a single focus, the personal power of the tsar, and from there radiated outwards as 'truth' through the sphere of influence of 'true' power to the 'true' unity of the people. [Szücs, 1988, p. 321.]

Russian expansion across the Eurasian plain coincided with, but differed from, the imperialism of Western Europe. The Western nations' colonial empires were largely overseas, with unmistakable distinctions between mother-country and colony. In the Russian case, the newly acquired lands, though peopled by non-Russians, were contiguous to and gradually merged with the 'mother-country'. In the conquered areas the previous leading strata were deported and a polity was set up that was a replica of the Russian state. Thus was created an ethnically diverse, but geographically and politically-united, empire, with the dominant Russian core surrounded by various conquered peoples on the borderlands.

For a long time the Russian state was successful both in resisting attempts at invasion and in expanding. During the nineteenth century the polity, based on large country estates tilled by serfs, showed signs of being in a crisis, and Russia began to lose to more effectively organized states. Two models were offered to solve the crisis: one by the Slavophiles, the other by the Westernizers. According to the Slavophiles, the Russians had a moral superiority over European peoples. The solution to the problems of Russia would be to go back to the roots of the Russian, Slavic culture and nation. According to the Westernizers, Russia needed Western, enlightened ideas and institutions (Westwood, 1981). Increasingly, the Westernizers adopted revolutionary socialist thought. One consequence is that, today, the blame for the failure of the Soviet model is attributed by the Russian Slavophile movement, Pamyat, to the model being a product of Western and Jewish influence (Koenen, 1990). The division between Westernizers and Slavophiles is still a key feature of Russian political thinking.

The Soviet Union

Besides the general features of the Stalinist model as described above, the Soviet version was characterized by a scheme for the development of the various nationalities. On this issue, history was prescribed to follow a three-stage development. The first stage was a flourishing of the national culture. This meant that those parts of the national culture deemed not to be contrary to the communist course were encouraged. Quite a few nationalities benefited from this stage in terms of getting a written language, books printed in it and schools established where the teaching was in their own language. The next stage was *rapprochement*. As the social system existing in the Russian republic was considered the most advanced, *rapprochement* in reality meant Russification. Under Stalin, initially the emphasis was on 'flourishing', but increasingly a harsh Russification became the dominant feature. According to the theory, in the final stage, when communism was reached, the national question would be solved by a fusion of the nationalities (Goldman, 1988, p. 9; Rywkin, 1982, p. 138).

Khrushchev's 'thaw' brought a partial relaxation of Stalin's harsh nationalities policies, and during the Brezhnev era, a policy of almost benign neglect of the nationalities question evolved, except for an even stronger push for making Russian a common language. Political elites from the indigenous nationalities were permitted to set up their own regional political machines within the party. They were allowed to control the economy, so long as they remained politically loyal to the centre. As leaders from a local nationality took control over local political and administrative affairs, they instituted policies aimed at increasing the educational, technical and administrative expertise of the indigenous people. Veritable fiefdoms emerged at the republic level, frequently marked by corruption and administrative inefficiency (Goldman 1988, p.11). Assisted by funds from the central government, vast irrigation schemes were constructed. For a long period, extensive growth was possible and the standard of living improved. The result has been termed 'welfare colonialism' (Rywkin, 1982, pp. 51, 57). It is traditional colonialism in the sense that an alien polity and culture have been imposed. However, there is also a welfare aspect in the sense that, although the standards of living in the Central Asian republics are among the lowest in the Soviet Union, there is not the widespread mass poverty characteristic of Western colonies.

The Brezhnev policy towards the nationalities was part of his administration's overall corporatist strategy. All the major interest groups were given increased funds, especially the military and heavy industry. Consumers were considered by increasing wages and by providing more investment for agriculture and light industry. Large funds were transferred to the non-Slavic republics and to clients in the developing countries. The different sectors of the state were to a large extent left to manage their own affairs. As the attempts at reform failed and resources and manpower became increasingly scarce, it was impossible to sustain the corporatist strategy (Bunce, 1983; Byrnes, 1983).

From reform from above to revolution from below?

When Mikhail Gorbachev came to power in 1985 he wanted to revitalize the economy through a traditional reform programme aimed at improving the performance of the system without changing the basic structures (Z, 1990; Simon, 1990). The campaign against alcoholism, sloppy work and corruption that was started under Andropov was intensified. He instituted quality control by state inspectors, regrouped ministries and replaced cadres on a scale not seen since Stalin. As a result, by late 1986 strong resistance to further changes, whether of policy or personnel emerged among the apparatus. The economy did not improve. Gorbachev was thus faced with the prospect of failure, if he did not take more radical steps.

Gorbachev opted for more radical reform. This started a dialectic of structural change and political mobilization that pushed the initial reform programme still closer to a revolution of Westernization. Gorbachev has been on a steep learning curve. Intentionally or unintentionally he has set in motion political forces that have obtained a momentum of their own: independent political forces are increasingly setting the agenda for further changes.

*The political and legal sector.*Gorbachev's answer to the crisis of reform was the campaign for *glasnost'* (openness). The idea was that a dynamic economy could not be built with a passive population. An active public was necessary in order to overcome the bureaucratic resistance to reform. In order to make the population, and especially the intelligentsia, an active political force, it was necessary that the public have some knowledge of the problems threatening the country (Z, 1990, p. 323). The public began to be informed about pollution, accidents, prostitution, poverty, the atrocities of the Stalin era, corruption and crime, all phenomena that so far had been reported only from the capitalist states. *Glasnost'* did not mean freedom of speech, as it was still the party that defined the limits to what could be published. However, these limits widened.

The next step was a campaign for democratization. In early 1987 it was decided that there should be two or more candidates to elections in the party and to the soviets. Formally the soviets directed the state administration, but since the days of Lenin these bodies had been totally controlled by the party. Now they were given a more independent role and more power. Thus the Supreme Soviet, the national parliament, was given some measure of legislative power, unlike its rubber-stamp predecessor. It was decided to have fixed terms for party and soviet posts. This was not democracy in the Western sense, as the candidates had to adhere to the programme of the communist party, only allowing for different interpretations of the programme, but it was enough to oust many of the old party bureaucrats. It also got a group of radical reformers elected, radicals who could demand an end to the party monopoly of 'truth' and power. In March 1990 the formation of other parties was allowed. The extraordinarily strong presidency also instituted in March 1990 could be seen as going against the general trend of Westernization. But whether the presidency will become a seat for a new tsar, or whether it will become a tool for protecting the still fragile democratic movement against a conservative backlash, is as yet impossible to say.

Another area where there have been politically significant moves is towards the rule of law (Bialer 1989, pp. 236–7; Vaxberg 1989, p. 111). In January 1990, the Soviet Union signed the Vienna Concluding Document, giving international law priority over domestic legislation. The Soviet Union has declared its readiness to submit itself to the jurisdiction of the International Court in the Hague and has signed the Optional Protocol to the International Covenant on Civil and Political Rights.

These changes have triggered a political mobilization of a previously very passive population. Unlike the East European states, there has not been a broad, uniting desire for Westernization pressing from below. Although there are nuclei of civil society (Lapidus, 1989, p.121–49), their development has been hampered both by centuries of absolutism and hostile propaganda against the West, and by the difficulty the media revolution had in penetrating the Soviet heartland. The result was that when the possibility for a democratic political life began to emerge, the public was torn by different ideologies: Slavophilism, Western, communist, social democratic, nationalist and many others. The attitude to *perestroika* among different strata of the population was very ambivalent (Zaslavskaya, 1988), and the constituency most likely to support and carry forward the revolution of Westernization was fragmented.

By mid-1990 it seemed that a revolution of Westernization was slowly gaining momentum in the political sphere, slowly uniting different political tendencies (Saslawskaja, 1990). The communist party and its affiliated organizations are shrinking and losing power. A wealth of independent organizations, national fronts and some parties have been founded. The elections to the soviets in spring 1990 showed a clear majority for Westernization in big cities such as Moscow, Leningrad and Sverdlovsk. But the trend towards Westernization was not consolidated. In the smaller provincial towns and in the countryside, the party still has strongholds. Another obstacle is that the logic of Westernization forces the Russians to face the descent of the Soviet Union from superpower status to the status of a major power. At the same time, two key problems for the future development of the Soviet Union, the nationality issue and the economy, have deteriorated sharply.

The nationality issue. The Soviet Union is organized as a federal state, with the territories of the major nationalities designated as republics. At present there are fifteen such republics. Many of the smaller nationalities have homelands in the form of autonomous republics, regions and areas within the Union republics, each category having a decreasing amount of local autonomy. National revival in the case of the Soviet Union thus means the revival of more than one hundred nationalities. If that was not a sufficient problem by itself, it also means the revival of national identities of peoples living inside other nations. The people most dispersed among the other nations are the Slavs, especially the Russians.

In 1979 the total population of the Soviet Union was 282.5 million. The three largest nationalities, all Slavic, are the Russians (137.4 million), the Ukrainians (42.3 million) and the Belorussians (9.5 million), together forming over 70 per cent of the total population (Goble 1990, p. 2; White *et al.*, 1987, p. 46). This picture of a clear Slavic majority in the Soviet Union is a static one. From a dynamic point of view, it should be noted that in the 1970s the rate of population growth of the Soviet Muslims was five times greater than the population growth of the Russians. The principal Soviet Muslim nationalities (in decreasing numerical order) are the Uzbeks, Tatars, Azerbaijanis, Kazakhs, Tadzhiks, Turkmen and Kirgiz. According to a Western estimate, by the middle of the twenty-first century, the Muslim population will rival the Russians for numerical dominance (Goldman, 1988, p. 47). At present, there are some 50–60 million Muslims in the Soviet Union. Most of them are concentrated in Central Asia in their own republics and unwilling to migrate, while the Russians are finding Central Asia less congenial and are migrating out. Combined with the a higher birthrate among the Muslims, the result is that the Muslim republics are becoming more Muslim (Goldman, 1988, p. 47; Krag, 1989, p. 82).

However, there are several difficulties in estimating the importance of the Muslim factor for the prospects of the Soviet state. The 10 million difference between the two figures for the numbers of Muslims reflects these difficulties. They are partly due to the fact that the Soviet Union was until recently offically an atheist state, where public statistics did not show numbers of believers of the different religions. The Muslims have different ethnic backgrounds and they belong to different strands of Islam; some are firm believers, others are not. Most are first of all nationalists. Probably the importance of the Muslim factor is still open in the way that it is dependent on the success or failure of creating a viable overall Soviet economy and a political system that leave greater scope for the free development of multiple identities. If these attempts fail, leaving the different parts of the Soviet Union in chaos, it is likely that the importance of religion and other ethnic factors will increase. So will the desire to establish ethnic contacts across state borders, as has been the case for other empires during times of rapid decline.

Under Gorbachev, to the great surprise of the Soviet leadership, the nationality problem has come more and more to the forefront. Since Gorbachev came to power, nearly 90 per cent of the demonstrators come from nationalities which total fewer than 10 per cent of the population (Goble, 1990, p. 3; Paul A. Goble is Special Assistant for Soviet Nationalities in the US Department of State's Bureau of Intelligence and Research). The Soviet leaders have been deceived by their own propaganda of the 'great unity' of the Soviet nations. In this, as in most other areas, the Soviet model for solving the nationality issue has accumulated huge problems. There are several reasons why the nationality issue will stay high on the agenda of the Soviet leadership in the coming years. To put in another way, it seems that no matter what strategy the Soviet leadership choses, it will be faced with severe difficulties for quite some time.

In many of the non-Russian republics, the nationality problems are growing worse, because of the fact that the economic and political crisis of the system has reached a critical point. The possibilities for continuing the previous 'welfare colonialism' have come to an end. Because of monoculture cotton growing (Rywkin, 1982, p. 47), huge, ineffective irrigation schemes and mishandling of agriculture in general, vast areas of arable land in the Kazakh-stan, Uzbekistan and Kirghizia have been destroyed. Since the 1960s, the Aral Sea, the fourth biggest lake in the world, has lost 60 per cent of its water, causing the spread of huge, saline deserts. In the autonomous republic of Karalkalpakia south of the Aral Sea, in some villages life expectancy is down to a mere 40 years (Ananjev, 1989, p. 17–25). Proceeding further along the same path is not possible. To get out of these dead ends will demand enormous investment, as well as imaginative new thinking and firm political will. However, given the broader crisis of the Soviet economy, the possibilities for transferring funds are very limited, if not quite non-existent.

As a remedy for the ills of the Soviet state, the leadership have embarked on Westernization. However, the process of Westernization is a threat to the present Soviet multinational state. In general, the right to national self-determination is accepted in the West as part of the idea of democracy. Westerniza-tion, therefore, gives legitimacy to a majority claim to national self-determination. At present there are strong separatist move-ments in the Baltic republics, in Georgia, in Moldavia, in the western part of Ukraine and in Azerbaijan. Westernization could also fuel the rising self-consiousness of the Muslims in Central Asia (Goldman, 1988, pp. 47–54). While the process of

Westernization fits well with the basic values of the population in the Baltic republics, this is not the case with many of the Muslim peoples (Arutyunyan and Bromlei, 1986; Gerner, 1988, p. 72; Gerner, 1989, p. 223). Anti-corruption campaigns and campaigns against nepotism and administrative inefficiency have hit the fiefdoms of the local elites in the Central Asian and Caucasian Republics built up during the Brezhnev era. They are fighting back.

Another potential strategy would be to use the extensive powers of the new presidency to suppress national unrest. Here the problem is that large-scale use of force would be unacceptable to the West and thus make the process of Westernization impossible. This is not to say that the nationality issue is bound to block the revolution of Westernization in the Soviet Union. Nor is it to say that the only solution to it is to shrink the Soviet Union to its Russian core. Most of the republics in question are landlocked, have few alternative alliance partners, and have obtained a higher standard of living and secularization than their non-Soviet Third World neighbours. Unless the situation in the Soviet Union continues to deteriorate, only a part of the local elite is likely to look to their neighbours for models to imitate.

A successful resolution of the nationality problem will demand innovative policies in many areas. These include taking the constitutional right of the republics to self-determination seriously; allowing those republics who want to secede to do so; making good the damage done by the Soviet-type system; and developing new production structures. However, so far Gorbachev has not been able to form a strong alliance with local Westernizers, who want to combine modernization with the national-cultural heritage. Neither has he been able to devise an economic programme that fits the local conditions.

In the economic sector, aside from the campaign for better discipline, Gorbachev has tried to improve the performance of agriculture and the service sector. Considering the experience of Hungary and China, reforms within these sectors could be expected to lead to a rapid growth. But these sectors in the Soviet Union have been mistreated for a much longer period, and the attempts have met with only limited success. The expansion of the service sector by establishing cooperatives has been met in the Soviet Union with strong, ideologically-based resistance. Likewise, the attempt to curb the role of the state central-planning apparatus, by enacting a law providing for more self-management and self-financing of enterprises, has failed in practice (Åslund, 1989, pp. 178–95).

These piecemeal reforms have brought the economy close to chaos (Schmeljow, 1990, pp. 22–9) In 1989, for the first time in fourteen years, the Soviet Union came out with a trade deficit (3.3 billion roubles), led by a sharp fall-off in energy exports and a jump in grain imports. Oil exports fell to 127.3 million metric tons from 144.2 tons in 1988, a drop of 11.7 per cent. Coal exports dropped from 39.4 million tons in 1988, to 37.5 million tons in 1989, a loss of 4.8 per cent. Total production for the first quarter of 1990 was 1.2 per cent less than for the same quarter of the previous year (*International Herald Tribune*, 9 April 1990, p. 7). One of the few encouraging items from 'The State Committee for Statistics' concerning the first quarter of 1990 was that the production of some consumer goods like colour television sets, tape recorders and sewing machines had gone up. This was partly due to the fact that the production for civilian purposes in defence industry factories had increased by 20 per cent (*Information*, 21 May 1990, p. 3). The income of the state has gone down, while its expenditures have gone up. This resulted in 1988 in a budget deficit of 11 per cent of GNP, roughly triple the US ratio of budget deficit to GNP (*International Herald Tribune*, 18–19 March 1989, p. 15; Shelton, 1989, pp. 3–77) As wages have gone up, the imbalance between the large amount of purchasing power and the very limited amount of goods has become worse. The economy seems close to a financial collapse. Distrust in the value of the rouble has resulted in hoarding of gold in Moscow (*International Herald Tribune*, 27 October 1989, p. 1; *Guardian Weekly*, 18 February 1990, p. 21). Having regard to the marketization of the economy, this is a very alarming development, as the means of payment is pivotal for a capitalist economy.

It has been decided *de facto* to accept private ownership, the market mechanism and integration in the world market (*Novosti*, no.110, December 1989). The revolution in the economic sphere has been decided, though it is still an open question as to when and how effectively the decision will be be implemented. If implemented what are the prospects for economic performance? In the first stages, a revolution will, by definition, create disorder in the whole system. For a new economic system to work, all the key links in it have to work, and this will take time. To learn new standard procedures to learn entrepreneurial skills will take time. The effects of many of the reforms will not have a positive influence on the economy until much later. Consequently the economic restructuring will produce pain, and lots of it, before it begins to generate widespread material rewards.

The problem of how the economic reform process acquires a self-reinforcing momentum is exacerbated by the fact that economic reform is closely linked to the nationality issue and to the political infighting connected with the overall revolution of Westernization. Thus the coal miners strike in the Soviet Union in the summer of 1989 seriously harmed the economy, but the strike was necessary in order to topple the conservatives in the party and state apparatus. Gorbachev tried to use the accelerator by encouraging the development of a mass movement, while at the same time using the brake by appeals to stop the strikes (*International Herald Tribune*, 17–26 July 1989, p. 1; and *Moscow News*, no. 31, 1989, p. 9).

On the other hand, some developments could have a positive effect on the economy within a fairly short period. One is to convert resources from military to civilian production (Cooper, 1989; Kincade and Thomson, 1990; Lemaitre, 1989a, p. 338). In considering this question, it should be kept in mind that the cost of the military is a very large part of the Soviet GNP: the prevailing estimate in the West is between 15 and 17 per cent. (Wilkinson, 1988, p. 41; European Strategy Group, 1988, p. 70.) This figure should be compared to 6.6 per cent for the United States (1987). Transferring resources, manpower and transport capacity from military to civilian use might, within a relatively short period, have a positive effect on some of the bottlenecks and critical sectors of the Soviet economy: the availability of consumer goods, transport and highly skilled young workers and scientists. Another resource that could be tapped is the vast scientific reservoir of talent in virtually every discipline. It can be leased cheaply by the West. Several Western firms and universities have already bought research in the Soviet Union (*Bloc, The Soviet Union and Eastern Europe Business Journal*, 11:1, p. 35). This is probably not enough to change the general picture. Even if the revolution in the economic sphere is implemented, it will take many years before the economy can recover.

The domestic–foreign link. Despite the fact that more and more evidence suggests that the new thinking is not a propaganda trick, many Western observers have found it hard to believe that there is a revolution unfolding in Soviet policy under Gorbachev. While Gorbachev started out by trying to revitalize socialism in Eastern Europe and to revitalize the Warsaw Pact and COMECON, he has in fact accepted the Westernization and dismantling of the Soviet-type systems in Eastern Europe. There have been deep cuts in Soviet spending on clients in the developing countries. The Soviet Union has made considerable unilateral troop reductions and has cut military expenditure. There is a logic connecting the domestic and foreign policy elements of Gorbachev's policy. A revolution of Westernization demands good relations and close contacts with the West. It is impossible to conduct such a revolution at home and at the same time have the West as the deadly enemy abroad. Good relations with the West are also necessary to overcome the political resistance of the Slavophiles. There is thus a close relationship between the domestic revolution and changes in foreign policy. This is another reason why the success of the revolution of Westernization is in the interest of the West (Lemaitre, 1989b, pp. 17-20; Petersen, 1990).

Success? Backlash? Muddle through?

In the preceeding section it was argued that successful Westernization is a 'package deal'. An interplay between the economic, political, ideological and legal elements of Westernization is necessary if development is to be sustainable. In the case of the Soviet Union such an interplay is not to be expected soon. Considering the very contradictory character of the processes unfolding in the Soviet Union, the following developments seem possible:

*Backlash.*The trigger could be a continued deterioration of the economy, ethnic unrest and political infighting. This would be a situation where it would be easy to put the blame for the crisis on the attempts at Westernization. Candidates to head such a backlash could be Slavophile organizations like Pamyat or part of the old communist elite. The conservatives within the party are already trying hard to play on Russian Slavophilism by putting the blame for the crisis on the attempts at Westernization. In the debate in the Central Committee in February 1990, Vladimir Brovikov, Soviet ambassador to Poland said:

Lately we have come to value the opinion of the West more than our own opinions. Let George Bush be; why are we always trying to prove he's for *perestroika*? And what *perestroika*? The *perestroika* that in five years has brought the country to an abyss of crisis and brought it to the point where we are under the sway of anarchy and the economy is in ruins and the morale is in crisis? . . . People are against all this and speak ever more loudly about it. . . . we have been witnessing for a long time the mistakes not of the Brezhnevian 'stagnation' era but rather the thin gruel of our own *perestroika*. We have brought the motherland to an awful state, turning it from an empire admired throughout the world to a state with an inglorious present and indefinite future. And all this to the great pleasure of the West . . . *International Herald Tribune*, 8 February 1990, p. 2

A retreat to the previous polity will solve none of the basic problems that the Soviet Union is facing. In terms of its internal socio-political cohesion, it will be a weak state, though probably left with enough military power to pose a threat to the surrounding countries. However, if confronted with a credible Western military deterrent, such a Soviet Union or Russia is likely neither to be expansionist nor able to re-establish dominance in Eastern Europe, perhaps with the exception of one or two states. Thinking in terms of correlations of forces is deeply rooted in Soviet strategic behaviour, and there can be no doubt that for quite some time the Western wind will prevail over the East.

Success. According to the main line of argument of this chapter, for the Soviet Union the only way out of the crisis is by being closely integrated with the West and by changing the domestic political balance towards a pro-Western stand. Even though such a Soviet Union or Russia would be a stronger state in terms of economic strength and political cohesion, for Europe it would pose a security threat no bigger than the United States, except for the fact that it would be geographically much closer.

Muddle through. Many developments could be thought of between the extremes of success and backlash: for instance, that the revolution is successful in some areas, like Westernizing the political institutions, the economy, and in conversion from military to civilian production; but unable to find a solution to the nationality issue. But for all these scenarios, compared to the 1980s, the Soviet Union or Russia would be a weaker state, and most likely a weaker military power.

5.3. Eastern Europe

The East European revolutions have been labelled 'moral revolutions'. Moral, because of their non-violent, unbloody, disciplined character. Moral, because more than anything else they were reactions against forty years of immoral rule: lies, corruption, dissimulation, time lost and lives wasted.

The wave of revolutions sweeping Eastern Europe and astounding the Western world in the late autumn of 1989 was predominantly a reaction by the peoples in the then Eastern, now Central, Europe against the forces that both prevented them from constituting their own societies and forced them into the straitjacket of a Soviet-type society. The revolutions might be seen as a reaction against the fallacy of the communist economic system. But above all, they were liberation movements with the aim of freeing individual and societal creativity, and expressing the societies' desire for the right to individuality. Until recently, influenced by the Polish case, experts on East European affairs believed that an economic crisis would be the trigger for social uprisings in Eastern Europe. The reason for the Polish, but not yet Czechoslovakian or East German uprisings in Eastern Europe, were, as late as the summer of 1989, interpreted as the presence or absence of a devastated economy. Because of the violent suppression by the Ceauşescu regime, Romania was considered an exeption to this rule. Thus, the best thing to wish for the politically suppressed Czechs and East Germans was that their economies would be less successful so that populations in these countries would feel 'pressed against the wall' and react with an uprising.

The future theoreticians on 'why people rebel' will have to note that economic conditions, whether good or bad, are just one of the triggers. 'Dignity of life' — possibly understood differently by different people — is no less important a factor. This is confirmed by the fact that in the spring of 1990 we are watching uprisings in those Soviet republics where the standard of living is the highest in the whole of the Soviet Union.

There are some common features among the Eastern European revolutions. First, it has been possible to set these revolutions on the world stage because the end of the twentieth century is dominated by widespread public access to information. This has been true for Western Europe for about a decade or so. In Eastern Europe, only a decade ago all typewriters had to be registered, and one of the actions in support of Solidarnosc was to smuggle daisy-wheels and IBM typewriter heads into Poland. As late as the summer of 1989 a well-informed Sovietologist summed up the difference between East and West as follows: 'Information is available but the *disclosure* [our emphasis] of that information is not permitted in many countries' (Dau, 1989). But, the future was just round the corner: also in political research! The same researcher continued: 'However, the breakthroughs in communication technology have revealed the absurdity of the situation, and may in the end be what statesmen will have to realize that they cannot fight'. Both Mary Dav and the then relatively unknown researcher, now vice-premier of Czechoslovakia, Valtr Komarek, put their hopes into the unprecedented escalation of science and the expansion of informatics.

Their hopes were not badly placed. 'Telerevolutions' was the term coined by Timothy Gorton Ash to characterize the wave of revolutions not even half a year later. And certainly they were. The TV and the press yielded protection. The Czech students were chanting 'The world sees you' to the riot police; the Romanian princesses were thanking the press for drawing the world's attention and thereby ensuring support for the demonstrators (*Berlingske Tidende*, 22 January 1990). It is difficult to tell whether the presence of the TV cameras had much impact on the behaviour of the security forces but it certainly did have an impact on the pride and confidence of those protesting against the regime. In Romania, the TV station was the coordinating centre of the uprising. In Czechoslovakia and East Germany, mass media were consciously utilized but did not acquire an equally central role. Before that, in Poland, Solidarnosc learned about the power of the world's attention: first during the strikes in 1980–1 and 1988–9, later when Solidarnosc won its own independent seven minutes every day on TV up to the Polish elections in June 1989. After the elections, the Solidarnosc press still plays an important role in Poland, and not only in its home territory. The Solidarnosc papers have also been studied by opposition intellectuals in the other East European countries, especially Czechoslovakia.

Direct contacts between the East European societies also played an important role for the planning and implementation of the uprisings. 'The fall of the Berlin Wall did not begin in Berlin, but at the Austrio-Hungarian border', it was stressed during a Polish discussion on German unification (Wojna, 1990). The Czechs watched the East Germans sleeping on the Prague streets waiting for exit visas to West Germany. Leaders of the Czechoslovak opposition took part in a Czechoslovak–Polish joint session in Wroclaw, during the summer of 1989. 'They returned very happy and full of hope' (Gammelgaard, 1990). The Czechoslovaks and the East Germans had learned many organizational techniques such as sit-in strikes, non-violent actions and round-table discussions from the Poles. They also benefited from some of the negative Polish experiences, for example the economic costs of a 'Polish style' revolution, labelled by Germans 'Polnishe Wirtschaft' (Ash, 1989b).

However highly we may honour the opposition movements in each of the former socialist republics, it is clear to all observers that the central precondition for all the East and Central European revolutions was the Soviet abandonment of the Brezhnev doctrine. Western observers began to get a sense of what was in the Soviet political pipeline by listening to Gorbachev's speeches in the spring and summer of 1989. Soviet acceptance of the Solidarnosc-led (i.e. not communist) government in Poland in the summer of 1989 was the first decisive proof of the fact that the Kremlin had both changed its policy towards its satellites and revised its security priorities drastically. What was at stake was no longer total control of these states' political systems. The Warsaw Pact's denunciation of the 1968 invasion of Czechoslovakia in the autumn of 1989 was a solid confirmation to the West, and to the rest of the East European societies, that the Soviet Union would not intervene if they decided to overthrow their communist leaders.

The question remaining is to what extent this change of Soviet policy was a reaction to pressure from East European societies? Or was it a carefully elaborated plan, as argued by one Polish sociologist (Staniszkis, 1989b). Staniszkis argues that the political leaderships of the East European states have long ago been transferred from the decomposing communist parties to an elite, a centre made up of the top echelons of the military and secret security forces for the purpose of administering the crises in Eastern Europe and preventing them from getting out of hand as happened in Czechoslovakia in 1968. Aware of the deficiencies of the centralized economic model, and being themselves trained for orientation towards efficiency, these leaders have, according to Staniszkis' theory, constructed a plan for modernizing the economies. To do this they need to attract Western capital. Since no Western capital would be channelled to the old mono-party centralized political and economic systems, it was necessary to abandon the Brezhnev doctrine in order to allow political and economic pluralism to those societies that desired these values, and to give a push to those that had not yet dared to cherish such hopes.

The success of the process of Westernization is highly dependent on the level of cohesion in each of the East European societies. Cohesion is understood here as the society's ability to withstand political and economic crises without falling victim to processes of atomization into alien social or ethnic groups fighting each other in violent uprisings which would result in little but increased poverty for the whole society. One of the means by which the Soviet-type system maintained control over the whole society was to inspire and provoke conflicts between ethnic or social groups such as Romanians against Hungarians, Christians against Jews, peasants against workers, workers against technocrats, and so on. This has been part of the official policy for decades. Every one of the East European societies now suffers from the effects of this 'educational process' on relations between different groups within society.

The transformation process from centralized economies and one party systems to democracies and full-scale market economies will be very painful in economic terms. This pain is likely to spill over into social and political relations within the East European societies. The reforms will test the level of societal cohesion, at the same time as the success of the reform processes is highly dependent on their ability to pass this test. One of the major problems arising in the economic sphere is unemployment plus the absence of a functioning social security system. This has been spelled out in nearly every analysis of the East European economic reforms (CIA Report, 1990).

This is not the place for a discussion about whether closing down state enterprises will automatically lead to huge unemployment rates. On the bright side, there is the possibility that a combination of foreign capital injection and businesses started by the new local entrepreneurs will provide jobs for those able to work under the new market mechanism. The problem will then be not with those sacked from the state enterprises, but with those who were so well adapted to the centralized economic system that for years they have been able to 'muddle through' within the framework of the old system. This might mean that they are today unable, or perhaps even unwilling, to change their habits and take on new tasks that will demand independent acting and thinking. These are the people who will not be able to obtain a new job, and who will form the cadres of the unemployed. Unemployment created by absence of jobs is likely to create economic and social problems. Unemployment in a situation where jobs in the new firms are abundant, while there is lack of qualified people (qualified less in terms of technical skills than attitude towards adapatation) to fill the positions is likely to create psychological lines of division in the population on top of the social ones. This is most likely to mean that the small group of efficient, 'hard working' people, in the Western meaning of this term, will be less prepared to fight for social security for those left behind, being thereby one of the factors creating further lines of division, further lowering the society's level of coherence.

In the political sphere difficulties originate from the fact that in order to carry out a thorough political pluralization it is necessary to inspire political initiatives among the population. After a long period of political suppression and the straitjacket of political uniformity, it is difficult to avoid a period in which all citizens are seeking their own individual political standpoints, distancing themselves from everybody else's. Whether or not a coherent system of political parties can form from the cross-currents of apathy, disorientation and liberation is an open question. Another danger is from irresponsible political leaders, eager to benefit by feeding prejudices and raising animosities on ethnic and social grounds, thereby contributing to further atomization of the society.

The East European revolutions can be ranged along a line reflecting the duration of the incubation period during which important segments of society, both within and outside the country, had time to work out possible alternatives to the communist programme. Alternative programmes discussed in the opposition *samizdat* press, however romantic and unlikely they might have seemed at the time, helped to make society think about alternative options and to reveal candidates for new leaders.

The extent to which it has been possible to carry out such discussions has been determined by a number of factors, efficiency of the apparatus of repression being one of them. Others are the economic and technical means available for organizing *samizdat* publications, the citizens' ability to travel abroad and thus receive stimulation, and the degree of the *émigré* groups' involvement in the home country's political and economic life.

For different reasons Bulgaria and Romania would be placed at the very end of such a line, having had virtually no preparation at all. In Romania, the main reason was the efficient functioning of the security forces. Other significant reasons for the absence of an organized political alternative to the Ceauşescu regime were shortage of money, inability to travel abroad, and lack of organized *émigré* groups that could take up political and economic discussions and project them back into the home country. Ranged further along the same line, Czechoslovakia, Hungary and Poland would be placed in that order. The Czechoslovak and Hungarian societies have been exposed to a more severe political control than the Polish.

The Hungarian economic reform meant some admission of the fact that the centralized economic system was not the absolute and only best way. Confidence in the state and its structures is anyway not a conspicuous feature of Hungarian society, among other reasons because of its experience during the Second World War when Hungary sided with Hitler, and suffered great numbers of casualties as a result. The fresh memory of the consequence of independent action in 1956 is another reason for not trusting the state's ability to manoeuvre in a tricky political situation. The revolution attempted in 1956 in Hungary, and the ensuing Soviet invasion, had a profound influence on later developments. It forced the Hungarian Communist Party under the leadership of János Kádár to a major rethinking of strategies and policies; it started thirty years of experiment with reform from above. As a result, Hungary is today in some respects in a more advantageous position than other East European countries. The service sector and agriculture are functioning fairly well, and in some areas industry is up to the world standard, especially in pharmaceuticals and software (*Bloc*, February/March 1990, p. 35).

In the case of Czechoslovakia there is also agreement about the necessity of market-oriented economic reforms as a means to get out of a similar impasse. There is, however, little agreement about the speed of the reform process. Part of the government, the minister of finance included, and the population seem to be in favour of rapid and radical reform. Other members of the Havel cabinet, for example the deputy prime minister, are more concerned with the social costs that a reform will force upon the population. The Czechoslovak population's socialist sympathies after the Second World War and the 1968 revolution's socialist slogans hint that left-wing political trends are likely to play a stronger role in Czechoslovakia than in Poland, where the threat to the government in power is rather on the right wing of the political spectrum.

In terms of political tradition, Czechoslovakia is in the unique situation of having had a functioning democracy for a couple of decades before the Second World War. Not a long period, but sufficiently alive in the memory of those living today to inspire a call for continuation of the 'European' tradition, as opposed to the use of violence. This, as well as the socialist sympathies and the respect for the working class, has influenced the '10 days revolution'. Decisions were taken in as democratic a way as possible, and it was seen to that each sub-group had a representative from the 'working class' (Ash, 1990a). The Czechoslovak revolution was the smoothest and the one that took the shortest time to implement. Its incubation period was also short. After the 1968 attempt at revolution the Czechoslovak people seemed to have turned inwards, occupying themselves with everything but politics. In a way this was a situation similar to the occupation period during the Second World War. In both periods the Czechoslovak people were very successful at muddling through, trying to avoid the provocation of those in power. This spared the country from political and economic losses, but did not create an oppositional tradition. Even the Czechoslovak exile publications, for example *Listy*, devoted many fewer of their pages to political and economic discussions than did, for example, the Polish *Kultura*, *Aneks*, and many others.

Possibly part of the reason is embedded in the interplay between the country's political situation and the character of the opposition. While the Charter '77 was a humanitarian organization in defence of human rights, in the case of Solidarnosc human rights was just one of a number of issues to be defended. Poland's political situation had changed the agenda. Human rights had been successfully defended in Poland by Solidarnosc's mother organization, the Committee for the Defence of Workers, established after the Baltic coast events in 1970. Towards the end of the 1970s it was no longer standard procedure to beat up political prisoners in Poland. Thus, the new oppositional movement could change focus from the rights of the individual citizen to the rights of the masses. Also the organization became a mass organization, a trade union aiming at influencing Poland's economic and political structures, as opposed to Charter 77's aim of ensuring the citizen's physical security within the existing structures. For the same reason there was a difference between the two organizations' 'foreign offices' in Paris and Stockholm. While Charter 77 aimed at informing the world about the atrocities committed in Czechoslovakia, Solidarnosc put all its efforts into maintaining contacts with political parties, trade unions, banks and other organizations in the West that were considered important for the new Poland after the revolution.

Of the three countries Poland had the longest time to prepare its change of political system. Polish society has historical experience and traditions for opposition, examples including uprisings during the times of Poland's partition, the resistance movement during the Second World War, and the uprisings in communist Poland. Poland also has the politically most active exile groups. One of the consequences of the long periods of occupation by foreign powers, and the society's oppositional response to the alien powerholders, is a specific attitude to the state and the government in particular. Since 'the government' was for decades, indeed nearly for two consecutive centuries, either directly an occupational power or considered to be the arm of an alien state, Poles have developed particular skills in ignoring the laws and rules or countervailing them directly. This does not make life easy for any government, including the current Mazowiecki cabinet. In a period with internal political debates and forces pulling in different directions, for and against market-oriented reform in each of the East European countries, the peculiar thing is that those in Poland aiming at starting private businesses or entering into cooperation with Western companies, tend to ignore the legal obstacles. To a lesser degree than their Czechoslovak counterparts do they seem to wait for political and legal approval of their activity. This does not make the country any easier to govern, and in the long run it might be a severe problem, not least for carrying out economic policy. But in the transition period the appearance is that more things are happening at the grass-root level in Poland than than in Czechoslovakia or Hungary.

At the government level the leaders of today have evolved from a decade's political actions, and from discussions in exile publications as well as local *samizdat* press. The close links to exile groups in the Western countries, especially Britain and the United States, have contributed to the fact that a great number of the present Polish political and administrative leaders have spent time in the West getting acquainted with the Western political and economic system. The long incubation period of the Polish revolution and the long fight have attracted the Western media's attention, making many of the present leaders well known to the Western public, and thereby smoothing the transition process.

Another line to be drawn is a line of transition from centralized to market economy. Somewhere down this line is a model of a centralized economy with market elements. That model had been attempted several times, most often in Poland, in efforts to improve the populations' living standards without changing the economic system. It was a half-hearted model that returned every time to the centralized economy. Starting from the centralized end it proved impossible to introduce only a few market elements at a time without their being quickly recentralized and 'eaten up' by the dominating centralized system. At first glance it might seem as if a discussion of a centralized model with a market mechanism is without relevance in a chapter on post-Soviet-type societies. No politician in the reform-oriented East European countries (at the moment defined as Poland, Hungary and Czechoslovakia) is advocating this model. The place that East European states will take along a line from centralized to market economies, perhaps trying to hang halfway, is determined by a host of factors. The Western interest in getting involved in one country rather than another is of crucial importance. The local society's ability to absorb the flow of capital and joint ventures is another. Here, an important role is played not only by hard data such as the economy's level of organization, the standard of the technical equipment, and so forth, but also by 'soft' factors, such as the society's attitude towards capitalism as such.

This attitude is in part a product of both communist propaganda and available information about the capitalist system: poverty versus glamorous living standards. But it is also shaped by the values predominating in the society, and these are often influenced by religion. Also important is the fear of loss of existing social security. Job security is probably one of the main issues. The individual East European citizen, who has never had the opportunity to prove him or herself in a market economy, is bound to worry about unemployment, even if he/she in principle agrees with the necessity to change the system. It is these factors, taken together with the duration of the incubation period and the existence of alternative economic models, that determine the society's ideological readiness to head down the winding and bumpy road towards a market economy.

Romania is a case where it is hard to see much readiness among the population to take the capitalist road. Neither is there much sign of structures able to incorporate foreign investment. Not surprisingly, Western firms heading for Romania are few and far between. The Romanian revolution does not seem to have been about changing the system. It was more a kind of palace revolution. Unfortunately, it has also been a feudal revolution with all the nasty problems that follow when isolated groups in a deeply suppressed society are grabbing for power. Romanian society is short of most of the types of networks needed for pluralist political and economic activity. The absence of civil society is a much bigger problem than reconstructing Romanian agriculture or industry. Agriculture might be solved within three years, industry within a decade, but the problem of building a society with democratic structures in Romanian political life might take twenty years (Brucan, Radio Free Europe Report, 21 March 1990). Romania has no democratic tradition and, what is worse, its population has been trained over one or two generations to be aggressive, suspicious and to inform on one another. This has inflicted deep wounds on the society that are likely to affect the country's political life.

The Bulgarian change of ruling elite is close to the Romanian case along the range of transition from plan to market. The elite is giving merely verbal declarations of change, and the society has not demanded a thorough market-oriented economic reform.

Hungary and Poland, and to a significant extent also Czechoslovakia, provide many instances of the population being in principle in favour of a market, yet still demanding defence of their individual rights. An example is provided by an interview with Geza Farkas, a Hungarian independent trade-union leader of 10,000 coal miners in the Pecs mining district. He expressed support for and commitment to a Hungarian transition to a market economy and opening towards world markets. Shortly after the interview he was to be found among the leaders of a strike against the introduction of a progressive tax system that would affect the bonuses that so far had helped to keep the miners' salaries above the average for a Hungarian industrial worker. He argued fiercely against the closing down of clearly unprofitable mines unless the workers were paid compensation and offered retraining courses (Srensen, 1990).

Given the dismal state of the economy in the previous Soviet-type systems, finding money for compensation to workers affected by closure of overgrown heavy industries will not only be very difficult, it also goes against the grain of the desired reforms. Citizens in some East European countries have more (or less) to lose than those in others. For example during the last decade or so in Poland one could hardly say there was a well-functioning health care system. It was also irrelevant to argue that under socialism Poles were able to rent cheap flats, because a newly married couple could expect to rent a flat only after waiting three to five decades from their wedding date. Poles thus seem least worried about the 'loss' of the social security system, while the Czechoslovaks still have some elements to defend. This difference affects attitudes towards future social security systems, and how speedily they can be expected to achieve Western standards. Because they have the least to lose, Poles seem to be the most pro-

capitalist of the East European countries. Good-will alone, however, is not a sufficient condition for success.

There is no dispute that the economy works better in Czechoslovakia and Hungary than it does in Poland. But Poles have
become the trading nomads of Europe, and during the last decade
have given up what some used to call the Catholic work ethic and
others saw as the result of decades of communist indoctrination
against capitalism. The networks and skills that Poles, and also
Hungarians, have developed while operating in the second economy are extremely useful for further operations in a proper
market, no longer a black market, as private entepreneurs.
Experiences from a black market are of course not directly
transferable, but they do reduce the individuals' fear of an
unknown system, which is vital for confidence in his/her ability to
survive within the new framework.

This may be one reason why Poland has attracted the majority
of foreign investment, despite the fact that Czechoslovak industry
and agriculture are better organized and better equipped in terms
of technology. In none of these three countries is there any
shortage of willingness to take risks, to start a private enterprise,
despite the fact that the legislative base is still ambivalent. The
Czechoslovak entrepreneurs not only have to struggle with the
bureaucracy and the legislative system. They have also to cope
with the mentality of the society that tends to drag Czechoslovakia back to the middle of the range, to the half-way
solution of a mixture of market and centralized system. The
present Czechoslovak government, composed of previous Charter
77 activists, seems to give more weight to the voices demanding
protection of individual rights, now seen as social and economic
rights, than to the country's economic reconstruction through a
market-oriented reform.

Recent trends in foreign investment are changing. Despite the
half-hearted reforms West German and Austrian investments
have been attracted to both Czechoslovakia and Hungary. The
reason could be that for major firms a bureaucratic system of
economic operation is much less of an obstacle than for the
smaller enterprises, which were some of the first to set out for
Eastern Europe. Historical links between these two states and the
German-speaking part of Europe does without doubt have
significant influence. The foreign investors attracted to Poland
are numerous, but the total amount of capital is increasingly
overtaken by the sums invested in Hungary and Czechoslovakia.
This means that although at the moment these countries are
behind Poland on the line of transition from a centralized to a
market economy, they may soon find that their 'backwardness'
was of benefit. Major Western capital appears to prefer to discuss

the terms of investment with one ministry rather than with a dozen decentralized authorities, however democratic they might be. This does not preclude development of a capitalist system. It is, however, more likely to be a corporatist kind of capitalism.

The vision is one of industrialized, redeveloped countries in Eastern Europe, reaching the level of Southern Europe in political and economic terms. Despite a number of problems, the societies seem determined to move forward along the road towards pluralist political economies. Their individual speed will be determined by a number of internal factors, above all the interplay between the political, historical and economic traditions and developments in each country. Each state's ability to move forward is determined by the degree of cohesion within its society. But external factors also play a role, and not only Western ones. Western capital, technology and organization is highly desired by all the Eastern European states, including Bulgaria, Romania and the Soviet Union. But both Western capital and willingness to engage in Eastern Europe are scarce. A competition has developed between the East European states to attract Western capital.

This is not only the healthy kind of competition, where the aim is to outperform other candidates. It is also the kind where dirty tricks are accepted in efforts to divert possible Western investors from the competition. One tactic is to create rumours about each other. For example there has been a rumour in the international financial world that the Czechoslovak crown would be inflated the week before one of the first private banks with Western shareholders capital was to open. The story, repeated by the bank's director, led, according to him, to hesitation on the part of Western investors. Another story is the Czechoslovak leader's description of Poland as not a European country. The aim of such a statement by Havel was also to distract Westerners from Poland and attract them to 'European' Czechoslovakia. Whether such efforts were successful is difficult to say. In the longer run, however, there is a danger that such a policy will discredit the whole region. In terms of economic reforms, divisions among the East-Central European states are just as damaging as divisions within them.

5.4. Outlook

All the leading parties in Eastern Europe and the Soviet Union are heading for some form of Westernization. Except for East Germany, it is still an open question whether the attempts at Westernization will succeed. They may result in changes that will only amount to reform of the old system. In some cases the attempt to change may produce disintegration rather than viable, functioning economies. All the ex-Soviet-type systems still have the most painful parts of their revolutions ahead of them. Even in Poland, where the unity against the previous regime was strongest, the political divisions are deepening in the face of the hardships of transformation.

Success or failure will depend on the ability of political parties and movements in the different Eastern states to devise adequate policies. However, because it is a revolution of Westernization, ties to the West will be of major significance. This makes the policy of the West very important. Through customs barriers and organizations such as the OECD, GATT, the World Bank and COCOM, the West can substantially regulate both admission to the world market and the availability of credits and technology. The West possesses such know-how as exists, albeit imperfect, about how to manage the complex interplay among a market economy, a democratic political system and a social security system. The West can facilitate learning processes and can make it easier to establish contacts between East and West at many levels, including people-to-people. Westernization being the desired goal, the West has great influence on the transformation process. These include such norms as peaceful conflict resolution, respect for human rights and rights to an adequate standard of living, even for those not in the work-force. The West has a strong financial and political position in relation to the East and Central European states. If its power is not used modestly, if insufficient room is left for adapting the basic elements of the Western political economy to the national historical-cultural roots of the individual nations of East-Central Europe, then in these communities anti-Soviet feelings could quickly be transformed into anti-Western ones.

Two strategies seem possible in relation to the transformation of Eastern Europe (Strange, 1990). They are likely to result in very different prospects for Europe as a whole. One is aimed at using Eastern Europe as a reservoir of cheap labour for assembling goods designed and marketed in the West. This strategy will result in a dominance–subordinate relationship similar to that between the United States and Latin America. It would probably cause continued indebtedness in Eastern Europe and tend to make the region unstable. The other is a 'Marshall Plan' strategy. The aim of this would be to integrate the East European states as equal partners in the European and world economies. A means to achieve this goal would be to use Western credits to encourage regional cooperation and trade. Other elements in such a comprehensive 'Marshall Plan' approach could be better access to Western markets, providing funds and know-how for retraining courses, and for the establishment of social security systems.

Given the size of the Soviet economy, a 'Marshall Plan' will have only marginal importance for it. The best the West can do in order to enhance the chances of success of the revolution of Westernization in the Soviet Union is to make it easy to establish ties to the West and to facilitate the learning process of how to manage a pluralist political economy. In addition, as a partner in the arms control negotiations, the West has some influence on the possibilities for cutting military forces in the Soviet Union. Agreements on arms reductions and defensive deployments are important for the success of the revolution in the Soviet Union, facilitating the conversions from military to civilian industry without giving rise to accusations of endangering national security.

Chapter 6
The Centre: The German Problem

The fall of the Berlin wall on 9 November 1989 marked a historic change in the European political landscape. As described in Chapter 5 Europe had already experienced profound changes in the East before this date, both in the Soviet Union and in Eastern Europe. But the opening of the border of East Germany, the break down of the communist regime and the process towards German unity added another dimension of change in Europe. The so-called 'German problem' had again been put on the European agenda. The consequences of the move towards unification between the two German states were to be great not only for the Germans themselves, but for the whole European development.

The events in Germany during the autumn and winter of 1989–90 came as an immense surprise to practically everyone, politicians and observers alike. Things moved with amazing speed. Up to the autumn of 1989 the situation was one in which the Germans were organized into two seemingly stable states, West and East Germany, both of which worked for improving their mutual relationship and relieving the consequences of their separation. By the spring of 1990, unification between the two states seems to be the only likely outcome. It is difficult to interpret this development and its consequences, but it is quite obvious that the changes which it brings about are of great importance.

Previous chapters have described how the European security complex is in a phase of basic change. A main thesis has been that in this phase of European history the 'overlay' of superpower dominance which has dominated security questions in Europe since the Second World War is breaking up. This gives rise to new problems and perspectives. It also results in the revitalization of problems, which in some aspects are old, but now appear under new conditions and in new forms. A main purpose of this chapter is to investigate how German unification is one of these latter issues.

The breakup of overlay does not mean that developments in the European security complex now happen independently of the superpowers. The withdrawal of the superpowers from Europe is only relative, not total. It is a shift from overlay to penetration. Thus an important task is to identify both the emerging, relatively independent European dynamics, and the new roles that the United States and the Soviet Union will play in European security in the coming decade and beyond. One relevant question for this chapter is how the future roles of the United States and the Soviet Union might develop in relation to both Europe and Germany.

Although the German problem is reappearing on the European agenda, the new questions concerning a united Germany in Europe are not taking the old form. The wish for or fear of a 'reunited' Germany, and worries over its possible role in European politics, are still part of the problems of the new German development. But one should be careful about thinking of the German problem in old ways. The current developments on the European scene have already profoundly reshaped the character of the questions related to Germany's future role in Europe. The German development will have central importance not only for the Germans themselves, and their Central European neighbours, but also for the whole European security complex. Consequently, the political strategies for German unification will affect decisively the political conditions of European states outside central Europe. The future organization of Europe, and also the distribution of relative power in all of Europe, are at play in relation to the German development.

6.1 The German Problem in the History of European Security

What is 'the German problem'?

How has the German problem been seen in the history of European security? The elements of the problem are diverse and complicated, but two essential aspects stand out. One relates the problem to issues of power and security, the other relates it to culture and ideology. The security aspect of the German problem is concerned with the power balance in Europe: how can the German people be organized politically without disturbing the balance of power in Europe and causing insecurity for other European states? The most traditional way of thinking about this question is to relate it to the fear of a reunited Germany. The cultural and ideological aspect of the German problem relates to the question: how can the whole German people, the German nation, enjoy the right to organize its political life as it itself wishes in free self-determination? As will be explored below, this question has elements of both national and democratic ideology. There is a close connection between a national and a democratic ideology, but they are not identical. Any discussion of the German problem should distinguish between these two aspects of cultural identification.

In essence the German problem is the task of finding a solution to both power-security and cultural-ideological questions at the same time. After the events of November 1989 these two questions take the form: (1) how is the relationship between the Germans in the two states to be organized, and (2) how is a unifying, and eventually united, Germany to fit into an overall European framework? As Hassner puts it: 'What kind of Germany would fit into what kind of Europe so as to be neither too strong nor too weak for the European environment' (Hassner, 1968b, p. 2)

Clearly, there are other important questions which are closely connected with the German problem, and which in some interpretations are seen as part of it. One is geopolitical, relating to the position of Germany in the centre of Europe and the German role that derives from this. Another concerns the issue of democracy in Germany. Seen in a historical context the Germans have had strong authoritarian political traditions and have had great problems in establishing a democratic political life for themselves. The history of West Germany has been an important and positive exception in German history, and the recent development in East Germany has been an exceptional change. For the first time in history the Germans have had a successful and peaceful revolution. Due to the problematic history of democracy in Germany, West German politics has been marked by a 'stability complex'. One thinks the patient is ill if he just sneezes!

It is a consequence of the double nature of the German problem that when seen from within it has not looked the same as when seen from the outside. In Germany the main content of the German question has been the division of the German nation and the lack of self-determination for the whole German people. (In Germany one tended to talk about the German 'question' rather than the German 'problem'). Thus the question was for decades closely connected with the lack of political freedom in East Germany. The political debate has been concentrated on the 'renunification' of the two Germanies. (The concept of 'reunification' is seen by many as problematic as compared to 'unification'. The concept is unclear because the whole German nation was never totally united. When much of it was united in the Wilhelmine Germany and under Hitler it comprised much more than the area of West and East Germany. Furthermore, the 're-'

tends to signal recreation of a kind of Germany we have seen before. It is unlikely to be in the German interest to create this image abroad (cf. Eppler, 1989).

Seen in the perspective of the neighbours to the two German states the main content of the German problem has been the historically founded and for many still remaining fear of the re-emergence of a united and powerful German state, which once more might change the balance of power in Europe. The external perspective is thus focused on the international setting for the German state or states and on the longer historical perspectives. (This is the context in which one has tended to talk about the German 'problem'. In this book we use 'German question' and 'German problem' interchangeably.)

The division between an internal and external perspective represents important tendencies in political debate and theoretical literature, but it should not be overemphasized or treated as representing mutually exclusive views. One might argue that both among the Germans and among the neighbours to the German states the best interpretations include both, seeing the German problem in security and in cultural perspective. The great challenge in the German and European development in the present phase is precisely to find new forms, and reach new understandings, which can overcome the division between the two aspects of the German problem.

The complexities involved in the German problem are demonstrated by the divisions over the names used for the two German states. Bonn has insisted on the name 'The Federal Republic of Germany' or just 'the Federal Republic'. One reason for this is the ambivalence contained in the Federal Republic: does it refer to *the* Federal Republic of (all of) Germany, or to the provisional Western state, or in some sense to both? This ambivalence was the preferred position for Bonn since the first meaning refers to the long-term aim and the second to the present status. 'West Germany' and 'East Germany' or the two acronyms (in German, BRD and DDR, in English, FRG and GDR) displayed too much parallelism (Grosser, 1988, p. 267). As long as Bonn used SBZ (Soviet Occupation Zone) for the Eastern 'state', one could accept BRD for the Western one. But when Bonn acquiesced to general terminology and adapted 'the DDR' (but *not* 'German Democratic Republic'), it was officially decided not to use 'BRD' in official communications (Brückner, 1979). Thus Bonn used, and asked its allies to use, the names: 'the Federal Republic (of Germany)' and 'the DDR'. The Russian term 'The Federal Republic in Germany' was resented by Bonn. In the summer of 1989, when Gorbachev visited Bonn, the Soviets introduced the name 'The German Federal Republic', a term which still contained important ambiguities. East Berlin has seen the terms 'West' and 'East' Germany as putting too much stress on two halves of a whole, and therefore preferred the full name 'German Democratic Republic' or in recent years, at best: 'GDR'/'DDR', which avoided totally any reference to 'Germany'.

This fight about names was of course also a fight over the question of whether the Western state was in some sense the truest representation of 'Germany' or whether it was just one of two or more states in 'Germany'. In this discussion we use the names East and West Germany simply because they are the most generally used, at least outside Germany. With the benefit of hindsight, and with an ever more real 'Germany' coming into existence, it also seems appropriate to use these terms.

On state and nation in the history of Germany

It is useful at this point to consider how the concepts of state and nation relate to German history. The Germans were among the last of the major European nations to form a nation-state. This meant that when the nationalist movement reached Germany during the nineteenth century, it did not find a ready-made nation-state. Where such states already existed, national movements expressed themselves in struggles for democracy based on the idea that the people should be sovereign. But in Germany this was not possible. The national question in Germany became a confused mixture of the desire to unite the many German states into one state, and the fight for a democratic form of government. These two purposes were sometimes in competition with each other (Gruner, 1985).

In the liberal movement in Germany in the middle of the last century there was a high degree of congruity between the national and the democratic cause. But when the democratic revolutions of 1848 failed in some German states, the forces favouring a democratic nation-state were severely weakened. In the last part of the nineteenth century it was the conservatives, in alliance with some national liberals, who dominated the national question. This movement expressed itself in the policy of Bismarck, and the creation of Wilhelmine Germany which triumphed in 1870. What resulted was a 'small' German nation-state, not including the Germans in the Austro-Hungarian Empire, and with only a rather limited form of democratic government.

The relationship between the fight for national unity and the fight for democracy thus became problematic in Germany (Craig, 1984; Grosser, 1988). It became part of the German political experience that the quest for nation and the quest for democracy could part ways. This tension was carried through into the post-1945 period. During the 1950s and 1960s a key argument of the CDU was that West Germany should not sell freedom for unity: i.e. should not make a deal with the communists for unification at the price of cutting links with the democratic West. This same argument still has echoes in the SPD's criticisms of Chancellor Kohl's precipitate drive for unification during 1990.

For Germany, there is an element of truth in Hans Kohn's distinction between Western and Eastern conceptions of the nation, with Germany belonging to the Eastern category. Eastern nationalism derived from the so-called 'romantic nationalism' of the early nineteenth century. Thomas Nipperdey (1986, p. 32) sums this up in two claims: (1) all culture is national, and (2) a nation is defined through the communality of its culture. Nation-states existed prior to this idea, but they did not rest on the powerful notion that a people naturally belong together because of a shared culture, history and language. Romantic nationalism developed as a reaction to the universalism of the enlightenment. It stressed the worth of unique and distinctive cultures, shaped by particular histories, and delineated by nationality. (Finkielkraut, 1987). In these terms, a nation is defined by objective historical and cultural factors. By contrast, Kohn's Western (mainly French) conception of nation is based on subjective factors. Here the ultimate basis of a nation is the choice of the individual to belong to it: Renan's famous definition of the nation as a daily plebiscite. These two views of the nation are reflected in two theoretical traditions of the state: French individualist and German organic (Dyson, 1980, pp. 157–83).

To begin with, the nation was seen by the romantics to be more important than, and even an alternative to, the state. Later (Hegel and all that) the romantic idea of the nation became the foundation for a strong idea of the state. Romantic nationalism first took root among the peoples that did not live in nation-states, Germans and East Europeans in particular (Nipperdey, 1986, p. 141ff.). But it did not remain confined to East-Central Europe. Even in France, romantic nationalism grew to challenge the individualistic Western view.

The Germans developed a particularly strong concept of state and nation precisely because they lacked a nation-state. This concept can work in two very different directions. On the one hand, it can underpin aggressive chauvinist policies in which a German state asserts the prior rights of an objective German nation. This quality is by no means unique to German nationalism, but manifested itself with particular brutality in the German case. On the other hand, it can inform a vision of a national culture realizing itself without a state to contain it: a

'*Kulturnation*', thriving in spite of, or even because of, the lack of a '*Staatnation*'. Many Germans developed a conception of culture and politics according to which the Germans were deeper and had a more inner-directed concept of culture and a more organic attitude towards society and state. This was compared with the individualistic, superficial, Western democracies. At the same time, however, Germany was seen as distinct from the mysticism and despotism of the East (Russia, Asia and the like). This pattern of thinking was powerful in the late nineteenth and early twentieth centuries and was part of the process leading up to Hitler.

These questions have deeply influenced the ways in which Germans have been thinking about their divided nation in post-war Europe. The range of possible solutions to the German problem is dependent on which understanding of nation prevails. Even after the unification of East and West Germany this question will remain, since the German nation extends well beyond the borders of the two German states. In the 1980s, several intensive debates in West Germany (*Historikerstreit*, Heidegger controversy, *Mitteleuropa*) can be interpreted as debates about whether West Germany had become and should remain a truly Western country. Could it, and should it cut the cords of its 'deviant' history (*Sonderweg*)?

The Greens were criticized for linking up to the earlier tradition when they orientated themselves towards inner development, and towards the romanticism of the German *Wald* (forest). *Mitteleuropa*, often presented by social democrats as a project for *détente* and enlightened reform policy on both sides of the Cold War, was vulnerable to the same criticism (Wæver, 1989a, pp. 314ff.; 1989b; forthcoming). The German right wing came up with ideas for re-evaluating German history and identity which also met the same attack: it is dangerous to start thinking again in anti-Western, 'in-between' terms. This counterattack was mainly carried out by left-centrists such as Jürgen Habermas and liberals such as Sir Ralph Dahrendorf. Their argument was that it was a decisive gain for Germans that their post-war identity had become adjusted to the 'normal' Western form. All attempts to find a special German tradition 'in-between' would undermine the democratic commitment of West Germany (Jahn, forthcoming). Robert Picht has argued that if one looks at opinion polls or concrete behaviour such as consumerism, West Germany has definitely become part of the 'normal' West (Picht, 1989).

The post-war concept of the state in West Germany has been one of controlling the state, of securing a balance between state and society. This balance is aimed at avoiding the excesses of a strong state (Hitler) as well as those of a weak one (Weimar)

(Holm *et al.*, 1989; forthcoming). To what extent are these changes away from traditional German state forms and national identities based on learning processes and societal evolution, and to what extent do they rest on a specific constellation of power where the international conditions made all other options impossible? In the first case, this political culture must be expected to stay. In the second case, there are more grounds for concern, since the post-war power structure that shaped and divided Germany is itself now breaking up. Habermas has argued (1990, pp. 62ff.) that West German pride has been displaced to the economic level (pride of the Deutschmark) because there was no nation-state to become nationalist for. But with unification there is a danger that the combination of Deutschmark pride with a revived nation-state pride will lead once again to arrogance.

These questions will be on the agenda in the coming years as all watch carefully the direction of German domestic politics and foreign policy. It is important to remember three things when observing this unfolding. First, that the specific German tradition is not only one of state-fetishism and great power behaviour. It is also one of believing in the inner qualities of the nation as separate from the political state. Second, the post-war period has marked a very sharp break with these German traditions and has taken West Germany on to the track of Western political 'normality'. Thirdly, this Westernization of German political culture has been articulated strongly as a desired aim, and in the debates of the 1980s seemed to win out. The Germans want to be Western rather than 'in-between', even if they also still want to be German.

On the history of the German problem in European security

The German problem has played a central role in the history of Europe. Twice in this century an expansionist German state has with violent means attempted to increase its power within Europe and in the world. Twice Europe and the world have for this reason experienced the catastrophies of war. And twice Germany has been defeated.

If we take a longer historical view, we can say that the whole history of European security has been closely entangled with the fate of the Germans. For centuries Germany was divided into a multitude of separate states and principalities. The great struggle in the Middle Ages was between the German emperor and the Pope. One of history's most destructive wars, the Thirty Years War, took place mainly in Germany and removed for a long time any basis for power concentration in the German area. For centuries Germany was divided into a multitude of separate states and principalities. In the 'European concert' which lasted from 1815 to at least 1856 two German states played a role as weak great powers in the multipolar international political system: Prussia and the Austro-Hungarian empire.

It is a commonplace to note that the position of Germany in Europe is marred by a weak/strong dilemma: a united German state will always be too strong to fit into a stable balance and too weak to stabilize Europe by dominating it. Actually this is not entirely true. At the happy moments of European history where the structure was stable, there was a solution to this dilemma. The 'Metternich system', which was partly responsible for the stability during the 'European concert', was in fact a dual system: a system for organizing the European state order, and just as important, a specific arrangement for the states in and of Germany. The latter part consisted of the *German Confederation*. In this strange construction, Austria was a member but only with its German third, the Polish provinces of Prussia were not in, but the

Netherlands were represented because of the possession of Luxembourg, and Denmark was included because its king was also ruler of Schleswig-Holstein. Prussia, the largest purely German state, had only one vote out of seventeen. It was theoretically possible that a grouping of states comprising less than a quarter of the population or resources of Germany could outvote the major powers, Austria and Prussia [Kissinger, 1968, p. 901] . . .

Under this arrangement, Germany was neither too centralized and powerful (which would trigger counterbalancing by France and Russia) nor too divided (which would invite constant pressure on Germany). This solution was secured in an over-all balance in Europe between Germany and East and West but also through the specific internal equilibrium within Germany which made Germany able to resist attacks from the outside but unable to become centralized enough to threaten offensively (Kissinger, 1957, 1968).

In the coming years a major issue will be whether there is a geo-political logic that, political and democratic rights and national self-determination notwithstanding, makes it unfortunate for all that West and East Germany (and Berlin) unite in one state. One part of this question will be the character and degree of federalism in Germany. To what extent does the democratic and federal charac-ter of West Germany and a coming 'Germany' modify the unfor-tunate geopolitical logic? (Holm *et al.*, 1989; Nipperdey, 1986 pp. 71–131). Does federalism in Germany actually amount to a modern equivalent of Metternich's arrangement? Will it be too weak in the real issues of high politics: budgets, exchange rates and military policy? Will the federative character be strengthened or weakened by unification? This latter debate is already vigorous in Germany.

One suggestion for handling the alliance dilemma for the territory of East Germany has been to set up a kind of home guard or territorial defence under command of neither NATO, the NATO member 'Germany', nor the no-longer existing East Germany, but under command of the *Länder* (constituent 'states'). Would this be, in effect, a move back to a Germany of local princes and overlapping authorities? Some people have expressed fear that unification could weaken the federative traits. The federation (*Bund*) would obtain more status as it moved closer to being a nation-state. It would also be strengthened by the sheer numbers of *Länder*, and by the relatively weak character of those yet to be re-established in East Germany. The mayor of Bremen suggested a reorganization into less and bigger *Länder* allegedly in order to strengthen the counterweight to the federal state power (*Frankfurter Allgemeine Zeitung*, 19 April 1990).

2. The Post-War Division of Germany: From Unification to Reassociation (1945–88)

Even during the Second World War the German problem, the problem of how to organize the future of the German people within the future Europe, was at the centre of the attention of the Allies. In the negotiations around the end of the war (especially in Yalta and Potsdam, 1945), one of the main questions concerning the future of Europe was the organizational problems related to Germany. This resulted in 'plans for Germany' ranging from total destruction to different concepts of a divided, non-militarized and non-industrialized country. (See for example Hans-Peter Schwartz, 1966.) But as the Cold War sharpened, the plans for Germany diminished in importance. By the time of the formation of the two German states in 1949 the German problem was overlaid, as was the rest of Europe, by the East–West conflict. During the period in which the Cold War dominated the organization of Europe, the German problem still existed. Beneath the cover of superpower overlay, it took different forms and underwent important changes. In the autumn of 1989, it once again resurfaced at the forefront of European politics.

The German problem in the 1950s

In the first decade after 1949 the internal aspect of the German problem — the question of German self-determination and the

unity of the German nation — was dominated by the enforced
division of Germany and the creation of the two German states.
The most central and often very heated debate in West Germany
during the 1950s was connected to the West German dilemma
between giving priority to West Germany's Western orientation,
which was preferred by the conservatives and Chancellor Konrad
Adenauer, and giving priority to the national question and 'reunification' (*Wiedervereinigung*), which was preferred by the social
democrats under the leadership (until 1953) of Kurt Schumacher.
The debate in West Germany during the 1950s between the two
policy lines concerned both the state's attachment to the economic
integration in Western Europe (participation in the Coal and Steel
Community and later in Euratom and the EEC) and, in a more
heated debate, the rearmament of West Germany and its attachment to NATO. The social democrats succeeded neither in
gaining government power nor in changing the government's
policy line, and in 1959 changed their position with their
Godersberger programme. In 1960 they accepted the Western
orientation of West Germany as a premise for their policy,
establishing an internal consensus on this, which lasted throughout the 1960s and 1970s, and with some modifications, throughout the 1980s.

The **Ostpolitik** and the German problem

An internal consensus was thus established on the Western
orientation of West Germany from around 1960. But another
disagreement, and another phase of the internal debate in West
Germany on the German problem, began during the 1960s in the
form of an increasingly important difference of opinion on policy
towards the East. The result of this disagreement did not become
manifest at the government level until the end of the 1960s with
the so called *Ostpolitik* of the Brandt–Scheel government. But the
roots of this policy were present much earlier in the 1960s, in the
building of the Berlin wall in August 1961, and in the interpretation by at least some politicians in West Germany that this
could be seen as a failure of the Eastern policy pursued during
the Adenauer period. The new Eastern policy might also be
interpreted as a reaction to the improved relations between the
United States and the Soviet Union which, especially after the
Cuba crisis in 1962, initiated the first *détente* period of long
duration between the superpowers (Nolte, 1974, pp. 473–589).
The new Eastern policy can be interpreted as the somewhat
hesitant adaptation of West Germany to this new international
détente.

The content of the new *Ostpolitik* was essentially a whole set of agreements between West Germany and the Soviet Union and the other Eastern states in the period from 1969 to 1972. The SPD's leader, Willy Brandt, had already attempted to introduce a new policy towards the East as foreign minister in the 'great coalition' between the conservatives and the social democrats in the period 1966–9, but without success. It was not until he took over the Chancellorship in the first social-liberal government in West Germany in 1969 that he was able to put the policy into effect. His government very quickly, and in an extremely intensive negotiation process, put the new policy through. The agreements with the Eastern states aimed mainly at establishing with them a common acceptance of the status quo in relation to the two German states, but without giving up West Germany's legal positions. The purpose of the policy was described, in the words of Willy Brandt: 'we had to accept the *status quo* territorially in order to dislodge it politically' (Brandt, 1978, p. 498).

The *Ostpolitik* can be seen as a policy by which West Germany 'Europeanized' the German question. By recognizing the existing order in relation to Germany, West Germany also recognized that attainment of unity could not take place through any separate German policy or without changes in the overall European order. This recognition in effect subordinated the goal of German unification to the broader goal of overcoming East–West differences. It also created possibilities for a specific West German policy towards East Germany. Thus this subordination of the goal of unification to a broader European goal, which was interpreted by many as giving up the unification goal, made room for a specific German–German policy. In effect, it divided the policy of unification in two, a European policy and a German–German policy. It established the view, which has been dominant in West Germany ever since, that it would be impossible to find a solution to the German problem independently from a solution to the East–West conflict. Since then, and until the present phase, the relationship between the two German states has been concentrated on improving relationships between the Germans in the East and the West within the framework of the East–West conflict. This policy of 'human relief' developed its own life and history, but it was not until 1989 that changes in the East–West relationship also changed the basic German–German relationship, thus vindicating the linkage of the East–West conflict and unification.

Whereas the new *Ostpolitik* was often seen outside Germany as a way of closing the German question, in Germany it was neither presented nor accepted as a 'less national' policy. It was sold on the argument that it was the only way to keep the nation alive and eventually to generate some movement into the frozen situation.

Thus, it was in no way part of a revision of the unification aim. The debate was on *means* to this end. However, the social-liberal governments were probably not unhappy with the frequent misunderstandings among neighbours and allies in seeing West Germany as turning from being a revisionist power into one supporting the status quo. The importance of these domestic discourses surfaced in late 1989, when it suddenly became decisive that parties pursuing *de facto* status quo policies had never argued against the aim of unification. They had only argued that prevailing conditions made it impossible to go for more than human relief. Even in the early Eastern policy it had been said that real unification was the preferred outcome. Except for the Greens, debates within Germany on German politics were debates inside this consensus (Meyer, 1989; Holm *et al.*, 1989).

West Germany's European policy developed into a general policy of European *détente*. It manifested itself in West Germany's engagement in the CSCE process, which can be regarded as a multilateral continuation of the *Ostopolitik*. It had considerable success in the early 1970s during the *détente* period, but ran into difficulties during the second phase of the Cold War at the end of the 1970s and the beginning of the 1980s. It was important, though, that the CSCE process never broke down completely, not even at the peak of the second Cold War in 1983–4. During the new *détente* towards the end of the 1980s the CSCE-negotiations were vigorously revived.

The revitalization of the German problem in West Germany in the 1980s

At the beginning of the 1980s, West Germany experienced a new internal debate on the German problem. With various aspects and nuances this debate continued all the way through the 1980s. The main lines of West Germany's position towards the internal aspect of the German problem were not changed from the 1970s. During the whole period it was clear that West Germany did not seek any special German way in relation to the German problem and that unification should be neither sought nor expected without amelioration of the East-West conflict in Europe. Thus, the reason for the new debate was not a changed view on the relationship between the German–German policy and the East–West problem. Rather, it arose from deep cultural factors relating to collective identity and new political factors.

The deep, cultural factors were an undercurrent of increasing problems relating to German identity. For the West Germans the substitute identities of economic growth and Europeanness were increasingly worn out, and in many different contexts questions of national identity started to reappear. West Germany (as all German states) has been hit by several rounds of self-doubting debates on national identity. But this one turned in a new direction. Identity in West Germany was found neither in the Federal Republic on its own nor in the contrast to East Germany, but rather as an image in which East Germany was seen as somehow the crucial factor for 'Germany' and thus for one's own identity, as German, in West Germany (Korte, 1988). Political problems were articulated as questions of identity, and the issue of identity found expression in concrete political issues and debates (Weidenfeld, 1983).

The major political factor was that at the beginning of the 1980s it was unclear how the new conservative-liberal government under Chancellor Kohl's leadership, which came into power in 1982, would deal with the Eastern policy previously followed by the social-liberal coalition. Although the CDU had sharply resisted the Eastern policy at the beginning of the 1970s the new government's policy was characterized by a remarkable continuation. This, on the other hand, disappointed important groups within the CDU, in particular the groups of refugees and those who had been expelled (*Vertriebene*), causing much internal political debate and provoking many 'Sunday speeches' in which some verbal compensation was given to these disappointed groups. It was the speeches for these groups which, in spite of the continuity of the Eastern policy, triggered a new debate on West German revanchism.

The severe controversies between the government and the opposition on the INF-issue also had a certain spill-over into the German question. This reflected a long-standing tendency for all great debates on West German security to end up being also debates on the future of the nation: and vice versa (Weidenfeld, 1983, pp. 32ff.). Clearly, the pro-INF policy in the debate on the stationing of new nuclear weapons in West Germany triggered the argument that this policy would spoil the possibilities for improved relations between the two German states. The more leftist policy of joint German–German security positions seemed to involve a 'two state patriotism', in effect affirming the division of the country. This led quite a lot of social democrats away from the previously shared aim of ultimate state unification (Brocke, 1985; Bredow and Brocke, 1986; Holm *et al.*, 1989).

In 1986–8, when the second phase of *détente* was developing, new possibilities arose. With the new policy in the Soviet Union, some people in West Germany, especially the social democrats, but also some on the far right, saw new possibilities for European development. Because of the linkage between Germany and Europe, this also meant possibilities for more mobility in the

broader aspects of the East policy and therefore also for the
Germany policy. Other groups, especially parts of the conservatives, saw another danger: that improved understanding
between the superpowers might endanger Western Europe's
security position, especially the position of West Germany. The
Reykjavik summit at the end of 1986, and especially the fact that
President Reagan engaged himself in a policy of nuclear disarmament which was not in line with the overall NATO policy, was
interpreted as a severe danger for West Germany. This argument
gained in strength when an INF agreement became more and
more likely. Yet the conservative resistance against this, and the
dangers for a new special threat towards West Germany (*Deutsche
Sonderbedrohung*), were put aside in the summer of 1987 in order to
keep internal agreement between the Allies. In a very complicated
way this debate realigned the internal criticism against external
forces, which threatened progress in the German–German
relationship. That this relationship was improving in this phase
was clearly demonstrated by General Secretary Erich Honecker's
visit to West Germany in September 1987.

A further new aspect in the debate in West Germany on the
German question became vital in the summer of 1989 when
reforms in Poland and Hungary were accepted by the Soviet
Union. This gave new hope not only for reform in East Germany,
but also for overcoming the whole East–West contradiction in
Europe. These hopes were nourished in June 1989 when Gorbachev visited Bonn. During this visit Gorbachev did not take as
negative a stand on the possible changes in the Soviet view on the
German question as he had done at the end of 1988, when
Chancellor Kohl visited Moscow. Thus by the summer the debate
in West Germany had a new perspective: preserve *détente* and
continue to improve relations with the other German state, but
also pursue development of better relations with the Soviet Union
and the Eastern European countries in order to create new
conditions for a European solution to the German problem. The
main interpretation of the German–German relationship during
the summer of 1989 was that the prospects for cooperation with
the East German government, in combination with the policy of
human relief which had been followed since the beginning of the
1970s, were good. As a leading analyst wrote in July 1989: 'The
real issue today — the 'new German Question' relates not to
reunification but to the evolving modalities of inter-German
détente and their implications for European security' (Larrabee,
1989, p. 3). Even in the summer of 1989 no one could foresee how
the German question would very soon be put on the European
agenda, not by West Germany or the West, but through the
developments in East Germany.

Seen in this light both the character of the German question and the relationship between the two German states underwent a profound change with the fall of the wall on 9 November 1989. Since this event the whole character of the German–German relationship has changed radically.

6.3 The Revolution in East Germany and the Process of Unification

The history of East Germany was marked by its struggle to establish itself as a normal state in the international community. One of its great difficulties in the 1950s was to be recognized by other states. It succeeded relatively well in this, although West Germany attempted to prevent it through the Hallstein doctrine, which said that West Germany would not keep up diplomatic relations with states that recognized East Germany.

The West German 'new *Ostpolitik*' was at first resented by the East German government under Walter Ulbricht, but in spite of this it was accepted by Moscow, and after a change in government in East Germany in 1971, which brought Erich Honecker into power, it was also accepted by East Germany. One of the consequences of the new Eastern policy was that West Germany gave up the Hallstein doctrine. This improved the standing of East Germany in international society. In the Basic Agreement of 1972 between West and East Germany (*Grundlagenvertrag*) East Germany was recognized as a state, although not a normal state, by the West German government. Willy Brandt's government insisted on the basis of 'two states, one nation' that East Germany was not a normal, foreign state. One of the indications of this was that so-called 'permanent representations' and not normal diplomatic representations were established between the two states.

Even after the shift of government in East Germany in 1971, the reaction to the Eastern policy of the social-liberal government in West Germany was a 'policy of demarcation' (*Abgrenzung*). In the 1970s the communist leadership in East Germany acted from the concept of 'two nations, two states', establishing the idea of a 'socialist nation' in the GDR and eliminating the references to the 'German people' in its official language. In 1974 the constitution of East Germany was changed accordingly.

During the 1970s and 1980s East Germany was generally recognized as a stable state in which the government through its very authoritarian means had control over the economy and the people. It followed a cautious cooperative line in relation to West Germany, continuing the demarcation policy but also maximizing the profits from small concessions to the West Germany policy of 'human reliefs'. Thus the rules for travel over the German–German border, for minimum exchanges of Deutschmark to Eastern mark, were used in bargaining with West Germany. Through this policy the East German government obtained large credits and other economic advantages from West Germany.

In the 1980s it was remarkable that East Germany followed a line which, compared to the line of most of the other Warsaw Pact countries, was relatively independent from the Soviet Union. At the beginning of the 1980s, when the East–West conflict sharpened, East Germany reacted with moderation. Right after the decision in West Germany in November 1983 on stationing of the INF missiles in West Germany, and the breakdown of the Geneva negotiations between the Soviet Union and the United States, East Germany reacted with a policy of damage limitation, trying to keep as much of the *détente* alive as possible. In the last years of the second phase of Cold War (1984–5) East Germany was, together with Hungary, considered to be one of the most progressive states within the Warsaw Pact.

East Germany continued this line during the new *détente* in the last part of the 1980s. A clear manifestation of the cooperative line towards West Germany was the visit of GDR's leader, Erich Honecker, to Bonn in September 1987. Cooperation went even further in this period in the different agreements which the communist party of East Germany formulated with the West German SPD on nuclear-free and chemical-weapon-free zones in Central Europe, and on 'a new culture of political conflict' in an age of common security.

Yet in relation to the Soviet Union, East Germany experienced increasing problems. These were not directly because of the general Soviet *détente* policy. They arose from the steadily increasing pressure for reforms in East Germany, which was nourished both by the internal reforms in the Soviet Union and by the reform process in other Eastern European countries, notably Poland and Hungary. These in turn were amplified by the influence from West Germany. Because East Germany did not give in to the reform pressure, in the late 1980s it was placed in the reform-resistant group within the Warsaw Pact along with Czechoslovakia, Bulgaria and Romania. It was this position as externally relatively well adapted to the international conditions in the *détente* period, and internally seemingly politically stable, but under increasing pressure for internal reforms, which developed so dramatically and surprisingly during the autumn of 1989.

The fall of the Berlin wall

The developments in the late summer and autumn of 1989, which led to the fall of the Berlin wall on 9 November, constituted a complicated set of events. Only in combination can these be seen as having caused the dramatic result. In some ways it was the stream of East German citizens attempting to reach West Germany via the West German embassies in the other Eastern European states that triggered the chain of events. Yet the many reasons why this became possible must also be seen as different factors of explanation.

Without attempting a detailed analysis, the following factors can be mentioned as important for the developments in East Germany in the autumn of 1989.

(1) The Soviet acceptance of non-interference. The signals sent by President Gorbachev more or less directly to the people in East Germany, especially during his visit for the fortieth anniversary of East Germany, indicated that the Soviet soldiers in East Germany would remain in their barracks if the demonstrations were directed towards *perestroika* and *glasnost'* in East Germany and not against the Soviet Union.

(2) The developments in Poland and Hungary. Generally the reforms in these countries caused pressure for reforms in East Germany. Of particular importance was the policy of the Hungarian government. When it was simultaneously asked by the governments in East Germany and West Germany respectively to stop and not to stop the East German citizens in their attempt to reach West Germany, it chose to let the East Germans go. After this it became impossible for the communist government in East Germany to control the 'voting with the feet' without increased oppression of the East German people.

(3) The influence in East Germany from West Germany, not least in the media. West German television can be watched all over East Germany. There is no doubt that the intense coverage in the West German media of the stream of refugees and their problems, and of the demonstrations in East Germany, contributed to an accelerating process of discontent and hope for reform in East Germany.

(4) Most important was the fact that the regime in East Germany had insufficient support among the people, so that, when the chance was given, there was a great willingness among people in East Germany to engage politically and demonstrate for reforms. Especially in the beginning this was a very daring undertaking and demonstrated a politicization of the masses

of East Germany. This cannot be explained without the other factors mentioned, but it also shows that the people of East Germany were not as conformist and not as politically demobilized as observers in the West had postulated for many years. Nevertheless, it should be remembered that the East German revolution, as most other revolutions, was initiated by demonstrations characterized by a high ratio of youth and outsiders. In the second round the controlling fear was removed and a wider spectrum of society participated.

There were profound reasons for the breakdown of the East German regime. Many of these were the defects of the 'soviet type of system', which were discussed in Chapter 5. In East Germany the reasons for the revolution have become much clearer in the light of developments after the fall of the wall. Most important was the lack of support among the people for the regime. Its moral bankruptcy had also become obvious. Other reasons were the bad state of the East German economy and the devastating ecological effects of the mismanagement of the economy.

The process of unification

The fall of the wall initiated what was in fact a domestic revolution in East Germany, but it also initiated a process in which it became gradually clearer from week to week that the forces for a new and independent East German state had to give in to the forces which sought a unification of East Germany with West Germany (a 'second revolution'). Thus the result of the fall of the wall was not only the revolution in East Germany, but also the process of unification which will result in the dissolution of East Germany.

The unification process, which started in November 1989, was not a result of political developments within West Germany, but of the developments within East Germany and in the relationship between East Germany and its neighbours. Yet the way in which the unification process developed is clearly dominated by West Germany, both by its official policy, and by the internal debates and interests within West Germany. Indeed, the whole way in which the German problem has been understood within West Germany during the Cold War years has now come into play in the broader game of Germany politics. In this course of events it has been very important that the political leaders and the public in West Germany have not interpreted the German question as closed, but have, in spite of the priorities given to European development, preserved both the understanding of

West Germany as a provisional state and the goal of national unity.

The constant stream of *Übersiedlers* from East Germany to West Germany, which did not stop after the fall of the wall but stayed at its high level of about 2,000 per day, put pressure on the Kohl government to act. The political situation in West Germany, with an election due in December 1990, made it impossible (within the existing domestic political discourse) for any major party not to declare itself for German unity. Thus the situation was characterized by a competition among the parties in West Germany to be most pro-unification. Despite the problems created by incoming East Germans nothing was effectively done to stop them from coming.

The policy of the Kohl government after the fall of the wall was laid down in the ten-point plan of 28 November. This plan foresaw a process of unification in stages, emphasizing the democratization of East Germany and the establishment of confederative structures between the two states. It stressed that the unification process should take place within a European context. Yet the fact that the Allies were not consulted in advance, and that the plan did not include references to the Allied powers in Germany, subtracted politically from this statement, as also did the fact that Kohl did not consult Genscher, his coalition partner.

The SPD reacted to the fall of the wall with a policy that stressed unity as the goal of the process. When the wall fell, the party was in the last phase of a great programme revision, aimed at finalizing a new policy in place of the old Godesberg programme from 1959. At its Berlin conference in the beginning of December 1989, the SPD completed this task, but the part of the programme which related to the Germany policy had to be taken out of the programme and replaced by an independent declaration. In this the goal of unity was given priority over a confederation between the two states. There was a marked difference of opinion within the SPD on this. One line, with a national emphasis, was advocated by Willy Brandt. Another, with a more pragmatic line, which was hesitant about over-hasty unification, was advocated by the SPD candidate for the Chancellorship in the 1990 election, Oscar Lafontaine.

Even in the early stages of the development after the fall of the Berlin wall the international dimension had a major impact on Bonn's policy. It can be argued that in November and December Kohl, Genscher and the whole establishment actually attempted to slow down the process of unification and keep it below the limit of the international right to interfere (Wæver, forthcoming). One might also find that the government in West Germany did not do very much either to stabilize East Germany, or to encourage the GDR-Germans to stay in East Germany.

Instead, it encouraged unification through massive engagement in the election campaign in East Germany and retained the special treatment (for example *Begrüssungsgeld*) of the Germans coming over from East Germany (Kelstrup, 1990b).

The amazing speed of developments in East Germany made it clear that the preference there was for speedy unification, and this quickly overtook the positions in West Germany. Thus a broad consensus on the general goal of unification emerged in both German states. The intermediate goal of confederative structures or a confederation dwindled in relevance. The Foreign Ministry eliminated 'confederative structures' and 'community of treaties' from official terminology in early February (*Spiegel*, 12 February 1990). Instead the practical political question became: how can the economic and social problems in East Germany be managed within a unification process? And what is the easiest legal way to unity? The first debate concentrated on the appropriateness of the early establishment of a monetary union between the two Germanies and on a wider economic union, which also specified the conditions under which West German capital could invest in East Germany. Soon fears in the East German population about the social and economic problems that could follow a monetary and economic union led to claims for the inclusion also of a social union between the two states. The discussion on the easiest legal way to unity concentrated on the question of whether it would be preferable to use paragraph 23 or paragraph 146 in the constitutional law. Paragraph 23 gives a possibility for other *Länder* than those constituting the Federal Republic to join the federation and thus adopt the legal system of West Germany. Paragraph 146 says that the constitutional law is valid until a new constitution is decided upon by the whole German people.

The political, economic and social problems in East Germany after the fall of the wall first led to round table discussions between the government of the 'reformed' communist party (which changed its name from 'SED' to 'PDS') and the opposition groups, and then, when the problems sharpened in the early months of 1990, to a coalition government including the oppositional groups and agreement on an early election. The election was held on 18 March after an extremely short election campaign. The result of this first free election in East Germany since 1945 was an overwhelming (and surprising) victory for the conservative 'alliance', which got 48 per cent of the votes. The East-CDU gained 41 per cent of the votes, the East-SPD got 22 per cent, the former communists, PDS, got 16 per cent and the Liberals 5 per cent. The East German people, by giving support to the Alliance, had voted for a speedy unification with West Germany.

The period from the fall of the wall until the early spring of

1990 was characterized not only by the revolution in East Germany but also by a deep crisis in East Germany which led to the process of unification. This process was mainly driven from within, but stimulated by the West German attitude towards unification. While a German–German unification process accelerated in the early months of 1990 the problem of relating this process to European politics was growing quickly. Thus the German–German unification process was soon followed by a parallel German–European unification process.

The German–European unification process: the two plus four formula (2+4=5)

As it became increasingly clear to the different actors that German unification was really on the agenda, it became equally clear that there had to be some negotiations about the international aspects of unity. In the beginning it was a German concern that this could turn into a reimposition of (symbolic) occupation. If the four met against the wishes of the Germans because they stated that Germany was overstepping the post-war line (and especially if the four met on their own), we would more or less be back in Potsdam, the nightmare of West German foreign policy. This possibility and fear very much structured the situation during November and December 1989.

When it became generally accepted during late January and early February, even by the Soviets, that unification had to come and that one could not blame it on Bonn, it became the interest of Bonn to get started with negotiations about the transference of responsibility for 'Germany as a whole' from the four powers to Germany. Negotiations could then be called not against Germany but as a symbol of the general acceptance of German unity as a reality in the making; i.e. negotiations to carry the process through to unity. It was important to the Bonn government that the negotiations should be 'two plus four', not 'four plus two'.

The shift in the Soviet attitude towards German unity became manifest when Kohl and Genscher visited Moscow on 10–11 February 1990. Shortly after, on 14 February, informal consultations between the two German states and the four at the edge of a CSCE-meeting in Ottawa on 'Open Skies' took place. It was agreed that negotiations should be initiated between the two German states and the four former allies on the external aspects of German unification. Thus the Ottawa meeting led to the so-called 'two-plus-four' formula. The Americans were awarded the honour for the agreement though it seemed to be one of the many successful moves by Genscher, as well as one among several cases of efficient cooperation between Bonn and Washington. At the first meeting (in Bonn, in early March) the Soviet diplomat did not accept the name 'two-plus-four' so the meeting was called 'the six'. The latter of course poses the problem that the six at some point will be only five. Regarding meeting place, it was also a sensitive compromise when it was decided to rotate among all six capitals. Bonn had wished to meet only in Germany.

Not all neighbours were happy about the initiation of the 2+4 negotiations (as they were still called in public). Several meetings in NATO, the EC and other forums were held in the spring of 1990 to coordinate attitudes. Poland demanded access to the 2+4 negotiations and this was supported particularly by France and the United States. The Polish concern was first of all the direct one that the four powers might (once again) sell out Polish interests. (Politics of status could also be involved since Poland sees itself as something like a number 5–7 in European rank: on the basis of population and historic symbolism, although not of economic weight.) For other countries such as Italy and the Netherlands, the quarrels might stem more from a concern that the '2+4=5' negotiations could be the embryo of a future European security council. The Italians could rightly claim that they have as much right to sit in such a council as the British have. The Dutch oppose this kind of great power directorate in principle.

A further question of far-reaching importance was the mandate for these negotiations. Should the six negotiate about unification *in toto*, or only about the external aspects of unification? The solution was the latter, thus the four have formally no influence or veto on the internal aspects of unification which are negotiated solely between the two German states. The set up was that the six and the two were expected to negotiate in parallel. The internal aspects were to be worked out by the two, the external by the six, with a certain synchronization taking place between these two processes. Then the agreement regarding the external side was to be presented for endorsement by the other twenty-nine states in the CSCE process during the autumn of 1990 at the 'Helsinki 2' summit. Because of the need for coordination of the two processes the four to some extent retained an indirect veto on the unification process.

This whole constellation meant that due to the unavoidable speed of the processes in Germany the external side of German unification would have to be agreed at least in its outline by late 1990. Since arrangements for Germany cannot in practice be separated from the new security order for Europe, this meant that decisive elements of the so-called new 'European architecture' were to be formed during 1990 under incredible time pressure. Of course, this could not mean a final answer to the future of Europe. History remains open. Even the competition among the scenarios of this book remains open. But, nevertheless, a number of central structural elements in the new Europe had to be fixed at the pell-mell speed of German growing together in order to keep up the balance between Germanization and Europeanization.

6.4 German–European Questions in the 1990s

There is a shared understanding in Europe about the necessity of tying Germany into European structures. However, the different powers have an interest in using different organizations for this purpose.

For France it is first of all a stronger EC that can make German unity safe for Europe (read: for France), but even this is not sufficient. For France a future Europe has to include a *grand dessein*, for France and for Europe. This is no longer the EC as an aim in itself. Now the meaning of the project is Europe plus Eastern Europe. One of the curious inversions of 1989 has been that France became the leader of the (political) *Ostpolitik*. In this view, the EC will remain distinct from the East but it will *act* for Eastern Europe. France will stand at the head of this project. Thus an expanded Eastern policy (*Ostpolitik*) and the actor capacity of the more narrow EC-Europe (political union) become two sides of the same coin (a French franc). The increased integration of the EC is necessary as French compensation for three reasons: as a direct rope to tie Germany, as a means to secure French competitiveness against a stronger Germany, and finally to give France a new role in a post-Yalta Europe where its mission and position can no longer be made secure by the cry: we want to overcome Yalta (Holm *et al.*, 1990).

The Soviet Union is probably the state that in influence and power stands to lose the most by developments in Europe and in Germany. The Soviet Union is also the arena in which Europe can lose most: unacceptable developments in Europe/Germany could be the final straw, added to the weight of economic chaos and disintegration of the state, that breaks the reform process in the Soviet Union. A change of policy in the Soviet Union could (see Chapters 5, 9 and 11) have major effects on developments in Europe. Both the Soviet Union and France could lose much if the present cooperative trend in European security management was undercut by a nationalist change of policy and by a revitalization of the old power-aspect of the German problem. The Soviet development, however, seems the more problematic since so many other developments put a strain on the legitimacy of the present leader.

Soviet reactions in November were relaxed: no alarmist warnings about stability or about the balance. The Soviet leadership seemed to have accepted the interpretation that it would be sufficient to apply the principle of self-determination together with the view that every state had a right to security. This would make a two-state solution for the Germans, with a reformed East Germany, the most likely. But the Soviet Union could not hold this position as actual developments in East Germany went in the direction of unity. Therefore they changed their position in January 1990, marked by Kohl and Genscher's visit to Moscow on 12 February. This was to some extent foreshadowed at the meeting between Gorbachev and East German Prime Minister Hans Modrow. What was new was a clear statement to the effect that the internal side of unification, including form and speed, was an internal German affair, whereas there had to be consultations on the external side.

The Soviet position in regard to a United Germany's position in the European security system was that Germany should be neutral. The Soviet demand for Germany to be neutral was not put with much force. For instance, Foreign Minister Shevardnadze remarked that this was the ideal solution but 'there were others, and Genscher had made some interesting suggestions' (*Süddeutsche Zeitung*, 12 February 1990). During the next month (at the Ottawa meeting and the first 2+4 meeting in Bonn), the Soviet Union was wavering on the question of German membership in NATO or neutrality. This might have been due to competing opinions in Moscow, or it could easily have been a tactical position in order to get a better bargaining position. The Soviet demand for Germany to be neutral is a major bargaining chip, which it can use in reaching what seems a more realistic, and in the last instance also preferable, outcome for the Soviets: an all-European system of collective security.

A new system of collective security in Europe could mean anything from a brand new, complete system of collective security to some significant strengthening and institutionalization of CSCE. The strictly military component could be a new mutual obligation among the CSCE (or perhaps only the 'European') states — or it could more realistically be in some way built on the existing alliance(s).

In fact the Soviet Union has been surprisingly slow or restrained in formulating concrete visions for an all-European security system. Such a system could even serve as a way to dress up neutrality. Among West German social democrats various expressions have been tried in the direction of giving Germany a position which is neither neutral nor a member of NATO. It means to go directly from the present situation to an all-European security system. More realistically the European security system could be a parallel evolution of the CSCE, a strengthening of the EC and a continuation of NATO. The French, the Russians and the Americans would then be soothed by different structures (EC, CSCE and NATO respectively) and these would only in a very partial sense be fused into one coherent construct. Each power could concentrate on the forum where it felt itself the most reassured and the most able to exert influence on Germany.

Why should it be necessary to have an all-European system of collective security? Why not just give concrete guarantees for Soviet security? Because for the Soviet Union the new security order has to be symbolic, as the control of East Germany was very symbolic. It was the main prize of their Second World War victory. Letting it go would be an offence to millions of dead Russians. 'As the colours and contours of Europe's political map are changing, the bones of Russian infantrymen stir in their unknown graves', Alexander Prokhanov wrote in the January issue of *Literaturnaya Rossiya* (quoted by Dashichev, 1990, p. 12). Equally symbolic would be the diplomatic victory of attaining the classical Russian and Soviet aim of a diplomatic system for managing European security including a leading role for Russia/Soviet Union.

Furthermore, the creation of an all-European system (European Common House) can with the present weak situation of the Soviet Union be seen less as the classical threat of Soviet influence in Western Europe and more as a way of retaining *some* influence in Eastern Europe. 'There will in any case be some sort of European Home, and a home in which the European part of the USSR will have a place is the only alternative to one from which it is shut out' (Shenfield, 1989, p. 8). Thus the option of gaining through the deal over Germany an all-European security order also serves a broader purpose as a way to stay in Europe — to avoid the present changes ending up as the formation of a clear-cut 'Poland to Portugal Europe' pushing the Soviet Union in all senses out of Europe. The Soviet system for 'the whole of Europe' could not win out as the only format for Europeanization, but it has a chance to act as counterbalance to the dominant mode of Europeanization.

The US interest is to secure a future political role in Europe which allows for some military and economic disengagement, while at the same time keeping good relationships with Western Europe, and especially with the united Germany. The immediate American interest is economic and, as is well known, trade and investment are the first casualties of conflicts. So for the Americans it would be dangerous if the process of the new European bargain should break down in any way and produce new conflicts and splits around Germany. These would mean renationalization and probably have negative implications for the international economy. A further factor behind the American support for unification could be that in the US perspective the unification is also interpreted in East–West terms, as a gain for the West. All together this has produced a constellation where the US government has functioned as mediator, and as the one of the four with the fewest 'vested interests'.

The British also seem to have limited interests in the German unification process compared to France and the Soviet Union. And that is exactly why Mrs Thatcher could dare to be so brutally negative, though at the price of losing influence over the whole European process.

Poland is of course the most threatened of all, but Poland is not a great power. It is a medium-sized power with an unfortunate location and a tragic history. In general Eastern Europe in the future will probably be an area of German economic dominance. This seems to be tolerated by most of the new elites but with the condition that the European structures be as strong as possible. Therefore in contrast to the Soviets, the East Europeans support the idea that a unified Germany should become and remain a member of NATO (cf. meeting of WTO foreign ministers in Prague, 17 March 1990).

It seems necessary that the main bargain in relation to the German-European unification process has to be made with Paris and Moscow in order to secure their acceptance of German unity. The issue is primarily for them so sensitive, that it could unleash reactions (due to *raison d'état* or domestic populism) that could in the end prevent or more likely ruin the harmony in unification. This is not a rational policy for France or for Russia and self interest should deter them from adopting it. But enough is at stake to pose the danger that they could turn in a nationalist direction as a reaction to their loss of position resulting from the recreation of a strong European centre. A process of unification forced through against the will of one or more of the four would be much less attractive to the Germans. First of all, because the new Germany would then be born into a Europe which was structured from the start as 'All against Germany'. Therefore the game for Bonn, and thereby the German-European question of the early 1990s, had to be how to secure a tolerable Europe for France and Russia, the losers of the post-war peace (Wæver, forthcoming).

The foreign policy elite in Bonn showed a considerable ability to think along these lines. Across the political landscape there was a willingness to think of the EC project in French terms (Glotz, 1990; von Staden, 1990; see further Holm *et al.*, 1990). For a long time the Soviets seemed unable to put forward clear plans for what had to be their interest: collective security arrangements for

Europe. Instead the foreign ministry in Bonn worked these out! (*Spiegel*, 12 February 1990.) The election manœuvres of Kohl did not always contribute to confidence in Paris and Moscow, but the ministry of foreign affairs as well as the broader establishment clearly worked on a model which was more than just any Europeanization of the German question: it was clearly a triple Europeanization. Processes in Germany (and thereby in Central Europe) would unfold very much in German colours, but Western Europe (EC) had to be built along the lines set out by France, and Germans were figuring out the all-European and disarmament arrangements in Russian.

Naturally, it is very difficult to find a solution which can give the needed security to all the actors concerned. One possible answer, and maybe the most probable, is the one described above: a new historical compromise emerges in Europe resulting in an economic and political structure in which the main concerns of the major actors are taken into consideration. Thus it is possible that the Germans will get unity and relatively positive economic possibilities in Europe generally (through the EC's internal market) and particularly in Eastern Europe. The French might get a much more politically integrated EC and also the desired all-European role. The Soviet Union (or Russia) might get an all-European security system and maybe other guarantees for non-exclusion (also economically) from Europe. And the United States might obtain a renewed political role in Europe and preserve a military presence on a lower (and less expensive) level, not least in a continued, but somewhat changed NATO.

It is not at all certain that such a historical compromise will come about. The German question functions as an accelerator, but at the same time as a potential brake, for Europeanization (both Western Europeanization and all-Europeanization). There seems to be in the present situation much pressure for a specific bargain where the different Europeanizations balance each other. One way of reading the rest of this book is therefore as pointing out where the risks are. The different ways in which this possible main scenario can go wrong (backlash in the Soviet Union, overwhelming dominance in the EC by Germany, and so on), point to the roots for the scenarios in the last part of the book.

Chapter 7
The West: Cooperation and Rivalry Among the Western States

This chapter discusses how West–West relations are developing during the breakup of superpower overlay. By 'West–West relations' we mean the relations within the Atlantic Community as well as the relations between the states within Western Europe. In both cases we deal with interstate relationships and with the international organizations of special relevance for the Western states. Thus NATO has a crucial function in the transatlantic relationship, and the European Community (EC) and other Western European organizations are central on the West European scene.

In Chapter 3 it was described how after 1945 Western Europe was partially dominated by its relationship with the United States. This chapter contains a more qualified interpretation of this statement. In the first part of the chapter we discuss the transatlantic relationship. We look particularly at Western Europe's security problems and the importance of the coupling of the United States to the defence of Western Europe. The main view is that in the history of Western Europe there has been a competition between Atlantic cooperation and specific Western European cooperation. In this competition the Atlantic line has dominated, especially in the security field. There have been only relatively weak moves towards clear Western European cooperation in the security area. In other areas the manifestation of Western European cooperation has been stronger. In the economic field there has been relatively far-reaching integration especially concentrated on the development of the European Community. In the discussion of the transatlantic relationship in the 1980s we distinguish between the tensions at the beginning of the 1980s and the improved relationship during the second period of *détente*. We stress that the United States' participation in the new international *détente* was combined with a positive American engagement in the *détente* and changes in Europe. Thus the revolutions in Eastern Europe were followed by exceptionally cooperative tendencies in the Atlantic relationship and by a changed stance for the United States in its policy towards Europe, most notably in choosing West Germany as its leading partner in Western Europe.

The second part of the chapter discusses tension and cooperation in Western Europe. We look at the old tensions in Western Europe and at the developments in Western European integration. In examining the integration process we put special emphasis on the new dynamism that has characterized the EC since the middle of the 1980s. We also deal with the developments in other Western European forums, with the all-European process, especially the CSCE process, and with the interplay between the all-European process and the development of the EC.

The third part of the chapter deals with developments in the present post-Berlin wall period. We examine the Atlantic relationship and the internal relationships in Europe in this period. As described in the earlier chapters this period is characterized by the revolutions in the East and the development towards German unity. The description in this chapter adds to these the new dynamism in Western European integration. The interplay of these developments raises many questions. What are the consequences of the diminishing Soviet military threat? How is a united Germany to be fitted into the organization of Europe and into the Atlantic relationship? What will be the interplay between the process of integration in Western Europe and the all-European development? We might interpret these problems as the relationship between a 'European house', a 'political (Western) union', the German problem and 'new Atlanticism'. The main concern in the chapter is with how West–West relations have developed in this period. What characterizes the Atlantic relationship, and what is meant by 'new Atlanticism'? We attempt to interpret this phase of Europe's development as tensions between new relationships and old institutions. The discussion of the possible developments of this tension will be continued in the scenario chapters on the future of Europe.

7.1 The Atlantic Community

The transatlantic relationship and Western Europe's security problems

The premiss for our interpretation of the history of Europe is that in the period after the Second World War the East–West conflict became dominant for Europe, which was subordinated to the bipolar structure. There is a very important difference though, in the way the United States organized its relations with Western

Europe as compared with the way in which the Soviet Union organized its dominance over Eastern Europe. Immediately after the war the American attitude was 'to bring the boys home'. The United States demobilized and started to withdraw its troops from Europe. Yet, as the Soviet Union established not only military but also political control in the East European countries, and further seemed to pursue an expansionist policy in Korea, the United States changed its policy and decided to return its forces to Europe. Moreover, in the sharpening East–West conflict both of the new superpowers drew important lessons from their experiences from the war. They both established forward defence in Europe. The Soviet Union established a glacis undoubtedly on the basis of the Soviet experience with the German attack on Russia in both world wars. The Americans drew lessons from Munich and Pearl Harbor in the establishment of a forward defence in Europe, a policy which later led to the rearmament of West Germany and its inclusion in NATO. Both superpowers formed their military strategies on the basis of the negative experience with appeasement strategy in the 1930s. This can also be seen as the basis for their deterrence strategies.

Immediately after the war the United States had a very strong relative position within the international system. During the war the dominant power centre within the West shifted from being mainly British to mainly American. The Soviet expansion after the war was a challenge to the new American hegemony.

In the immediate post-war period, Western Europe's security problems were dominated by the Soviet threat. This meant that Western Europe felt the need for an American engagement in Europe as a counterbalance to the Soviet forces in Eastern Europe. Since then Western Europe's main security problems have had a double nature. One part has been how to deal with the Soviet threat under conditions of geostrategic asymmetry, which place the two superpowers at unequal distances from Europe. The other part has been how to secure, and how to deal with, the American engagement in the defence of Western Europe. This problem of coupling and de-coupling the American engagement in Western Europe has been an important aspect of Western Europe's security since the onset of the Cold War.

The problems related to the American engagement in the defence of Western Europe, and to the fears of de-coupling, became more important when Soviet nuclear weapons were added into the strategic equation during the late 1950s. The emergence of the balance of terror created an important nuclear dilemma in the transatlantic relationship. Seen from the American side the United States' engagement in Europe ultimately demanded the problematic commitment to engage in strategic nuclear retaliation in case of Soviet aggression against Western Europe. This would with near certainty provoke a Soviet counterattack on the United States with devastating effect. Seen from the European side the dilemma was that an American commitment requiring eventual suicide was not credible. This created recurring doubts about the credibility of the American nuclear guarantee (Buzan, 1987b, chs. 10–12; Snyder, 1984; Jahn *et al.*, 1987).

The many developments in the strategic relationship between the United States and Western Europe after 1945 can be interpreted as different ways in which the United States established its forward defence in Europe, and in which Western Europe tried to secure the American engagement in the defence of Western Europe. Thus it might be seen as ways in which the two parts, the United States and Western Europe, tried to overcome their respective dilemmas. This holds for the rearmament of West Germany, the stationing of tactical nuclear weapons in Western Europe in the 1950s, the German debate on nuclear weapons in the 1950s, the strategic debate on massive retaliation, the MLF-debate, the change to the present NATO strategy of flexible response, the withdrawal of France from the integrated defence cooperation within NATO, and the debate on the non-proliferation treaty.

On the historical development of the transatlantic relationship

In the history of the transatlantic relationship after 1945 it was not evident at all times and for all actors that the defence of Western Europe should be organized on the basis of Atlantic cooperation. Since the war there has been competition between a West European and an Atlantic orientation.

In the military field the Atlantic cooperation was institutionalized in the Atlantic Alliance (NATO) in 1949. An attempt to organize clear Western European cooperation was the plan for a European Defence Community (EDC) from 1950. After the negotiations on the EDC plans had made them more Atlantic in their orientation and secured American support, they failed in 1954 because of opposition against them in the French parliament. This failure led in 1955 to a strengthening of Atlantic cooperation by the inclusion of West Germany in NATO. With this move, the dominant orientation and organization for the defence of Western Europe became the transatlantic relationship. Attempts to build up cooperation among the Western European countries in the military field have reappeared from time to time. One was the withdrawal of France from military integration within NATO in

1966, which can be seen as a protest against the Atlantic dominance in the defence of Western Europe, and allegedly also against
the lack of credibility of NATO's new nuclear strategy, flexible
response. Others were the revitalization of the WEU in the 1980s
and the inclusion of discussion on security policy within the
machinery for European political cooperation (EPC). These
tendencies have not been able to challenge Atlantic dominance in
the military field.

In the economic and general political sphere the relationship
between the West European and the Atlantic orientation was
different. From the beginning the United States supported the
establishment of open markets in all the countries participating in
the Marshall Plan. The attempts to create economic cooperation
between the West European countries were supported by the
United States. A specifically West European development
succeeded in the 1950s in the establishment first of the Coal and
Steel Union and then of the European Economic Community and
EURATOM. This process of 'narrow' Western European integration accelerated in the early 1960s, but by the mid-1960s ran
into a severe crisis. This was partly overcome by the beginning of
the 1970s in a process which broadened the character of the
integration. This included acceptance of new members and the
establishment of European Political Cooperation, combined with
new initiatives for deepening integration, such as the plans for the
establishment of a European Economic and Monetary Union
(EMU, the so called Werner plan). Yet the EC, and especially the
plans for deeper economic cooperation, ran into difficulties when
the Bretton Woods system broke down in 1971, and these
difficulties grew with the oil crisis two years later. Western
European integration stagnated during the 1970s, and it was not
until the mid-1980s that it gained new dynamism.

In spite of the periods of stagnation, economic integration in
Western Europe has been a success. The growth of the Western
European economies in the decades after the war was so successful and sustained that Western Europe grew relative to the United
States. The rising strength of the EC on the world market led to
tensions over economic issues with the United States. This was
the case during the late 1960s, when the EC Commission
attempted to pursue a more active, regulatory policy, and at the
beginning of the 1970s, when differences emerged between West
European and American interests over the oil crisis. Again in the
late 1970s tensions arose between Western Europe and the United
States, this time because of European dissatisfaction with United
States economic policy, a tension which was manifested in disagreements between Chancellor Helmut Schmidt and the American Presidents Jimmy Carter and Ronald Reagan.

The overall consequence of Western Europe's development in the decades after the Second World War was a growing in-congruence between the military and economic positions of Western Europe in the international system. Military cooperation was organized on a transatlantic basis in NATO. And while the general framework for international economic cooperation was the American-dominated Bretton Woods system, a more concrete and institutionalized cooperation in the economic field was orga-nized among the main states in Western Europe in the EC. Transatlantic tensions in the military field related mainly to nuclear dilemmas and strategic questions, and to the question of burden sharing. They were primarily conflicts within NATO. In contrast to this, tensions in the economic field took place between the EC and the United States.

The hegemonic or near-hegemonic position of the United States after the war was based on the relative dominance of the American economy, and the shorter-lived American monopoly on nuclear weapons. The general trend in the relative international position of the United States in the decades after the war was a relative decline in hegemonic power. Economically, the US share of the GNP of the world in 1950 was estimated at 34 per cent, its share of the global industrial production at about 60 per cent, and its share of total foreign currency reserves at about 50 per cent (Senghaas, 1986, p. 32). In 1980 the corresponding figures were 23 per cent, 30 per cent and 6 per cent (Senghaas, 1986). The forecasts are that the US share of the global GNP in the year 2000 will have diminished further to 17–18 per cent. The reason for this relative decline has not been the development of the Soviet Union, but the relative economic growth in Western Europe, Japan and, more recently, Southeast Asia and other newly indus-trializing countries. From the late 1950s the United States also lost relative power in the military field as the Soviet Union developed a nuclear second strike capacity. The change in power relations in the military field, which led to nuclear parity between the superpowers, was recognized in the SALT I agreements in 1972.

During the 1960s and 1970s American leaders were confronted with the problem of managing the relative decline in American power. One had, as formulated by Paul Kennedy, to ask the question: 'What do we do as the first generation to have to manage America's relative decline?' (Kennedy, 1982). This can be seen as the main problem in American foreign policy in recent decades. For example Stanley Hoffman in *Primacy or World Order*

tried to show that the United States had a choice between a classical policy of primacy and an innovative policy of world order, made necessary by the transformation of power in the atomic era and in the age of economic interdependence, and by the huge risk of violence and chaos present in the international system. (Hoffman, 1983, p. 1).

The foreign policies of the American administrations in the 1970s can be seen as different ways of adapting to the growing complexities of world society and of finding 'an innovative policy of world order'. Thus the foreign policy of Richard Nixon and Henry Kissinger recognized the political-military interdependence with the Soviet Union and gave priority to a differentiated and multipolar-orientated diplomacy, although one characterized by a relatively narrow priority to geopolitical and military considerations. The foreign policy of the Carter administration went even further in attempting to adapt American foreign policy to the 'emerging complexities' of the international system and to follow a foreign policy which, at least in theory, was based on a broad concept of interdependence. In practice the foreign policy during the Carter administration was not so clear, and can be interpreted as alternating between a new orientation based on interdependence and the old traditional American foreign policy of 'leadership', which dominated especially in the later part of Carter's administration. (See for example Senghaas, 1986, p. 35ff.)

The foreign policy of Ronald Reagan in his first period can be interpreted as aimed at the re-establishment of the 'American primacy' in the international system. The idea of emerging complexities and interdependence was put into the background and military strength and geopolitical options received priority. This resulted in a new policy of strength, ideological confrontation and tendencies towards unilateralism (the interventions in Grenada and Libya). Also in the economic field Reagan's policy was for 'a strong America'. This had severe consequences for the American balance of trade and sharpened the disagreements in the economic field between the United States and its Western allies.

The continued Soviet armament in the 1970s, especially the steadily growing number of intermediate-range nuclear missiles (SS-20s), caused great concern in Western Europe, not least in West Germany. This concern resulted in a call for a new American response to what was seen as a growing Soviet threat towards Western Europe and especially as a risk of de-coupling due to loss of escalation dominance. The West Europeans, not least Chancellor Helmut Schmidt, were at least partially responsible for NATO's 'dual-track decisions' in December 1979 in which it was decided to station new intermediate-range nuclear missiles (INF) in Western Europe, unless there was within four years an agreement with the Soviet Union to eliminate this new threat to Western Europe. In the late 1970s and early 1980s the West Europeans were thus pressed by what was considered a growing Soviet threat. But at the same time the revitalization in the late 1970s of the old American policy of military strength created severe difficulties and dilemmas for the West Europeans. Most parts of Western Europe, particularly West Germany, still adhered to a *détente* policy. As a consequence Western Europe experienced a repoliticization of security issues, growing peace movements and rising public interest in security issues, especially after the NATO dual-track decision of 1979 and the election of President Reagan in the autumn of 1980.

This new security debate included heavy public criticism of the United States in Western Europe and caused new Atlantic tensions. The attempts in the 1980s by governments in major Western European states to lean more towards a clear West European orientation in the security field can be seen in the light of these new Atlantic tensions. Yet the attempts to intensify security cooperation between the Western European countries, first in the EPC and later in the revitalization of the WEU, did not have much success. Atlantic tensions in the early 1980s were high because of the United States' sensitivity towards public opinion in Western Europe. Janet Finkelstein has argued that United States needs Western Europe to legitimize its international policy as being something more than American unilateralism. Because of the American distaste for *national* power politics, it has been necessary to present the actions of the United States in the name of 'the West' or 'democracy'. A major controversy in the early 1980s therefore was the American criticism against the Europeans for lack of moral support. 'The USA claims that its global strategy represents something other than its own interests, and in the view of the US the only authority competent to validate this claim is Western Europe. But such an "authority" is resented' (Finkelstein, 1989, p. 96).

As mentioned earlier Western Europe experienced great difficulties in its economic development in the 1970s. The economic crises at the beginning of the 1970s, which were dramatically worsened in 1973 by the oil crisis, hit Western Europe very hard. The economic crisis lasted throughout the 1970s, furthered by the second oil crisis in 1978–9. These economic difficulties caused a stagnation within the EC which lasted throughout the 1970s. In the 1970s severe economic tensions developed between the EC countries and the United States, mainly because of the economic policy of the United States and the fluctuations of the dollar. One consequence of this was that West Germany gave up supporting the dollar and together with France initiated the European

Monetary System (EMS) at the end of the 1970s. At the beginning of the 1980s the relative economic stagnation in Western
Europe continued. One of the main economic debates in Western
Europe during this period was on 'Eurosclerosis': the fear that
Europe would fall behind in the new technological revolution and
lose its relative position in the world economy. These fears were
the main driving forces behind an attempt in the middle of the
1980s to give a new impetus to the process of European integration. This led to the plans in 1985 for the creation of an
internal market before the end of 1992, the so-called '1992
project'. In 1988 and 1989 this was expanded further with plans
for the establishment of a monetary and economic union (the
Delors plan). Thus it was not before the end of the 1980s that
the element of pure West European cooperation, which had been
latent in the European Monetary System since the end of the
1970s, was picked up again and integrated in a new dynamism in
the EC.

On the transatlantic relationship in the second phase of détente

The second phase of *détente* began after the Reykjavik summit in
October 1986 and ended in late 1989 when *détente* turned into the
end of the Cold War. One important development in this period
was the change in the foreign policy of President Reagan. *Strategic
Survey 1986–87* (IISS, 1987, p. 5) described the development of
American foreign policy in 1986 in this way:

President Reagan began the year with the confidence that derived from
his extraordinary popularity at home and substantial approval from his
allies abroad . . . As the year wore on, however, his Administration began
to look less in control of its policies, reacting to the outside challenges
with uncertainty and in the end failing to cope . . . The sum of the year's
activities, misadventures and revelations left the Administration with its
foreign-policy goals undermined, and the President's own authority and
credibility damaged.

President Reagan managed to get out of the foreign policy crisis
in 1986 through a remarkable shift to what was in reality,
although the term was avoided, a new *détente* policy. The first
result of this was the summit in Reykjavik in October 1986.
Although final agreements were not reached, this meeting
marked a consensus between the two superpower leaders on the
goal of nuclear disarmament. The Reykjavik summit and the
succeeding Soviet concessions paved the way for the INF agreement late in 1987. At the same time the change in American policy

towards the Soviet Union, and especially President Reagan's stand on nuclear issues, caused severe uncertainty among the Allies. His proposals were not consonant with the nuclear strategy of NATO, and the United States had not consulted with its European allies beforehand. Thus, the major Western European states, especially West Germany, only supported the INF agreement after hesitation and difficult internal debates. Western European hesitations about the concrete steps towards the new *détente* — a *détente* they had themselves advocated — must be interpreted in the light of the fundamental Western European fear not only of the Soviet Union, but also of being de-coupled either from the United States or, through an exclusive cooperation between the superpowers, from influence on developments affecting Europe. Nevertheless, as the new *détente* unfolded, these fears were calmed. Work within NATO on a new comprehensive concept for security and disarmament was part of this process, and the result was that a common Atlantic *détente* policy developed in the late 1980s.

It was important for Europe which foreign and European policy the new Bush administration would choose when it came into office in January 1989. There were clear indications beforehand that Bush would continue the American policy from the late Reagan period. Yet, through the developments in Eastern Europe, especially in Hungary and Poland early in 1989, there were new questions about how far the new administration would go in a *détente* policy. President Bush hesitated for some months before a new policy became clear. This period saw a new transatlantic conflict in the security area: in April–May differences arose over the modernization of short-range nuclear missiles (the SNFs) in Western Europe. The government of West Germany took the extraordinary step of challenging the United States severely on a security issue. It turned against a modernization of the SNFs before the next West German election in 1990, and argued for negotiations with the Soviet Union on tactical nuclear weapons. The reasons for the change of attitude in West Germany were quite obviously of an internal political character: fear of a new modernization debate and vulnerability because of the government's poor electoral prospects.

The conflict over modernization in the spring of 1989 was solved by President Bush at the NATO summit in May 1989. In effect Bush's proposals for this summit initiated a new line in the United States' policy towards Europe. Without reiteration of the concrete American proposals we can interpret this policy as containing the following main elements: (a) an active engagement in the new *détente* in Europe, also in the changes in the East (cf. the

American engagement in the CFE negotiations in Vienna and Bush's travels in Hungary and Poland in July 1989); (b) indications that the United States will, with the continued *détente* in Europe, gradually reduce its military presence in Western Europe (a line which has since been expanded); and (c) a certain shift in the relative weight which the United States put on the position of West Germany in Europe. This last point was indicated in June 1989 when, during his visit in Bonn, Bush spoke of West Germany as a 'partner in leadership'. The increased priority to the Washington–Bonn relationship has been more manifest subsequently both in American attitudes towards the developments in Eastern Europe and in American policy towards the process of unification after the fall of the Berlin wall. One might add as a fourth element in the European policy of the Bush administration: (d) American acceptance, and even encouragement, of more Western European initiatives in European affairs combined with the view that this must be followed by changes in the relative burden sharing within the transatlantic relationship. This willingness of the United States to play, but only to play second violin, in relation to the development in Eastern Europe was demonstrated at the Economic Summit in Paris in July 1989, where it was decided to let the EC administer Western support for these countries.

7.2. Tensions and Cooperation in Western Europe

The history of integration in Western Europe

The history of the 'European idea', the vision of a united Europe, is centuries old. It had support in important political circles before the First World War and in the 1920s. During the Second World War both anti-fascists and fascists fought in the name of Europe. For the resistance movements and in the oppositional press during the war a united and democratic Europe was a strong vision (Thompson, 1982). The aims of political consolidation and economic construction were added to the new federalism which increased in strength and experienced a rebirth after the war.

In Western Europe a key goal for those adhering to the idea of European federalism was that what in 1949 was to become the Council of Europe should develop into a supranational organization. Opinion was split between federalist plans from France and Belgium and more minimalist plans, in particular from Britain. This split parallels the later difference between EEC and the European Free Trade Association (EFTA) in their attitude towards political integration versus free trade. Because of these differences the Council of Europe was not shaped as a supranatural body and did not initiate a major process of integration.

With the advent of the Cold War and the division of Europe and Germany, the plans for an all-European unification became unrealistic, and the hopes for unification were concentrated on the unification of each part of Europe. Each offered a strong motive for the other. On the Western side after 1947 the United States engaged itself actively in the strengthening and also the unification, of Western Europe. In 1948, a narrow organization had already been formed by five countries in the area of security and defence: the Brussels Treaty. This organization, comprising Britain, France, Belgium, the Netherlands and Luxembourg, was quickly overtaken by the formation in 1949 of NATO. In 1954 the Brussels Treaty changes into the Western European Union (WEU) also including West Germany and Italy. But this move was only to pave the way for the inclusion of West Germany into NATO. The WEU remained marginal until the beginning of the 1980s, when it gained importance as a possible vehicle for the revived interest in European security cooperation discussed above.

The most important development towards Western European integration, the process of forming the European Communities, got started in 1951 when six countries (France, Belgium, the Netherlands, Luxembourg, Italy and West Germany) signed the treaty of the European Coal and Steel Community in Paris — the first supranatural organization in Europe. Jean Monnet's original idea of a sectoral integration with supranatural powers, which was manifested in the Schumann plan, aimed first of all to overcome the old enmity between France and Germany. But it was also part of a gradualist and sector-specific approach towards general European unification. The major motive was political: to guarantee a lasting peace between France and Germany. War between the two should be made not only 'unimaginable' — but also materially impractical. The plan was also brought forward for economic motives: among other things the French steel industry needed safe supplies of coal. The gradual expansion of the economic integration continued with an important step forward in 1958, when the EEC and EURATOM were formed.

For West Germany European integration had a special dimension as the new substitute for nationalism. This worked in a double sense: substituting emotionally as an object for attachment, and politically as a possible vehicle for reunification. To Adenauer the cooperation in Western Europe offered some very attractive benefits. It was an element in the policy of tying West Germany to the West and it constituted the core of his policy of strength. The attractiveness and dynamism of Western Europe would sooner or later pull the Soviet satellites (and East Germany in particular) out of their Soviet orbit.

During the following years, the European Communities were consolidated and extended into further areas. But the process of creating a unified Europe was also marked by political differences. The most typical source of conflict was French suspicion that the Germans were too dependent on the United States. The major transatlantic controversies were played out with the United States and France as the main combatants, and West Germany as the major variable (Grosser, 1980). This led to important conflicts in cooperative endeavours outside the communities. The most conspicuous of these had been the aborted attempt to create a European Defence Community (EDC) during 1950-4. This showed the French ambiguity in particular since the French ended up opposing their own initiative because of its extensive infringement on French military sovereignty. Instead the process led to Germany's entrance into the Brussels Treaty and NATO in 1955.

Another of these conflicts was the 1963 Elysée Treaty. The Bundestag added to the agreement between de Gaulle and Adenauer a Preamble, partly drafted by Jean Monnet, which offended de Gaulle because of its emphasis on transatlantic relations (Grosser, 1980, pp. 104ff.). The treaty thus signified both the early and far-reaching attempts at Franco-German cooperation, and the political limits to it. A major disagreement was the sensitive issue of the United States. This was expressed in the 1960s and early 1970s in West Germany through a debate within the Christian Democrats between Atlanticists and Gaullists (cf. Nolte, 1974). After a renewed French attempt at establishing leadership of the Western European unification project with the proposals from the Fouchet committee (1961-2), the French under de Gaulle turned increasingly towards pure intergovernmental cooperation. This was unacceptable to the smaller EEC countries so long as Britain could not join as a balancer against Franco-German domination. Without Britain the small remained dependent on supranationality.

Among the controversies of the 1960s should be mentioned French (de Gaulle's) opposition to British membership, allegedly because this would be to give the Americans a vote inside the community. (All was seen as part of Kennedy's 'grand design' for an Atlantic partnership.) This 1963 refusal led at first to a strengthening of counter-integration in EFTA. The French line culminated from 1965 in crisis, with a French walk-out in 1966 ended by the so-called Luxembourg compromise institutionalizing a national right to veto. With this the EEC merged with the other communities in 1967 to form the EC, though it seemed to be stuck at a low point of progress.

The social-liberal Brandt government in West Germany from 1969 was less supportive of the idea of supranational Western European integration than its predecessor. Consequently, the all-European orientation and a confederal view on the EC played a comparatively larger role for the West German government from the end of the 1960s (Kelstrup, 1988). Brandt and his people 'stressed the role of the nation-state for the Central European peace order' (Hacke, 1988, p. 169). Eventually in 1973 the EC was enlarged when Britain, Ireland and Denmark joined. In the 1980s the 'Southern Enlargement' followed, and Greece (1981), Spain and Portugal (1986) became members. In the early 1980s it became a common assumption that the EC was like a cyclist: it had to sustain the momentum of integration, or fall; in this case not to the ground, but at least to the base line of a customs union (Kaiser, et al., 1983). The stagnation of in-depth integration, which had dominated the 1970s, continued and a new pessimistic debate on the lasting weaknesses of the European economies ('Eurosclerosis') developed. Also at the level of culture, ideology and identity it was generally assumed that Europe was in a steady process of losing dynamism (Hoffman, 1979).

The image of the EC came to be dominated by the unsuccessful (or overly successful) agricultural policy and the growing bureaucracy in Brussels. Surprisingly, there was some success in foreign policy. The European Political Cooperation (EPC) had been set up through decisions taken in the early 1970s, and had originally an independent and clearly inter-governmental status. EPC worked well in the early rounds of the CSCE as well as on some issues of regional conflict (Middle East, Central America, Southern Africa). In these more symbolic areas, as well as in the community-based issues of foreign economic relations, the EC/EPC became increasingly seen by the outside world as one actor. This development was contrary to the theories of functionalism and neo-functionalism that were associated with the development of the EC. These theories foresaw a gradual expansion of integration from within, but in this area it seemed to be high politics that pulled low politics towards some dynamism. This development was more in accordance with the tradition of political realism, where mutual recognition plays a key role in how states are constituted. The EC seemed to become a political reality for itself when it did so in the eyes of the others. This points to the possibility that the development of Western European integration can be explained to a considerable extent by its position and role in the international system. The history of integration should not be written solely as a slow internal process of learning the 'necessary' cooperation and overcoming nationalist inertia, but as a dialectic

between this process and the pressures on Europe from other-
actors, notably the United States, to pull itself together.

Under conditions of solid overlay, the United States pressure
for unity in Western Europe helped in forming a core community
in the economic area. Foreign and security policy was much more
difficult to integrate since the American dominance in this field
was too direct. Important questions of high politics were kept as
national decisions. These issues were played out within NATO,
where the key issue was how each of the European members
related to the United States (cf. Snyder, 1984). Not until the first
half of the 1980s did international developments produce the
conditions for European integration extending decisively into
security and foreign policy. A Europe under pressure from a re-
intensified Cold War in the early 1980s was followed by a certain
vacuum in the late 1980s. The result of both situations was
attempts during the 1980s to articulate 'a European voice' (cf.
Holm et al., 1989, pp. 45ff.; Wæver, 1989a). Especially in Bonn and
Paris this necessity was claimed across the political spectrum,
though with different messages to be spoken by the new voice.
But actually increasing cooperation among the EC countries
proved more difficult since the project had to be 'positive', not just
reactive. This experience probably gave important stimuli to
France and West Germany to re-evaluate their overall strategies
for Western Europe.

One result was the need felt during the early 1980s in several
EC countries for a new initiative to expand EC integration.
Several attempts were made, among them the Genscher–Col-
umbo plan, and a French *relance européenne*. In June 1983 the
European Council in Stuttgart adopted a declaration about the
political finality of the community. Most important was the
meeting of the European Council in Milan in 1985, which adopted
the plan for an institutional reform of the EC (the Common Act)
and the plan for '1992', the single integrated market. In a
masterpiece of symbolic politics a name and a deadline for this
relaunch of old ideas was fixed. Suddenly a political reality was
created — 1992 — and all actors in international as well as
domestic politics had to relate to it. It has been said: '1992 certainly
is going to happen — the question is only *when*'. Though it is rather
unlikely that the total programme will be implemented by 1992,
the project has had a self-reinforcing effect, and got well under
way very fast. In 1989 it was extended by the Delors plan for an
Economic and Monetary Union (EMU). The EC has with difficulty
agreed on the initiation of its first phase. Early in 1990 these plans
were supplemented by a French-German proposal for a 'political
union' of the EC. Greater difficulties, especially with Britain, are
to be expected in regard to these initiatives, but certainly the EC

has undertaken significant new initiatives and created bold new-prospects for itself.

By the beginning of the 1990s, the fear of Eurosclerosis had been forgotten and energies inside and outside the community had been redirected towards preparation for, and support of, a great leap forward. By its nature, the 1992 project has created pressure for yet further integration. Because of the different economic strengths and levels of social security within the EC, the creation of a real European common market would have quite strong, and quite different, effects on each of the states. This fact creates pressure for a still broader project including social, environmental and democratic extensions within the EC (see Chapter 10).

National interests: the continuation of differences

Growing cohesion in the EC notwithstanding, Western Europe is still marked by internal patterns of conflict and cooperation. The most discussed axes of bilateral (and sometimes trilateral) coope-ration are the Franco-German (sometimes Franco-German-Spa-nish or Franco-German-Italian) and the Franco-British nuclear 'axes'. The WEU was relaunched in 1984, but it was not clear whether this move was strategic or merely tactical with increasing security cooperation in the EPC as a long-term aim. The latter seemed to be the aim of Mitterrand, whereas Chirac opted for the WEU as a lasting framework. At the time the EPC was preferred by the German government (Schmidt) but later on the German government seemed to be more in line with French thinking, wanting defence as a part of the general project for Western Europe, i.e. inside the EC. Yet Genscher has also signalled preference for the WEU, in order to keep the EC more compatible with countries like Austria and, maybe, former Warsaw Pact countries. In practice the relaunched WEU has made only limited progress. It has not yet taken any planning or organizational role. Not has it concretely organized much defence. It has mainly been a useful paper option.

In the run up to 1992 there seem to be two main conflict lines in the community: French versus British approaches to integration/free trade, and French versus German visions for Europe. The British government fears that the French approach to integration, supported by the European Commission (Delors), will lead to a reimposition of 'statist' economic policies by Brussels. A free market is better created by the market, the British Conservatives claim. After some concessions to the British the train seems now firmly on the French and Delors tracks. Pressure for social extension of the 1992 project and the pressure generated by

German unification have both led to devoted activism by most other member states in the direction of deepening integration within the EC.

The Franco-German difference in regard to the future of Europe cannot be explained purely in relation to Western European cooperation. It relates to deep-seated concepts of state, nation and 'Europe'. (An analysis of this has been presented more extensively elsewhere: Holm *et al.*, 1989, 1990, and forthcoming.) In French and German thinking 'Europe' is linked to the fate of the nation in different, almost opposite, ways. Metaphorically, one could say that Germany is interested in the inner side of Europe, whereas France is interested in its outer side. For Germans the big issue regarding Europe is whether relationships in Europe can be changed so that Germany's nation, culture and economy will be able to unfold with less hindrance from the East–West division, and from other borders. For France the main issue is whether the sense of France and its mission can be regained through the constitution of a Europe able to act and be respected in the eyes of others.

It is in Germany's interest to clear the way for processes that will assemble the nation. In spite of the clear wish for a unified German state, there has been a tendency in German thinking for there to be less focus on 'formal' questions like states and borders. After all the substance can be obtained without the formalities. Before the dramatic changes of 1989 there was a tendency on the German centre-left to think about unification without state unity. Unity could be obtained in culture, in common policies of *détente* and reform, and economically. This logic is still relevant since it covers also the relations to other areas in Central Europe. Even those areas that no longer have German populations still have a link to German culture and latently to the German economy. For these relationships to develop in the post-Cold War era means downgrading the importance of borders. Half a century ago a similar German concern led to attempts to move borders. In the 1990s this seems an impossible way to obtain anything in Europe and so similar basic concerns are given a different outlet. For both national (i.e. minority) and economic policies it is, according to this German view, constructive to de-emphasize the dividing character of borders.

Political thinking in France shows an opposite picture. Politics, according to this view, must be about the state, about an actor, coherence, will. In most variants of French thinking the state is centralized, demarcated by clear borders and endowed with a certain mission. If Europe is to become a political reality it will have to take on these qualities. Under de Gaulle the concept was a 'Europe of the Fatherlands', thus respecting the full sovereignty of the 'nation-states'. In 1982–3 there was a dramatic change of French policy on Europe. France started to work for the EC to obtain a state quality on as many questions as possible. The underlying reason for this was French concern with position in the world: or lack of it. France has become too small and its mission must be taken over by Europe. The French concept of the state is repeated at the level of Europe, so the turnabout of 1983 is based on a continuity at the level of political thinking. Europe must now be what France should be (and shall somehow remain!). This includes a political and defence identity, civilizational values and status recognition by the world.

The Europe France thinks of is Western Europe. Only Western Europe can attain these qualities and become coherent enough to act decisively. Thus it is unacceptable to the French to have a Europe with an unclear border and unclear membership. The Germans, it is often feared, want a Europe which in a very unstatelike way, just fades out somewhere to the East, a Europe which would never be able to act in unity. Increasingly Eastern Europe enters into the picture. It is, however, important to notice the way Eastern Europe is included in the French Europe project: not as a part of the European Community, but as the mission for it. Eastern policy becomes increasingly important since the essence of the European project is the political actions of the EC in the name of the Eastern Europeans.

The most clear expression of this changing emphasis in French Europe policy was President Mitterrand's New Year speech (1989–90) in which he presented a vision of a 'European Con-federation' for all of Europe (except the Soviet Union, at least in the first phase). This is probably not to be seen as a retreat from the EC project but as an attempt to give the EC a new purpose, a larger meaning. The *grand dessein* is not of the EC, but Europe, and France is to lead the *Ostpolitik* of the EC. (What a change from 1988 when the French started to talk about *Ostpolitik* without any idea what this should mean!). The French stress on the EC's *Ostpolitik* is very logical: it is the only way to counterbalance German economic dominance in Eastern Europe. German firms act without a covering policy, their expansion grows from *laissez faire*, i.e. as a non-state process. French compa-nies do not have the strength or the motives for the same investment. Thus, the less political help there is towards Eastern Europe, the more German economic dominance there will be. The place to be for France is therefore in the forefront of the EC's *Ostpolitik*.

In this interpretation the French Europe is created on top of political structures and institutions; the German Europe evolves between them. A very important issue is whether and how it is possible to find a compromise between the French and the German views. It can be argued (Wæver, forthcoming) that after the fall of the Berlin wall there has been a pressure for Bonn to adapt to French concepts for Europe. Bonn has to buy the support of Paris for German unification. In order to make the overall change in Europe stable there has to be a certain balance between German and French gains. The Germans get one major aim: unity. More than that, they are destined to get a fair share of economic expansion into Eastern Europe. German dominance in Eastern Europe will grow automatically, therefore EC *Ostpolitik* is an issue first of all for France (and for the smaller member states).

For France current developments are critical. Basic dilemmas are put out in the open: France cannot but support changes in the East since these represent French values. However, the change in Europe towards unification of and regional dominance by Germany is not wanted. Post-war French identity has rested on the difference from Germany: on France being fully sovereign, one of the four occupation powers, and nuclear. Now Germany becomes a normal state and France is thereby diminished. Nuclear weapons seem to be of decreasing importance, and the mission of being opposed to the Yalta division equally irrelevant. On this basis French policy is not stable. The Germans are well aware that their own gains will be precarious if they are not able to secure a lasting and valuable position for France (i.e. a strong and active EC) as well as securing for Russia a new security and a new presence in Europe in exchange for the one lost together with the control of Eastern Europe. Therefore, the Germans are working now on EC deepening as well as 'a system of collective security in Europe'.

Whereas West Germany previously tended in the direction of EC enlargement, this is now downplayed in contrast to the show of reliability in respect of deepening (cf. debate in the *Bundestag* on 14 March; *Das Parlament* 30 March 1990). Developments in the 1980s have strengthened French and West German wishes for cooperation in security and even defence. It has become a generally recognized rule in Western Europe that progress in the EC depends on Franco-German unity. In security matters a more independent Western Europe was seen as developing around the Bonn–Paris axis. The special relationship was not always welcomed by all other states, but in the security establishments (European as well as American and Soviet) the Franco-German cooperation in security and defence was studied very carefully as the possible seed from which a West European army could grow.

What has been achieved was mainly symbolic (a common brigade, that cannot yet agree on common food). It has been easier to agree on the extremes: grand statements of objectives on the one hand, and narrowly specific concrete measures of cooperation on the other. The difficulty has been in making the political dimension operational: on shared conceptions of European security, strategy and institutions. Prospects for the Paris–Bonn axis seem at present both promising and sombre. A paradox is unfolding in that the establishment in both countries is well aware of the importance of their mutual relationship and therefore they do their utmost to enlist from their national community signs of goodwill and support for the other's policy. At the same time mistrust has increased in both countries, especially, as discussed above, during the first two months after the fall of the Berlin wall. It is impossible to predict whether the pressures will generate a qualitative jump in the direction of deepened cooperation or whether it will result in a break. This question is closely linked to the more general question of the different possible scenarios investigated later in this book.

7.3. Old Institutions and New Relationships

On the development in the West–West relationship after the fall of the Berlin wall

European development entered a new phase with the fall of the Berlin wall. European development was influenced not only by changes in the East, but also by the unification process in Germany. This had profound implications for both the Atlantic relationship and the interrelationships in Western Europe. The new developments have put the existing institutional structures in Europe under pressure: Europe is experiencing great uncertainty about its future organization.

American reaction to the revolution in East Germany, the breakdown of the Berlin wall, the following uncertainties in East Germany and the process of German unification can be seen as a continuation of the policy towards Europe which President Bush initiated at the NATO summit at the end of May 1989. The United States has, under the label 'new Atlanticism' engaged in the political changes in Europe. At the same time the United States has gone further ahead in its proposals for reduction of its military presence in Western Europe. The third part in the changed profile of the American policy towards Europe was the upgrading of West Germany to a 'partner in leadership' and this also has developed further in regard to the process of German unification.

There was close, though not unproblematic, cooperation between the American administration and the government of

West Germany in the phase immediately after the breakdown of the wall. It caused some difficulties that Chancellor Kohl consulted neither the United States nor the other NATO allies (nor Foreign Minister Genscher) before he formulated his ten-point plan for German unification on 28 November. Despite this, there has been general American support for the unification process. President Bush quickly supported Chancellor Kohl's ten-point plan. At the NATO summit in early December 1989 he reaffirmed America's long-standing support for the goal of German unification and enunciated four principles for American policy towards German unification: (1) that self-determination must be pursued; (2) that unification should occur in the context of Germany's continued commitment to NATO and an increasingly integrated European Community with due regard for the legal role and responsibilities of the allied powers; (3) that the moves towards integration must be peaceful and part of a step-by-step process; and (4) that on the question of borders support for the principles of the Helsinki Final Act should be supported (Baker, 1989). In later phases coordination between the two governments was close. For example, West Germany and the United States cooperated closely in preparing and negotiating at the conference in Ottawa in February 1990.

The old institutions under stress

The breakup in the East and the process of German unification have massive implications for the present institutional structures in Europe. The existing institutions are under the stress of adapting to the new relationships that are developing in Europe. Of particular importance are the two military alliances (NATO and the Warsaw Pact), the European Community and the CSCE.

The Warsaw Pact has been severely undermined by the political and military development in the Eastern European countries. The revolutions in these countries have brought new political forces to power and the cohesion of the past, which was problematic earlier, has been evaporating rapidly. In negotiations with the governments of Hungary and Czechoslovakia, the Soviet Union has agreed to withdraw all its troops from these countries before 1992. The developments in East Germany after the March 1990 election clearly point to a situation in which East Germany cannot any longer be expected to remain a meaningful member of the Warsaw Pact. This means that the Warsaw Pact is effectively dissolved as a military alliance, although it still exists on paper. The Eastern European states will still need to regulate their military relationship to the Soviet Union, but whether this will take place within some adapted form of the Warsaw Pact or in arrangements for each state is very uncertain.

NATO is also severely challenged, but very differently from the Warsaw Pact: its problem is adaptation, not survival. One important challenge to NATO lies in the fact that the threat from the East must be regarded as having disappeared or at least diminished considerably both in a political and a military terms. This calls one dimension of the existential basis of NATO into question. At a minimum it points to a reorganization of NATO's political and military functions. Politically, it is necessary to re-evaluate the goals and tasks of the alliance in relation to the basic treaty obligations of its members. The political functions of the alliance will probably grow and it will be of special importance to develop the cooperative aspect of NATO in relation to the East. One key question is whether even a more political, less military, NATO will still have as a central function the exclusion of the Soviet Union from the Western 'club'. Militarily, a thorough rethinking is necessary. But this is constrained both by the vast inertia of existing military capabilities and arrangements and by the lack of any clear political vision of what the future political and military functions of the alliance will be. All that can be said for certain is that NATO will continue to exist for a long time because it would be too risky to pull yet another prop out from under the European security order, but that it will be a very different NATO from the one that held the Western position during the Cold War.

These problems are inseparable from the other important challenge of NATO, which comes from the German unification process. This challenge is one for both the short and long term. What place will a unified Germany have in NATO? This problem is at the centre of the '2+4' negotiations on the European aspect of German unification. It is a main political problem in the shaping of the future security arrangements in Europe, because of its importance for the future of the alliances in Europe.

German unification also has important military aspects. The unification process has immediately provoked a series of paradoxes. How is it possible to keep tactical nuclear weapons which only are usable against the people with whom you are uniting as fast as possible? How is it possible to keep a forward defence to a border that is disappearing? Can a united Germany be a member of both alliances at the same time? Can East Germans become soldiers or officers in NATO? Is it really possible that after the German monetary union, West Germany will pay to keep Soviet troops in East Germany? The paradoxes are many especially, but not only, for the Germans. NATO is challenged in its fundamental military strategy. It does not make sense to have a forward defence of NATO with a unified Germany and Soviet withdrawal from Eastern Europe. Neither do NATO's tactical nuclear weapons and short-range nuclear missiles in Germany make sense. The unification of the two German states implies that NATO's whole military strategy has to be changed. Depending on the political solution found to the position of a unified Germany in the alliances, the military arrangements in NATO, particularly the military integration within NATO, have to be redefined, or perhaps discontinued.

The new challenges to NATO, including the problem of the meaning of the military defence in post-Cold War Europe, are so great that one might without exaggeration talk of a crisis in the organization, although a very unusual one. The present crisis is not, as most earlier NATO crises were, a transatlantic one. On the contrary, the transatlantic relationship is in better shape than it has been for a long time. The active American engagement in the political processes in Europe can be seen as a major resource for the alliance in overcoming the present form of crisis. The proposed and planned reductions of American forces in Europe are of a magnitude which in other circumstances would have triggered a deep transatlantic crisis. But the American cooperation in the transformation of Europe, especially with West Germany, has such as positive effect on the relationship that European concerns about American disengagement are overcome. This aspect might prove important to the 'crisis of meaning' in NATO, renewing the alliance as a framework for the transatlantic relationship and for 'keeping the Americans in', and for keeping them politically engaged in the all-European process.

The EC is also challenged by the development in the East and by the unification of the two German states: indeed, the development in Eastern Europe can be seen as a tribute to the progress of the EC. Practically all the Eastern European countries have sought closer collaboration with the EC. In many interpretations the magnet of the EC development has been mentioned as part of the explanation for the breakup in the East. There is no doubt that the EC already has had, and will continue to have, great influence on Eastern Europe, but the reverse is also true. For example, the EC has been strengthened by taking on the international role of coordinating the support for Eastern Europe from the Western countries, including the United States and other countries outside the EC.

In contrast, the German unification process might be a more profound and problematic challenge to the EC. Much points to the situation in which East Germany is uniting very quickly with West Germany. For the EC this implies that East Germany will very soon become part of the EC within the framework of a united Germany. All the problems concerning the inclusion of

East Germany in the EC will have a high priority on the Community's agenda. West Germany will give high priority to the development of the unification process and thus to the negotiations on German unification. The process of incorporating German unification into the EC could easily confront the Community with a heavy agenda of difficult issues at a time when it is already under pressure to pursue deepening (Kelstrup, 1990c).

One consequence of the clash between Western European integration and the German unification process might be that the internal dynamism of the EC will break down. The progress towards the internal market could either be blocked or lose momentum. Problems arising from the integration of East Germany into the Community could create new political cleavages. These dangers are somewhat offset by the fact that it is quite clear to almost all the main parties in the EC that this danger exists. It is therefore not impossible that in rising to this challenge the EC might release new integrative forces. Already important actors, especially the European Commission and France, have reacted to the dangers for the EC with more urgent proposals for accelerated integration. For France and several other member states, German unification is only tolerable if the EC is deepened. This seems to be well understood in the foreign ministry in Bonn and in the Chancellor's office (Holm *et al.*, 1990; Wæver, forthcoming). The response to the danger of blocking or of a severe slow down of the integration process is to propose fast and radical steps forward towards political union in the EC.

Thus German unification triggers proposals for fast steps towards a more supranational EC. France and the Commission have put forward such proposals. In April 1990, the West German government reacted to criticism of its reluctance towards integration with reinforced support for faster integration. The most remarkable proposal for this was the Kohl–Mitterrand plan for political union in the EC, which was accepted in principle by the European Council at its meeting early in May 1990. The question for the EC's future is whether integrative forces will prevail or not. This will be answered not only by the interplay of internal forces in the EC, but also by the external pressures that demand the construction of a European international actor. We will return to this in the discussion of the scenarios for the future of Europe.

The CSCE-process survived the second Cold War and experienced great progress during the second *détente* at the end of the 1980s. A very important agreement was reached in Vienna in January 1989. One result was the initiation of negotiations on reductions of military forces in Europe between the two alliances within the CSCE-framework (the CFE negotiations). Another was further progress on human rights. Many conferences were planned within the CSCE, giving a growing importance to this process. While the military alliances are in crisis, and the EC is under pressure, the CSCE seems to be doing rather well. New possibilities open up for it, and many things points to more importance for the CSCE process. The CSCE will probably have a greater political role in the future, and also be more institutionalized, and be assigned specific functions in regard to conflict management and confidence building. One possible development is that the CSCE will be expanded as a cornerstone of a new organization for collective security in Europe. Its economic functions might be expanded, furthering East–West relations in the economic and technological field. This aspect of the CSCE, long dormant, was revitalized at an impressive CSCE conference on economic relations in Bonn in March 1990. The human rights issue could also take on a new role for the CSCE. Instead of being, as before 1989, a tool for opening up the closed communist regimes in the East, it could become the place to press for greater Western openness to East Europeans. In this third area the CSCE could become the watch-dog securing decent EC policy towards its East European periphery — its outer concentric circles.

The old CSCE may fade as the new one comes into place. The old was dependent on being not institutionalized, and thereby retaining a dynamic from the force of constant concessions. The different actors had different hopes for the CSCE but for these different reasons they all attempted to keep the process alive. In order to do this the different states took turns to present their demands. Under Cold War conditions, the old CSCE would probably have died if it had been institutionalized (Jopp *et al.*, 1987; Nielsen 1988). Now, however, there is a need for new institutions where the CSCE can be a useful building block (and name). Yet the price for this might be the loss of the old CSCE conference diplomacy and the flexibilities which it gave.

Other European organizations are also under pressure. One is the Council of Europe, which gains a new status because of the developments in Eastern Europe. Most of the Eastern European countries have joined the organization as observers and have applied for full membership. Much points to an important function for the Council in the area of human rights. Another is the Western European Union (WEU). During the 1980s, this organization has been 'revitalized' several times as a forum for security cooperation between the Western European states. It might acquire new functions in a European security system, though it is very uncertain what these might be. A third is the Nordic Council, which finds itself facing a delicate new role dealing with the attempted secession of the Baltic republics from the Soviet Union.

On the other hand the revolutions in the East and, the ending of the Cold War relieve the Council of the problems that arose from the fact that some Nordic states were neutral and some were members of NATO.

New relationships

It is one thing to describe how old institutions are under stress from new developments, but quite another to analyse what the response to the new pressures will be. What are the effects of the European institutions being under stress from the new relationships that are still developing? This question cannot be answered simply by analysing each institution or by looking at the intentions of the individual actors. It is also necessary to try to interpret the pattern and dynamics of the whole European development.

A likely result of the ongoing negotiations is that we get a united Germany in NATO, probably with some prolonged stationing of Soviet troops in East Germany, and that as part of the same arrangement we get some form of all-European security system. Such a system would have the function of counterbalancing the influence that the West would have in Europe in the economic and political spheres. There are many uncertainties as to what such an all-European security system will look like. Because of the necessary speed in its construction process (driven by the pace of German unification) it will be necessary to build it on the basis of existing institutions. As indicated above it is very likely that the CSCE will have the major role.

If such a development takes place, it means that the two main processes in Europe will be a deep political and economic Western Europeanization with the EC at its core, and a less intensive all-Europeanization in the security field. While the EC would be the core of the politico-economic process, NATO would be an essential part of the military security one, i.e. a part of the new all-European security construct along with the CSCE. This would inevitably lead to a fundamental restructuring of the relationship between the Western European versus the Atlantic orientations in European politics. Atlanticism now means something completely different from what it was in the 1950s. Then it referred to an idea of community, a reference to a sense of belonging. Monnet and others were distrusted in Europe for being too American, and in the United States for being too European, and it was true: they really were Atlanticists. Now Atlanticism is not a serious contender for organizing Europe, or attracting primary loyalties, or establishing an international political actor. It is an attempt to add to the great European bargain an American link, a continued presence on the continent, a continuation of NATO, and a strong link to the economy of Germany and the EC.

The whole field of Atlantic and alliance issues is very paradoxical at present. Many commentators talk about current changes as if the fulcrum of re-structuring was in 'West–West relations', i.e. the possibility now of developing the long-discussed second pillar of NATO. But the whole concept of 'West–West' is becoming questionable. 'West–West' was only meaningful because the security political universe was first divided into 'West' and 'East'. These could then be subdivided. If there are two centres in the West, we can talk about 'West–West' relations but only until the day when neither one or the other 'West' is defined first in relation to East. This is even more clear in the East, where 'East–East' relations are becoming absurd as the one East (Eastern Europe) moves towards Western Europe. Czechoslovakia is today first of all 'Europe', then maybe something more specific (East-Central Europe, for instance) but it is no longer primarily a part of the 'East'.

The talk about European architecture can also be misleading, since it suggests one unified construct and gives the impression that the security structure will form 'Europe'. Of course security and politics should never be seen as in the last instance separable (Hassner, 1968a and b), but it might be useful to differentiate just a little. Basic stability will rest upon a balance of imbalances: an all-European security system with a latent Russian heavyweight, and political and economic dynamics coming predominantly from the EC and floating in the direction West–East (with Eastern Europe as periphery to EC and Russia as the periphery of the periphery). In the military security field, there will increasingly be only a negative system: a safety net. The arrangements for this will not, as in the past, be what 'organizes' Europe. They will secure a continued United States presence (NATO), as well as guarantee Soviet security. In the political process of forming a 'new Europe' the main pillars will not be NATO and the Warsaw Pact, but the EC and possibly the Soviet Union (the different ways to 'mix' the roles will be the basic issue of the scenarios).

To the extent that the all-European systems does not come into being in the grand bargain there will be a Soviet pressure for more immediate security guarantees, i.e. an East European buffer and continued control of the Baltic Republics. There is a certain parallel between the Russian and American positions of trying to secure a future presence in Europe. The Soviets are trying to convert their former status in Eastern Europe into a generally recognized presence at the High Table of European security. The Americans are concerned (as are many Europeans) that the United States not get squeezed out by the process of Europeanization.

The Americans and the Soviets could end up playing each other into this game. The CSCE structure is a necessary element in Soviet access, and this automatically includes the United States. From the American point of view the decisive factor is to keep NATO alive, and this goal might well be served best by integrating the alliance into an all-European security system, i.e. the Soviet project.

PART III - THREE SCENARIOS FOR THE FUTURE OF EUROPEAN SECURITY

Chapter 8

Introduction: The Main Variables Affecting Europe's Security

The final step in this study is to try to pin down the necessary conditions for alternative evolutions of the European security complex. This requires linking together the systemic issues raised in Chapter 2 (distribution of power, density/interdependence, international society), the historical issues outlined in Chapter 3 (the European security complex and the breakup of overlay), the definitional questions addressed in Chapter 4 (what and where is Europe), and the internal dynamics of changes explored in Chapters 5-7 (East, Central, West). Will the present resurgence of Europe prove to be a temporary aberration, a mere interlude before a new suppression of the security complex by a re-imposition of overlay and a new round of Cold War? Will the breakup of overlay signal the emergence of a European pole of power, thus transforming the European complex into a single major actor on the world stage? Will it unleash old historical forces that will reconstitute the complex in some form reminiscent of its pre-1939 dynamics?

To answer these questions one needs to reduce the vast mass of facts to a limited number of clear main variables that define the necessary conditions for each line of development. By 'main variable' we mean factors so central that significant changes in them require major reconsiderations of what is both politically possible and politically likely. Using these main variables, we intend to construct the three scenarios for the evolution of the European security complex mentioned above: Cold War III, an integrated European pole, and the political fragmentation of Europe into a reconstituted security complex. Each of these stems from plausible differences of outcome in one or more of the main variables. To the extent that this exercise is successful, it should reveal the tendency of the current developments, as well as the scope of changes necessary for a shift from the fluid status quo of the immediate post-Cold War situation into any one of the scenarios. Since the scenarios inevitably excite strong and controversial differences of preference, this analysis should reveal some important things about the scope of political choice available in the shaping of Europe's future.

The first section sets out these main variables and relates them to the three scenarios. The second section picks up some of the threads from the discussion about the definition of Europe in Chapter 4, and follows them into the question of what role the East-Central European states will play between the centres of power located in Western Europe and Russia.

8.1 Power, Fear and Interdependence

As argued in Chapter 4, the primary context for European security has been the East–West rivalry and the three subpatterns within it. The East–West framework is breaking down, and the forces within the sub-patterns are jostling for influence in a new pattern. Thus the actors within the East–West framework, though not the framework itself, remain the relevant context for European security. Because Europe's position and identity are so much up in the air, the transformation of the old order must remain the central focus of European security, at least for the short, and probably medium, term. Only major, and rather unlikely, pressures from the South, or unexpectedly rapid global ecological crises (warming, disease, mass migration) could change this emphasis. Within the decaying Cold War framework, the future of European security hinges on the interplay among three principal actors, the United States, the Soviet Union and Europe itself, and three key variables, power, fear and interdependence. There is also a question about the ability of existing political processes to handle the scale and pace of the changes now sweeping Europe.

We use power in the broad brush sense adopted by both Realists and Neorealists (Waltz, 1979, pp. 131, 192). In this meaning, power is aggregated and refers to relative capabilities across several sectors including military, economic, societal and political. To be powerful means to possess a broadly-based, relatively large and at least reasonably up-to-date economy. It means controlling advanced technology and supporting a sufficient military establishment to sustain at least a plausible self-defence against other powers. And it means having sufficient socio-political cohesion so that these assets can be maintained, controlled and their influence turned outward. Central to this conception is that the locus of power is a cohesive, centralized political entity.

The first question is therefore how powerful the three principal actors are in relation to each other, and secondarily how powerful they are within the international system as a whole? The answers to these questions will be much shaped by internal developments within each actor, and the outcomes are significant for the distribution of power discussed in Chapter 2. In the case of Europe, and increasingly also of the Soviet Union, there are major uncertainties about their internal relations and overall political cohesion. In theory, the answer for each actor could range anywhere along a scale from very strong to very weak. The Cold War regime was shaped by a pattern in which the United States was very strong in every respect, and the Soviet Union was strong politically and militarily. Europe was initially very weak because of the disruption caused by the Second World War. It remained relatively weak in relation to the superpowers because of its political fragmentation, but it grew strong in economic, and to a lesser extent military, capabilities.

As the Cold War ends, there is no reason to think that the United States will remain anything but very strong in all respects. It will stay the strongest of the great powers even though it ceases to be a superpower. The term 'superpower' should, like 'empire', soon disappear from daily usage. It will take on a historical meaning specific to the unusual structure of the Cold War era in which two big states dominated the power structure of the international system. While the United States remains a useful constant in the present fluid situation, there are big question marks over the power prospects of Europe and the Soviet Union.

In the case of Europe, the question of power is made complicated by the absence of a European state. Traditionally, the defining condition for power status is the existence of a state. But for this analysis the *sui generis* entity of the EC must also be allowed, despite the difficulty that it is precisely the degree of its integration that determines the level of its power. There is no question that the combined economic, military, societal and political assets of Europe are sufficient to support a world class power. The only issue is whether these assets will come under cohesive political control, or whether they will remain fragmented, and mutually cancelling, in the traditional anarchic state structure. To the extent that Europe coheres politically, it becomes powerful. To the extent that it remains fragmented, it remains no more than an interesting cluster of several second-rank powers. Between these two clear extremes lies the grey zone occupied by the EC. Within this grey zone the political actions of the EC and its members are driven by the position of Europe within the global balance of power, as well as by the balance of power dynamics within Europe. To the extent that Europe responds more to the external than to the internal power dynamics, it can be considered a pole of power within the international system even though it is not yet a single state.

As things stand at the beginning of the 1990s, Europe hangs in the balance. It already has a degree of economic integration and institutionalized political cooperation sufficient to mark it off as an entity much more substantial than a mere alliance. But its military, and to some extent even its political, integration is still deeply bound up with the United States. It is not clear whether the turbulence of the post-Cold War events will accelerate or disrupt the development of greater European cohesion. As of 1990, Europe could go one of three ways. It could stay roughly at its present level of cohesion, though almost certainly widening the membership of its core institutions. It could react to the breakup of overlay either by pushing the development of its own cohesion, as the French want to do, or by reasserting national interests in a less cohesive Europe, as the British government of Mrs Thatcher seemed to intend. Which of these trends dominates, and how far it goes, depends among other things on reactions to the outcome of German unification.

The Soviet Union seems condemned to get weaker, the main question being how far this process will go. Its economy is clearly unable to support its present military strength. The economic and political reforms necessary to remedy this situation are so large as to be revolutionary, and their outcome is uncertain. Already the reform process has led to military cuts, economic shrinkage and a great weakening of central political control. In the short and medium term, these trends look very likely to continue. The economy cannot be reconstructed easily or quickly and must have resources from the military sector. Economic reconstruction cannot occur without political and societal reconstruction, both risky processes that threaten the cohesion of the Soviet state/ empire. Shorn of both its dominating military might and its ideological cohesion, the Soviet Union is left competing in the sector where its hand has always been weakest, the economy. It is not inconceivable that the Soviet Union will break up, leaving Russia as one of the lesser great powers. As Europe struggles to overcome a counterproductive fragmentation by seeking greater integration, the Soviet Union struggles to overcome a counter-productive over-centralization by seeking looser political forms. The outcome of these two processes will determine the distribution of power that shapes the future of European security.

The variable of fear is more straightforward than power, in the sense of not raising complex definitional issues. Fear is about threats of attack or unwanted domination, and therefore relates closely to the idea of polarization. It stems in part from the way in which the domestic characteristics of states respond to each other.

There may be historical enmities and territorial disputes, as between Greeks and Turks, or ideological incompatibilities, as in the Cold War, that makes the existence and wellbeing of one polity threaten the legitimacy and stability of others. Fear is also mediated in important ways by the character and quality of international society, and for great powers, by the distribution of power. A strong international society reduces political fears between states by definition. The distribution of power can determine rivalries regardless of history. In a two-power system, the two powers will almost certainly be rivals, a logic illustrated by the relationship of the United States and the Soviet Union during the Cold War. When three or more powers exist in the system, patterns of fear are less determined, more flexible and arguably less intense.

The Cold War pattern was one of high fear between the United States and the Soviet Union. Europe was quite literally split on this issue. Western Europe mostly shared the United States' fear of the Soviet Union, and most of its states consequently subordinated themselves to the United States in NATO. Eastern Europe was forcibly aligned with the Soviet Union by the imposition of communist governments. Western Europe's fear of the United States under these circumstances was both genuinely low and necessarily dormant, though reactions to threats from its financial and corporate hegemony, and to some of its military and political policies, were far from negligible. Eastern Europe was in a curious position, with most of its peoples fearing the Soviet Union, and most of its governments depending on Soviet support.

With the crumbling of the Cold War and the rise of the EC, not to mention the rise of other power centres in Japan, China and India, new relational possibilities emerge. The logic of multipolarity suggests strongly that the level of fear between the United States and the Soviet Union, and thus also between East and West more generally, should drop as bipolarity decays. Evidence from the domestic events starting in the late 1980s also points in this direction. As overlay breaks up in Europe, a more three-cornered pattern of relations emerges to replace the intense bipolarity of the Cold War. The effect of this shift away from bipolarity in the East–West context is enhanced by the broader shift towards a polycentric system created by the rise of great powers in Asia. Between the United States and the Soviet Union the level of fear can only drop as a more diverse set of great power relations pulls their attention away from each other, and as the military capabilities of the other become a smaller part of the threat spectrum that each faces. How far the fear of the old superpowers for each other will decline is an open question. But if present trends in the winding down of strategic arsenals, and towards the elimination of serious ideological differences, continue, then both structural and domestic factors make possible a transformational change from intense fear towards something close to indifference. This change is restrained by the deep institutionalization of the rivalry in both countries, and by the impact that outcomes in Europe have on their security perceptions.

Between the United States and Europe, there are no strong grounds for thinking that fear will rise much above existing low levels. The operation of the fears that do exist will be less constrained than it was under Cold War alliance conditions, but this loosening will be offset by the reduction in United States–Soviet tensions which were the source of many European fears of the United States. Trade rivalry and its associated fears and disputes will continue, and may grow, but Europeans should have less reason to fear the strategic policies of the United States. It is almost inconceivable that Europe and the United States will move towards positions in which they pose military threats to each other.

Between Europe and the Soviet Union there is still uncertainty, although here too the main prospect is for a substantial reduction in tension. During the late 1980s, fear of the Soviet Union was dropping dramatically in both Eastern and Western Europe. This was partly because the Soviet Union appeared weaker, but mostly because its domestic changes made it less threatening. The main threat to Eastern European peoples dissolved when it became clear that Gorbachev had abandoned the Brezhnev doctrine. This of course raised a strong threat to the communist governments from their own populations, but the rapid removal of these governments during 1989 quickly resolved this anomalous alignment of threats. The main threat to Western Europe, already declining since 1988, waned rapidly as soon as the collapse of communist governments in Eastern Europe began to construct a substantial political buffer between the EC and the Soviet Union. By mid-1990, the withdrawal of Soviet power from Eastern Europe looked irreversible, the question being whether and how much of the Soviet Union itself would break away to add to the emergent security buffer. A major reduction in fear from Cold War levels thus looked secure. Whether the progress to date can be pushed further depends on how the crisis within the Soviet Union develops. If its attempt at pluralist reconstruction is successful, then fear could continue to ebb steadily. In the longer term, the construction of a security regime between the Soviet Union and Europe could even pave the way for its eventual inclusion into the Western security community. If the Soviet reforms lead to chaos or reaction, the fear will stabilize at some moderate level determined by the perceived probability that the internal troubles of the

Soviet Union would spill back into Eastern Europe. Soviet fears of Europe will hinge on the German question and the way in which NATO responds to the collapse of its principal *raison d'être*. Paradoxically, Soviet fears could be heightened by the withdrawal of United States' forces if this seemed likely to unleash a resurgent Germany.

Like power, the variable of interdependence can be conceptually tricky. Like fear, it has to be applied to the interactions of units rather than to the units themselves. It can be tricky because interdependence may vary markedly between the same two actors according to what sector one examines: economic inter-dependence may or may not line up with military interdependence. Since military interdependence is largely covered in the variable of fear, we will use here a narrow interpretation of interdependence as primarily an economic phe-nomenon, which eliminates most of these problems. Even with this narrower view one has to proceed cautiously. Interdependence tends to have a positive image. It points towards integration and so is associated with mutual interest and restraint on conflict. But like most things in economics, interdependence is marked by uneven distribution. In this view it points towards power differentials, dependence, and the fear of exploitation. There is also some tendency for the pattern of interdependence to correlate inversely with the pattern of military fear: when fear is high, interdependence will be low; unless fear is low, interdependence is unlikely to be high. Low fear may be accompa-nied by low interdependence when states are indifferent to each other across the board, as in the case of Chad and Paraguay. When interdependence is high, it puts a constraint on fear because of the way interdependence works to restrain the use of military force. This last point is particularly important for Europe, since it provides a strong barrier against any return to the unrestrained intra-European military rivalries of the pre-1945 era.

Under the Cold War regime, interdependence between the United States and the Soviet Union was extremely low (Waltz, 1979, ch. 7). Both joint gain and exploitation were avoided by keeping the two economic systems separated from each other. Between Western Europe and the United States it was high, with large-scale trade and investment. Within Western Europe, it was very high, the more so as the EC developed a common market. Between Eastern Europe and the Soviet Union it was fairly high, although the peculiarities of socialist economics worked against the development of efficient trade and finance mechanisms, and in many cases against the evolution of a division of labour. Between Western Europe and COMECON it was fairly low. There were a few major trade and investment deals, such as the gas pipeline, and the transfers of old car production technology by Fiat, and the major round of loans during the 1970s *détente*. Where interdependence existed, it tended towards a financial and technological dependency of East on West. In economic terms, Eastern Europe was anyway so small as not to count for much.

In the post-Cold War era, interdependence between the United States and Europe seems most likely to remain high. It might diminish somewhat if the drift towards higher levels of protectionism continues, but the web of trade, investment, finance and corporate linkage between the two is so dense as to create powerful pressures against any major 1930s-style breakdown of economic relations. This relationship is typical of those amongst all the major capitalist centres in which international capital is much more strongly placed in comparison with national capital than was the case during the 1930s. Within Europe, the very high level of interdependence is a major driver of the EC's integration process. Given the disastrous condition of most of the Eastern European economies, and their near desperate desire to associate themselves with the West, Eastern Europe seems fated to endure a period of dependence on the West in general, and the EC in particular. Only the political goodwill and fellow-feeling generated by the transition from communism to pluralism stands in the way of exploitation, perhaps reinforced by the chaos power of the Eastern Europeans to create instability in close proximity to the EC.

As the Soviet Union follows Eastern Europe towards market economics and pluralist politics, there is a reasonable possibility that interdependence between the West and the Soviet Union will rise. Europe and, possibly, Japan will be the central players in this process. For reasons of history and geography, the United States is likely to be a more peripheral player, particularly so if it continues to see the Soviet Union as its principal nuclear rival. The political issues raised by interdependence with the Soviet Union are much more difficult than for Eastern Europe. The economic condition of the Soviet Union points towards a dependency relationship that would be extremely humiliating for an ex-superpower. The size of the Soviet Union makes it a potential drain on resources, and when combined with its uncertain domestic prospects, a risky investment. And just beneath the surface lurks the naked question of power: is it in the interests of the West to help a country that has been the main source of threat to it for forty years? For these reasons, there will be strong temptations (on both sides) to go slowly in the construction of economic interdependence, particularly so if Europe and the Soviet Union define themselves as distinct from each other. Many in the West will prefer a weak Soviet Union, and will be able to count on its intrinsic inability to compete, rather than on specific exclusions, to keep it that way. There will also be a lobby in the Soviet Union that, China style, will prefer poverty and backwardness to dependence. The counter-pressure will come from those on both sides who want to reduce the threat from the Soviet Union by integrating it into the Western economic and political systems.

To sum up, some of the three main variables look quite stable, and others are at the centre of the current changes. In terms of power, the United States looks stable in a context of mild decline. Both the EC and the Soviet Union are much more mobile, their outlook depending on the respective processes of integration and disintegration. Europe could get much stronger, and is more likely to hold position than to decline. The Soviet Union will almost certainly decline, the question being how much.

In terms of fear, the picture is one of all round diminution from the configuration of the Cold War decades. The big reductions in fear between East and West that occurred during the late 1980s look stable, though their final resting point will depend on many things, not least the process of arms reduction and re-configuration towards more defensive military postures on both sides. As military and political fears decline, there is some scope for increase in the economic sector. Between the United States and the EC these should be manageable. Within the EC they depend on the outcome of the German question in relation to the process of European integration. Between East and West there will be strong fears of dependence on the Soviet side, and fears of risk, both economic and strategic, within the West.

In terms of interdependence, the picture is also mixed. The United States–EC relationship looks like remaining stable at a high level. Between the United States and the Soviet Union, interdependence will rise somewhat from a very low level, but perhaps not much in the short and medium term. Between Europe and the Soviet Union there will also be a rise from a low level, but whether this rise is large or small is uncertain. It will certainly be large between the EC and Eastern Europe, but may be much slower to develop with the Soviet Union.

Despite the breathtaking scale and scope of the changes under way in East–West relations there are none the less several substantial nodes of stability. Some directions of change are fairly predictable, and only a few factors, albeit central ones, still look open to a wide range of possible outcomes. The major uncertainty is in the power variable, where only the position of the United States is stable. By simplifying the process of change in this way, it becomes possible to organize a systematic discussion of the major possibilities inherent in the European security complex. If one takes the Cold War structure and the overlay of the complex as a starting point, then three main logical alternatives present themselves. First is that the current process of change collapses, resulting in a return to overlay and East–West Cold War. Second is the replacement of both overlay and the European complex by a new European actor constituting a pole of power centred on the EC. Third is that the breakup of overlay unleashes the historical dynamics of the European security complex, which thus picks up from where it left off in 1939, or possibly 1914, though under the rather different military, economic and political conditions of the 1990s.

Possible fourth and fifth scenarios in which a divided overlay is replaced by the domination of Europe by one or the other superpower are so unlikely as not to justify elaboration. Western Europe is already too strong to allow United States' domination, and such a scenario anyway does not reflect any powerful drive within the United States. Soviet domination was long feared, but after its withdrawal from control of Eastern Europe during 1989, and given its rising internal problems, the Soviet Union is too weak to pose this threat. Although it is still a formidable military power, arms reductions and redeployments are rapidly dismantling any realistic possibly for it to invade, or threaten to invade, Europe.

The next three chapters take up these alternatives in detail, but it is useful first to sketch how the three variables discussed above fit into, and condition the probabilities of, the main scenarios.

(1) Cold War III?

This scenario is about the reimposition of overlay on Europe. Its main requirement is a major reversal in the current trends towards a general lowering of fear between East and West. Such a reversal would require either a massive change of policy in the Soviet Union, such as an attempt to use military power to reassert control over Eastern Europe, or an aggressive attempt by the West to exploit current Soviet weakness. Either type of action would be filled with dangers under present conditions. It would also require a reversal of the trends towards a stronger Europe and a weaker Soviet Union, such that the United States was forced to continue to support Europe as part of its own forward defence against the Soviet Union. This scenario would foreclose any major changes in the low level of interdependence between the Soviet Union and the West.

Figure 8.1 – The Main Variables and the Main Scenarios

	Power			Fear			Interdependence		
Scenario	US	WE	SU	US/SU	US/WE	WE/SU	US/SU	US/WE	WE/SU
Cold War III	H	L	H	H	L	H	L	H	L
Pole	H	H	L	L	L-M	L-M	L	H-M	M
Fragment	H	L	L-M	(fear rises within WE)			L	H	L-M

H = high level; M = medium level; L = low level

(2) The Triumph of Integration: Western Europe as a Pole

This scenario is about the replacement of the European security complex by an actor sufficiently integrated to constitute a pole of power in the international system. Its key is a Europe grown much stronger in relation to both superpowers, but particularly the Soviet Union. The key to Europe's strength is the degree of its political cohesion. There is room here for a variety of mixtures between stronger Europes and weaker Soviet Unions. It requires a general reduction in the level of fear all round. Only in the very extreme and unlikely case of a much stronger Europe (one integrated up to the level of a single state, and therefore a great power) and a much weaker Soviet Union (disintegrated down to its Russian core), is the distribution of power a sufficient condition for this scenario. There would be a great increase in interdependence between Western and Eastern Europe; some, but much less, between Europe and the Soviet Union; and perhaps some decline in the high level between Europe and the United States.

(3) The Triumph of Anarchy: Fragmentation

This scenario is about the re-emergence of the European security complex. The necessary conditions for it are a reversal of the trend towards a stronger Europe, plus a decline in fear between both the United States and the Soviet Union, and Europe and the Soviet Union, sufficiently large to enable both superpowers substantially to disengage from their rivalry in Europe. This does not mean that either country would no longer have national security concerns in Europe. Where fear would rise is inside Europe, pushing a return to some form of balance of power behaviour amongst the European powers. A weak Soviet Union would facilitate the scenario. Its most likely triggers are either reaction against an overmighty Germany, or a breakdown of the adaptation mechanisms in NATO, the EC and the CSCE in the face of changes too big and too fast to handle collectively.

The linkage between the variables of power, fear and interdependence and the three scenarios is summarized in Figure 8.1.

8.2 From Front Line to Buffer Zone

During the Cold War era Europe, and particularly Germany, played the role of front line in the superpower rivalry. High levels of threat and tension produced a hard, militarized boundary between East and West. Now the rapid drop in Cold War tensions since the late 1980s gives the Europeans much more room for manoeuvre than they have had since 1945. With the ending of the Brezhnev doctrine, the subsequent collapse of communism in Eastern Europe, dropping arms levels on both sides and the winding down of the Soviet commitment to forward defence, the security problem in Europe becomes easier to solve. The events of 1989 have already opened up a political buffer of non-communist states between Western Europe and the Soviet Union. Events within the Soviet Union itself point towards eventual secession of some of the western and southern republics.

As suggested above, the breakup of overlay focuses attention on the changing relations of power, fear and interdependence among the United States, the Soviet Union and Europe. The relative weakening of the two superpowers, the relaxation of their rivalry, and the specific drop in both the power and the ideological threat from the Soviet Union, all work to raise the prominence of Europe in the East–West equation. Indeed, this process does not have to go very far before the East–West equation itself is replaced by a three-sided one in which Europe becomes in some form the third pole. In either configuration, East–West or tripolar, the end of the Cold War also brings into focus the ambiguity about the definition of Europe discussed in Chapter 4. Between a rising centre of power in the European Community, and a shrinking one in the Soviet Union, a political and strategic space is opening up. The hard, confrontational lines of the Cold War are rapidly transforming into a broad zone of disengagement. In some form, this zone seems almost certain to be a feature in all of the scenarios for the future. This makes it worth examining is some detail. As overlay weakens, the problem is how to transform East-Central Europe away from the role of an impermeable forward-defence shield, and to integrate it into a permeable buffer, which both insulates Western Europe and the Soviet Union from each other (where this continues to be necessary for security), and also connects them to each other (where possible and desirable). The post-war experience of the Nordic countries offers a useful model of how such a permeable buffer might be organized over the next decade.

The Nordic Security Model

On the European mainland, the Cold War saw the creation of a closed, heavily militarized and politically divisive boundary line in central Europe. Instead of a line, the policies of the Nordic countries resulted in the creation of a space between the super-powers in the form of a layered buffer zone. On the eastern side was Finland, which is neutral, has a formidable reputation for the vigour of its territorial defence, but also has a treaty of 'friend-ship, cooperation and mutual assistance' with the Soviet Union. This agreement dates from 1948, and was part of the settlements of the Second World War (in which Finland had fought the Soviet Union). It requires Finland to defend its own territory against all attacks and provides that the Soviet Union might assist in this, but only in a manner to be agreed by the two countries. It also provides for negotiation between the two if a threat of attack is observed (Finnish Commission, 1985, p. 249). The agreement is a substantial caveat to neutrality, but is the price paid by the Finns for their political independence from the Soviet Union. As a practical matter, Finland has deployed a territorial defence whose primary mission is to deter attack from the Soviet Union, but which poses no offensive threat to it (Bjøl, 1983, pp. 10–16).

In the middle of the zone is Sweden, which mounts a robust territorial defence and a strict policy of neutrality. Sweden's policy and the structure of its defence arrangements, which include a substantial indigenous arms industry, make clear that it will in principle resist aggression from any quarter, and that it offers no threats to anyone who does not threaten it. On the western side of the Nordic buffer stand Norway and Denmark, both members of NATO, but with qualified alliance policies, sometimes referred to as quasi-neutral, involving major restrictions on the peacetime basing of both foreign nuclear weapons and conventional forces on their territory (Bjøl, 1983, pp. 16–38).

These three layers are all mutually supportive. Finland would have been very hard pressed to remain neutral if Sweden had been a full front-line member of NATO. Similarly, Norway and Denmark would have found it more difficult to sustain their qualified alliance policy without the insulation provided by Sweden and Finland. Having Norway and Denmark within NATO has, *inter alia*, increased the credibility of the Alliance's claim to be a purely defensive organization, though this gain is often over-shadowed by complaints that Denmark does not contribute its share to the Alliance. Taken together, these three layers form an integrated whole which has successfully created a band of military and political insulation between East and West throughout the difficult decades of the Cold War. Levels of defence expenditure in these four countries are within the norms prevalent in Europe, though Finland and Denmark are on the low side (IISS, 1989, p. 224). In the context of the Cold War, the Nordic zone provided an area of relatively low militarization and tension, and also a modicum of East–West trade and contact. It is no accident that so many of the major East–West negotiations took place in Stockholm and Helsinki. For the Nordic countries themselves, the buffer role provided a way of meeting the security demands of both superpowers without having to suffer the many in-conveniences, indignities and costs of permanently stationed foreign military forces. With their variations on the themes of self-defence and part-alignment, the Nordic countries have avoided both the pitfall of being seen as weak, and the self-defeating consequences of being seen as provocative. This arrangement allowed the Nordic states to play a useful role for both sides in East–West relations. It also allowed them to max-imize their domestic freedom and disengagement from Cold War militarization within a situation that was by any definition highly constrained.

It might be argued that the Nordic buffer only worked because of peculiarly favourable conditions, and that it therefore has nothing to offer as a model for mainland Europe. Finland was extraordinarily lucky to escape the fate of Soviet occupation that befell other European allies of Nazi Germany. The Nordic states themselves were all strong states, with high levels of socio-political cohesion, and thus capable of managing the difficulties of a middle strategic way. In addition, relations among the Nordic states constituted a security community. The absence of military and political security problems within the Nordic group enabled them to construct a stable zone between the two sides of the Cold War. The Nordic area was mostly not as strategically vital as the central front, which made it easier to insulate. But even this argument had less force during the 1980s, when the Nordic states found themselves squeezed between the Soviet strategic sanctu-ary in the Barents Sea, and the aggressive forward posture of the United States' maritime strategy (Joenniemi, 1986, pp. 57–67).

While exceptional factors may in part explain the unique

position of the Nordic states during the Cold War, the post-Cold War era opens up Nordic-type opportunities for many states whose options were previously restricted by their locked-in position in the East–West confrontation. Gorbachev's policies are well on the way to eliminating ideology as a security factor in most of Eastern Europe. Both superpowers are seriously committed to making major reductions in their forward defence postures in Europe, and the unification of Germany will anyway knock the props from under the whole idea of forward defence. The East-Central European states are already largely removed from the arena of ideological competition, and are well on the way to reconstructing themselves as buffers rather than shields. The Soviet Union's remarkable acquiescence in this process reflects its own spectacular diminution in sensitivity to political threat resulting from its abandonment of rigid views on the meaning of socialism. Germans are anxious to reduce the heavy militarization, particularly nuclear, that their front-line role has necessitated. Conditions in East-Central Europe are making an extension of the Nordic security model not only attractive, but increasingly feasible.

Do the makings exist for a broad, layered zone in which a mixture of neutrals, semi-neutrals and qualified allies would lie between the major military forces and political centres in the Soviet Union and Western Europe? Such a zone would be designed to reflect lowered ideological tensions and to help institutionalize the less confrontational military posture appropriate to post-Cold War relations. Its strategic function would be to put a broad zone of disengagement between Soviet and Western military power in Europe. That zone would be filled with states prepared to offer robust territorial defence to any illegal military movements. Its political and economic function would be that of a semi-permeable membrane, allowing the desired degree of both exchange and insulation between East and West.

One way to think through the transformation of the Cold War boundary from a narrow line to a broad zone is in terms of the gradations of alignment suggested by the Nordic model. If hard, narrow boundaries require fully committed allies, then soft, broad ones require a range of alignment postures running from full neutrality or nonalignment (Sweden, Austria, Switzerland, Yugoslavia), through degrees of qualified neutrality (Finland) and qualified alliance (France, Romania, Denmark, Norway, Greece, Spain) to full alliance (most other central front members of NATO and the Warsaw Pact).

Full alliance means political commitment plus some level of political cooperation, plus willingness to have allied forces permanently stationed on one's territory during peacetime. Britain,

West Germany and Belgium have been the exemplars of this policy within NATO, and Poland, East Germany and Czechoslovakia within the Warsaw Pact. During the Cold War, the term 'Finlandization' was predominantly used to convey a negative condition and was often held up as a warning to Western Europe of its likely fate in the absence of American protection. 'Denmarkization' was used to indicate an irresponsible, free-riding ally. But in the new environment now unfolding, Nordic models may well become attractive to many Central and Eastern European states. It is worth noting that Finno-Soviet relations have been a historical success for the Soviet Union, and therefore provide both a positive image for reorienting relations between the Soviet Union and Eastern Europe, as well as a model of how to meet Soviet military concerns.

Full neutrality or nonalignment means the adoption of classical European-style neutrality. It requires strict denial of any military alliance or alignment with the major powers. Unlike Finlandization it does not require economic balance between East and West. It specifically excludes institutionalized rights of military transit or basing for other powers under any circumstances, the objective being to reassure neighbours that one's territory will not become a source of either indigenous or foreign threats against them. This type of neutrality is best served by the mounting of a territorial defence that is at least in principle *tous azimuts*, and which is non-offensive in the sense of not confronting neighbouring countries with major threats of invasion or bombardment. The purpose of such a defence is to deter aggression both by denying transit routes to foreign forces, and by raising the cost of attack above the likely benefit of occupation.

The essentials of qualified neutrality as exemplified by Finland can be summed up as: (1) deep and unequivocal political neutrality accepted as a condition of domestic political independence and freedom from foreign bases; (2) some attempt to keep economic balance between East and West; (3) firm territorial defence as for full neutrals; and (4) consultative arrangements with a great power neighbour which envisage both discussion in the event of major deteriorations in the military security environment and support should military threats arise that might overwhelm the territorial defence of the qualified neutral, and so raise the prospect that its territory might become a base for threats against the great power. Consultative arrangements along these lines would be a politically vital reassurance measure both *de facto* and *de jure* in transitions away from the present forward defence arrangements. But if the post-Cold War security order in Europe stabilizes at low levels of political and military threat, they might be expected to atrophy *de facto* over the long term. Qualified neutrality is aimed at meeting the needs of a particularly insecure great power neighbour. To the extent that the overall security environment itself generates a low level of fear, the distinction between full and qualified neutrality diminishes. This, indeed, was the direction of Soviet-Finnish relations after Gorbachev's visit to Helsinki in 1989.

Qualified alliance involves political and military alignment with a major power, and is therefore not a form of neutrality. But as with qualified neutrality, a key objective is to ensure that the country remains free of foreign military forces unless a major emergency requires their presence. Alliance is therefore firm on the political level, but qualified on the military one. There are elements of neutralism in the desire to offer reassurance to the enemy by maintaining the less-provocative military posture implied by the absence of permanently stationed allied forces. This stance inserts a partial buffer between the direct confrontation of opposing great power military forces. Existing practice offers a range of possibilities for implementing qualified alliance policy. The minimum conditions are a political commitment to the allied cause and agreement to avoid peacetime stationing of foreign military forces. Options for military cooperation vary from the rather minimal ones that France practised under de Gaulle, and Romania under Ceauçescu, where even allied transit rights were in question, to the rather extensive ones that have marked Norwegian policy. Minimum military cooperation involves little more than an undertaking to fight on the same side if it comes to war. Maximum military cooperation involves both fitting the country's military forces, command structures and doctrines into those of the alliance and participating in the continuing joint planning and exercises necessary to maintain coordinated military efficiency among a group of countries. Transit rights and reinforcement plans are central to military cooperation, and, in this sense, qualified alliance is a way of keeping immediate threats to the enemy low during peacetime, while holding the option that they may be quickly raised if war seems imminent. Qualified alliance offers a possibility of moving away from all alliance and thus of adapting to and supporting less stressed politico-military relations, while maintaining familiar elements of political and military stability.

The question is whether, and in what way, post-Cold War conditions in Europe offer prospects for an extension of the Nordic-type zone. Might it be possible to extend this principle southwards through Eastern and Central Europe, to create a permeable buffer zone stretching from the North Cape to Crete? The precise answer to this question depends on which of our three scenarios best represents the outcome of events in Europe.

If there is a return to Cold War, then the buffer would have to be constructed between NATO and the Soviet Union, and the conditions for it would bear some resemblance to those faced by the Nordic states during the Cold War. Under these conditions, there is a danger that it would become a kind of grey zone of intervening competition, somewhat along the lines of the inter-war years. Some states might have their internal stability harshly tested. If the EC coheres sufficiently to become a pole of power in the international system, then the buffer would separate the Western European core and the Soviet Union. Since this scenario requires low levels of fear, the buffer would exist in relatively benign conditions acting as a reassurance factor in a relationship from which much of the tension had been removed, but where a degree of separateness was still desired by both sides. The former East German territories might become part of a broader dis-engagement zone. If Europe fragments, then the buffer becomes important between Germany and the Soviet Union, and much would depend on the character and policy of Germany. Under these conditions, groups or alliances of states within the buffer might well play a role in the balance of power. A Nordic/Baltic group and a Danubian/Adriatic one might become players in a revived European security complex, though again the dangers of competitive intervention could arise.

Some of the component parts of an extended buffer zone already exist in the form of states with longstanding policies of neutrality. These include Switzerland and Yugoslavia, which took up neutrality by choice, and Austria, which was neutralized as part of the arrangements that ended post-war military occupa-tion. Swiss neutrality reflects an earlier age when the locus of conflict was located in Western and Central Europe, and Switzer-land is anyway too deeply embedded geographically in Western Europe for its neutrality to make much contribution to an East-Central European zone. Austria and Yugoslavia are much better placed geographically, and provide well-established and usefully contiguous nodes of neutrality around which a permeable buffer might be constructed.

After the events of 1989, several other countries seem firmly headed towards neutrality. Both Hungary and Czechoslovakia are well on the way to achieving complete withdrawals of Soviet troops, and have adopted neutralist-style foreign policies. Hung-ary was never as crucial to the central front as the countries to the north of it were. To the west and south it borders on neutrals, and might also do so in the east if Romania took that path. Czech-oslovakia, despite its frontier with West Germany, was much less strategically important than East Germany and Poland. Romania was fortunate enough to be located in a strategic backwater, and was able to be a qualified ally even under Ceauçescu. Its post-1989 politics are still unstable, but neutrality is a distinct possibility. Albania could easily adapt its present isolationist stance towards a form of full neutrality, thus completing a core of neutral states conveniently insulated from Western Europe by the Alps and the Adriatic.

Several countries might be attracted by qualified alliance status: political commitment, but no stationing of foreign military forces. Of the Warsaw Pact members, Poland and probably Bulgaria are obvious candidates. Should the three Baltic republics succeed in reasserting their independence, some form of qualified alliance might well be a necessary condition for reassuring the Soviet Union. On the Western side, Greece and Turkey are possible candidates for this role.

Poles might prefer neutrality, but they are stuck with Stalin's legacy which moved their post-1945 boundaries well into what had for a long time been German territory. So long as there is any uncertainty in Poland about German intentions, the maintenance of a link with Moscow will have compelling attractions. With a united Germany almost certainly part of NATO, Poland's options will be very strongly affected by the particular arrangements made to make the former East German territories into a disengagement zone. For obvious reasons, this option is most likely in the fragmentation, and possibly also in the Cold War III, scenarios, both of which pose the danger that this zone will break down. Bulgaria's geostrategic importance was low even during the Cold War, and will decline further if it becomes embedded in an East-Central European buffer zone. Its traditional close ties to Moscow point to continued alliance in a context that would not require any permanent stationing of Soviet forces in the country.

Greece has long been uncomfortable with its role in NATO. Because of rivalry with Turkey, and in consideration of its neighbours, Greece has never shared NATO's view that the Soviet threat is the primary one. American bases are deeply controversial in national politics, and the country has already adopted Gaullist postures of military distancing from the Alliance. The political left is hostile to NATO because of past Anglo-American interventions in Greek political life. For all of these reasons, Greece would almost certainly welcome a permanent loosening in Alliance commitments. It might even prefer qualified neutrality, but that option is constrained by its important geostrategic position in relation to Soviet access to the Mediterranean. More subtly, Greece might well not want to abandon its alliance links because a complete exit from NATO would leave it more exposed to Turkey. Qualified alliance would fit comfortably against neutral Yugoslavia and Romania, and a similarly postured

Bulgaria.

Turkey's position is unique. It is not obviously part of Europe in cultural, ethnic or geographical terms, though it could conceivably become so if it is ever accepted into the European Community. In regional security terms it forms the boundary of indifference where the dynamics of the European and Middle Eastern security complexes stand back to back (Buzan, 1991a, ch. 5). It plays an important role in NATO because of its crucial geostrategic position athwart the exit from the Black Sea. During the Cold War, this location made its membership in NATO vital to the United States' ability to retain naval dominance in the Eastern Mediterranean. Like Western Europe, Turkey also came under direct threat from Stalin's Soviet Union during the immediate post-war years. If the Cold War continues to fade, the need for close association with NATO should decline. As for Greece, qualified alliance might become an attractive option as Cold War tensions drop all through East-Central Europe. If the outcome of its relations with the European Community turns negative, then a shift towards neutrality might become appropriate. Turkey is well able to adopt territorial defence, and a robust neutrality would in many ways suit its difficult position at the juncture of the Western, Russian and Arab/Islamic worlds.

For both Greece and Turkey, decisions to move away from full alliance would be affected not only by the uneasy state of their relations with each other, but also by the dynamics of Soviet-American relations concerning naval power in the Eastern Mediterranean. Both might wish to retain association with NATO as a means of constraining their own dispute. To the extent that naval rivalry in the Mediterranean remains a serious security issue, both will also be constrained in their choices by the sensitivity of their strategic location at the exit from the Black Sea. Either of these issues could swing the balance towards continued association with the Western alliance, and it seems certain that the United States, the EC powers, and probably also the Soviet Union would not want to see either Greece or Turkey move into a position in which Balkan instability became more likely.

Putting all of these countries together produces a band of disengagement that stretches from the Nordic countries to the Aegean Sea. Many of the states within it either have, or are well-suited to adopting, non-provocative territorial defence policies. Their adjacency makes them potentially mutually supportive as the Nordic countries have been, though the central and southern parts of the zone do contain some significant trouble spots. Ethno-territorial problems between Albania and Yugoslavia, and Romania and Hungary, and instability in the Yugoslav federation might create problems within the zone. But these are essentially local issues, and would not necessarily compromise a policy of self-defence and political independence within the broader European context. One solution is that the restructuring of East-Central Europe has to be a joint project between East and West. Joint project does not necessarily mean an explicitly negotiated deal. It might best be done by reciprocal unilateralism within the broad framework of a common understanding about what needs to be done (such as either supporting Yugoslavia, or helping it to disintegrate peacefully). In one form or another, this buffer zone of states seems likely to be a feature in all the post-Cold War scenarios.

Chapter 9

Cold War III?

This scenario supposes that the great thaw in East–West relations that marked the closing years of the 1980s is but a temporary phenomenon, and that the pattern of broad-spectrum East–West rivalry somehow reimposes itself on Europe, if not the world. The major requirement for such a turn of events has to be a return of high levels of fear between the Soviet Union on the one hand, and Europe and the United States on the other. In power terms, it requires that the United States remain strong, which seems highly likely under any scenario. The power requirements for Europe and the Soviet Union allow for some variation. At a minimum, the Soviet Union must remain militarily strong enough to threaten invasion of Western Europe and nuclear bombardment of the United States. That posture could be sustained either by a resurgence in Soviet development which revitalized its economic base, or, perhaps for a time, by a return to the Brezhnev policy of squeezing a weak economy. The scenario is easiest to imagine if Europe remains relatively weak. For that to occur, the integration process would have to falter, or lapse back into 'Eurosclerosis', and the EC consequently fail to develop sufficient political and military coherence to look after itself. This provides the most obvious 'correlation of forces' that would make Europe seem vulnerable to Soviet threats and in need of United States' protection. A Cold War III scenario is possible with a stronger Europe if the Soviet Union was also powerful, and the level of fear was high. In all of its variants, this scenario envisages a continuation of the earlier Cold War pattern of interdependence: high between the United States and Europe, and low between both of them and the Soviet Union.

In order to keep this scenario distinct from the others, it is important to set some limits around what 'Cold War III' does and does not mean. Cold War implies the continuance of domination by the United States and the Soviet Union over European security. It is thus about the maintenance of overlay. Cold War also implies confrontation across a wide spectrum of issues: not just a balance of power rivalry, but one involving societal, political and economic challenges as well as military ones. It is therefore hard to imagine Cold War without a strong element of ideological difference between the rivals. Excluded from it are both a rivalry that centred on Germany and the Soviet Union, which would fall into the fragmentation scenario (Chapter 11), and one that centred on Europe and the Soviet Union, which would fall into the European pole scenario (Chapter 10).

The question is what kind of events could trigger a sufficient turnaround from the apparent collapse of Cold War in 1989 and the first half of 1990, to precipitate a return to Cold War? If this happened, how would Cold War III differ from rounds I and II? Since, this scenario requires a rather sharp change in current trends (as of May 1990), the easiest way to explore it is to look at the possible developments that could act as a trigger. Such developments might originate in either the West or the East.

9.1. Cold War Triggered by the West

The West could trigger a new Cold War by being too aggressive in exploiting the opportunities offered by the withdrawal of Soviet control from Eastern Europe, and by seeking to exploit the current domestic troubles of the Soviet Union to weaken its international position still further. Neither of these developments seems at all likely. Eastern Europe is already nearly free. Its governments are no longer in thrall to Moscow, and its peoples would fiercely resist any reimposition of Soviet control. The Soviet troop withdrawals now being negotiated will destroy whatever remains of the system by which the Soviet Union used the Warsaw Pact Organization to deny most Eastern European governments control over their own armed forces (Jones, 1984, pp. 109–10). So long as this trend prevails in Eastern Europe, the main reason for Western aggression against the Soviet Union is gone. The mainstream tendency in both Europe and the United States is to support Gorbachev's revolution. As the cautious and extremely diplomatic Western response to Lithuanian attempts to seize independence demonstrated, there was no sign up to the middle of 1990 that the West was seeking to push Moscow to the wall. The mainstream tendency showed sensitivity to the fragility of Gorbachev's position, and a hands off attitude towards the domestic turbulence within the Soviet Union.

It is extremely difficult to foresee circumstances that would produce consensus between the United States and Europe in taking an aggressive stance towards the Soviet Union provided that the Soviets themselves did not become aggressive. Bellicose behaviour by either Europe or the United States in the absence of such consensus is forestalled by the great breach that it would open up between them. Such moves by either side unsupported by the other would lead into the fragmentation or European pole scenarios. But although highly unlikely, this scenario of unified Western aggression is not wholly impossible. The policy decisions for it would have to be made by the United States and Germany and would be along the following lines.

If Western aggression was aimed at maximizing the disintegration of the Soviet Union — perhaps to carry the crusade against communism to completion, perhaps to eliminate the Soviet Union as a world power — then the leading actor would have to be the United States. The motivation for such a policy would have to come from the American right, and would be an extension of the thinking that underlay the Reagan administration's policy of bankrupting the Soviet Union by forcing it to compete in a high technology arms race. Necessary elements in a renewal of this policy would be continued military pressure on the Soviet Union, and a refusal either to negotiate arms reductions or respond to unilateral Soviet arms reduction initiatives. A United States pursuing this line would also seek to deny the Soviet Union access to Western capital, organizational technique and technology, which would mean keeping it out of the organizations (IMF, World Bank, GATT, EC) that embody the Western economic regime. It would also meddle in the turbulent ethnic politics of the Soviet Union, promoting an aggressive Wilsonian policy of self-determination in order to encourage separatism and generally trying to drive Russia back to its eighteenth-century boundaries.

Given the speed and depth of developments in Eastern Europe, the scope for Western aggression against the Soviet Union in this area has all but disappeared. The Soviet Union has already conceded a rapid unification of Germany. Since it seems to hope itself for Western assistance with its own reconstruction, it can hardly oppose the penetration of Western capital into Eastern Europe. There is still scope for action hostile to the Soviet Union's prestige and military position, and if this was to be exploited, then the leading actor would have to be Germany. The key question is what the military arrangements will be once East Germany unites with the Federal Republic. It now seems virtually certain that a united Germany will remain in NATO. Although the Soviet Union still resists such a move, it will eventually have to accept this. Several clear options for saving Soviet face exist: (1) negotiating a new European security regime within the CSCE; (2) negotiating the phased draw-down of Soviet forces in Germany;

(3) not extending the NATO front line to the German-Polish border; and perhaps (4) reducing, or phasing out entirely, allied nuclear, or even conventional, deployments in Germany. But if German unification proceeds without regard to Soviet interests, demanding rapid withdrawal of Soviet forces and replacing them with a strong German or NATO military presence, then it could provoke a Soviet reaction. If such an assertive German unification was accompanied by a revival of Pan-German territorial claims, then some Eastern European countries, notably Poland, might well seek to draw the Soviet Union into their defence. Although Gorbachev has undone much of Stalin's work, the old dictator's trick of moving Poland westward at the expense of Germany might yet come to haunt the construction of a new security order in Europe.

These German and American scenarios would have to be pursued together. They might be seen as one possible development of the elevation of Germany to being the senior European NATO partner of the United States that took place at the end of the 1980s. They would amount to a major assault on Soviet security.

Both scenarios are conceivable, but both carry such high costs and risks, and require such big changes from present norms and trends, as to make them unlikely. Since the Soviet Union is already in headlong retreat and has made many irreversible concessions, it is hard to see how such policies could be justified except in terms so extreme as to be well outside mainstream politics in both Europe and the United States. As communism visibly unravels even in Moscow the idea of an anti-communist crusade becomes harder and harder to sustain. Consequently, it is not at all easy to see where the political coalitions necessary to implement them would come from, or how they would gain power. Even if they succeeded in both Germany and the United States, the result would put huge and quite possibly unbearable strains on NATO.

The scenario would require the accession to power of the far right in the United States, a sustained willingness to ignore the impact of high military spending on both the deficit and economic competitiveness in general, and a reversal of the benign attitude towards Gorbachev. So long as Gorbachev continues on his present course, the justifications for such a costly and risky policy would be very hard to find. Since Gorbachev is accomplishing voluntarily the withdrawal, arms reduction and political reform measures that reduce the Soviet threat, it would be almost impossible to sell such a policy as in any sense defensive. An obviously aggressive policy would create crises in Washington's relations with both Europe and Japan, and would be unlikely to command a consensus in domestic politics. It would forgo the benefits of arms reductions and the possibilities of expanded trade and investment, as well as exacerbating budgetary problems. It would also require keeping alive the nuclear confrontation, with its risk of accidental war.

The German element in the scenario also carries high costs and risks. It presupposes that the Germans virtually exclude the Soviet Union from the unification process. This would require a major reversal of existing policy and, among other things, would leave hanging the awkward question of the status of Berlin, which is still legally under four-power control. A German-American consensus to squeeze the Soviet Union would almost certainly not find support in the rest of Europe. It would put at risk the whole construction of the European Community and raise fears of a resurgent German great power. Indeed, it virtually requires the emergence of Germany as a headstrong great power and so would be most likely to trigger balance of power responses leading to the fragmentation scenario. Again, the domestic political sources for such developments are hard to envisage. Mainstream sentiment in both parts of Germany is strongly committed to reducing the militarization of the country and enjoying the fruits of lowered tension. Because of its long years on the front line, the German body politic seems much more aware than most of the highly interdependent nature of security. The idea that Germany must not be the cause of a new war is strongly embedded, as is the idea that German unification can only flourish in a Europe that is also in some important sense unified. As the German writer Martin Walser put it: 'the more Europe absorbs us, the more pleasant it will be to be a German' (*Economist*, 12 November 88, p. 66). German society, as French, is deeply penetrated by the lessons of the wars that shattered the operation of the pre-1945 security complex in Europe. It is almost inconceivable that Germany would embark on a set of policies likely to recreate a configuration in Europe with alarming similarities to that of the late nineteenth century.

For all of these reasons, a return to Cold War as a result of Western initiatives seems deeply unlikely.

9.2. Cold War Triggered by the Soviet Union

Because the Soviet Union is undergoing considerable socio-political instability, any return to East–West Cold War seems more likely to be triggered by the Soviet Union than by the West. Here also, however, it is hard to find plausible policy lines that are likely to reconstruct the Cold War. By definition the situation in the Soviet Union can generate more options because it is already

turbulent. By comparison, politics in the West is relatively stable
and slow moving: even in Germany the process is one of absorption of the East into Western norms. The very fact of this
continuity is what makes the scale and speed of change required
for Western aggression against the Soviet Union appear so
unlikely. This is not to argue that the Soviet Union is indeed likely
to trigger a new Cold War, merely that conditions make it easier
than in the West. For such a thing to happen, there would have
also to be major changes in current Soviet trends in one of two
directions. The first involves political continuity, the change being
that Gorbachev's attempts to restructure the Soviet Union finally
begin to pay off, rather than, as during their first few years,
adding to economic inefficiency and failing to contain political
unrest. The second requires political change, specifically an abandonment of Gorbachev's attempt to Westernize the Soviet Union,
and its replacement with a more Slavophile, or possibly Stalinist,
regime.

The path to Cold War III through political continuity is long,
and extremely uncertain. It requires reduced tension and
increased transaction with the West for a longish period. It also
requires that the Soviet Union not succumb to domestic violence
in the process of economic and political restructuring. The key to
it is a reform of the Soviet Union so thorough and so successful
that it recreates not only the economic and technological foundations of Soviet power, but also revives communism, or finds some
'third path', as an ideology sufficiently different and credible to
challenge Western liberal democracy. That is a lot of 'ifs'!

On the power side, a return to Cold War would require a
success of *perestroika* that placed the productivity, efficiency, and
technological quality of the Soviet economy on par with those of
the West. This itself would require a transformation of *perestroika*,
which has so far added to economic and political disarray, without
yet generating an economic revival (*Economist*, 28 April 1990,
'Survey of Perestroika'). Assuming that all of these difficulties
could be overcome, and that *perestroika* worked, the Soviet Union
could, if it chose, once again mount a threat to the West by
building up modern, large-scale military forces. But as Paul
Kennedy argues at length, power in the international system is
relative, not absolute (Kennedy, 1988). On this basis, it is impossible for the Soviet Union ever to recreate the preponderant
position it held after the Second World War, no matter how
successful its internal efforts at reconstruction. The simple fact is
that at the end of the Second World War, the country was
surrounded by areas of weakness and instability that magnified its
own power. But since that time, old centres of power in Europe
and Japan have recovered, and new ones in China, India and

among the Asian NICs have arisen. Now, and for the foreseeable future, the Soviet Union will be surrounded by areas of political, economic, military and societal strength. Given its advantages of good resource endowments and a well-educated population, the Soviet Union could still become a very formidable power, though only if many things went right that are now going wrong, and only after a considerable length of time. It is the prospect that all of these 'ifs' might work out well for the Soviet Union that sustains an interest in the West in not giving Gorbachev much help. While the West has no interest in the collapse of his project, neither does it have much desire to see it succeed too well.

On the ideological side, the question of how reform communism would relate to the West after the success of *perestroika* is a tricky one. The recasting of article 6 in the Soviet constitution early in 1990 removed the right of the Communist Party to rule, thus opening the way to political pluralism. This makes possible two ideological routes to a successful reconstruction. By the first route, the Communist Party loses power, and the government of a successfully reconstructed Soviet Union is not communist at all. This virtually eliminates the ideological grounds for a return to Cold War. The second route assumes that the Communist Party not only wins the competition for power, but also proves capable of rectifying its own distortions and finding a workable and distinctive formula for an alternative political economy. Would it then reassert the Marxist challenge to capitalism? Here the question is how distinctive such a reform communism would be from social democratic forms of political economy that now fit comfortably within the West. The current leaning of the Soviet Union towards socialist pluralism and market economics suggest that it might not be different enough to reconstruct either the challenge or the fears of the old Cold War. The dictates of economic and political efficiency will shove the Soviet Union powerfully towards pluralism, and the pursuit of *perestroika* requires the development of wide-ranging contacts with the West.

By either route, a triumph of the Westernizers in the Soviet Union would thus be more likely to clear the path for the association of the Soviet Union with the Western great power security community, than it would be to reconstruct conditions for Cold War. It is deeply unclear exactly how a successful *perestroika* could lead to a renewed Cold War. It might even be argued that in order for the Soviet Union to meet the power condition of a return to Cold War, economic reconstruction along the lines of pluralist political economy is a necessary condition. If true, that would mean that the power condition for a return to Cold War by this route could only be achieved by making ideological reforms that would largely eliminate the political grounds for a new Cold War. This would be true regardless of whether Soviet reconstruction was led by the communists or by some other party. For *perestroika* to remake both the power base and the ideological difference necessary for a return to Cold War would require the invention of a new and effective kind of political economy, markedly different from, and structurally incompatible with, capitalism: the so-called 'third path'. Such a development is currently nowhere in sight. A Soviet Union functioning efficiently along social democratic lines, whether in communist clothes or not, would possess neither the military power nor the degree of ideological difference necessary to sustain and justify a new Cold War.

The other route to Soviet-triggered Cold War is somewhat more plausible because of the current fluidity of events in the Soviet Union. It requires political change, specifically, as said above, abandonment of Gorbachev's attempt to Westernize the Soviet Union, and its replacement with a more Slavophile or Stalinist government. This route does not presuppose the need to maintain open relations with the West. It is most likely to arise as a reaction against the failures of *perestroika*, and particularly against the threat that the political forces unleashed by *glasnost'* will break up the Soviet Union. The increasing fragility of Gorbachev's middle-ground position by the spring of 1990 made such a reaction increasingly plausible. He was squeezed between a backward-looking right fearful of national disintegration, chaos and loss of personal, ethnic and national position, on the one side, and a radical left wanting more and faster reform across a wide spectrum of economic and political issues on the other. With *glasnost* breaking up the country faster than *perestroika* was putting it back together, Gorbachev looked increasingly vulnerable. The fact that the country looked even less governable without him than with him was the last bastion of his centrist position. But the fact that governability itself loomed increasingly as the central question raised the prospects of the right as the likely successors to Gorbachev.

Nevertheless, given the widespread acceptance of the need for reform in the Soviet Union, a simple return to the political economy of Stalinism seems unlikely. Even the military can see that a return to the old ways would not address the fundamental economic weakening that is undermining the foundations of Soviet military power in comparison with the West. With the Soviet economy already smaller than Japan's, and within statistical sight of slipping behind Germany's, even the most hawkish and reactionary circles cannot escape the need for reform. However unlikely, a Stalinist reaction cannot be ruled out so long as the Communist Party and its bureaucratic apparatus remain in being, though the continued operation of Gorbachev's political reforms, particularly the revision to article 6, makes this option increasingly difficult. Since it could not solve the problem of the Soviet Union's relative decline, such a regime is unlikely to last long.

A more likely route is a change of course (with or without a change of leadership) necessitated by the mounting political disorder within the Soviet Union. It is becoming rather easy to envisage circumstances in which the survival of the Soviet state displaces most other issues on the political agenda. When added to widespread economic and ethnic discontents, Gorbachev's policy of *glasnost'*, plus his apparent personal dislike of the use of force to solve political problems, have opened up the many fault lines in what is still as much an empire as a state. As the Soviet government faces an increasingly daunting array of secessionist movements and inter-ethnic civil wars around its fringes, it will have to make some extraordinarily difficult political choices about how to handle them.

If *perestroika* can be made to work, it might just be possible to loosen the federal structure enough to maintain the strategic unity of the Soviet state. But if it does not, or cannot keep up with the rising tide of separatism, then the Soviet government will have to choose between a negotiated decolonization of its inner empire, and an extensive resort to force to keep the state together. The decolonization option would be hard to stop once begun. If it led to independence not only for the Baltic, Central Asian and Caucasus states, but also for the Ukraine, the Soviet Union would in effect be dismembering itself as a superpower, though even Russia alone would still be a great power. In a counterpoint move of historic irony, the Soviet Union could find itself falling apart at the same time as the EC was increasing its cohesion. The interplay of this giant double act would change the power structure in such a way as to push events in the direction of the European pole scenario in Chapter 10.

The resort to force in order to preserve the Soviet state might well look more attractive than dismemberment, despite its obvious costs. It is entirely plausible that a government refusing to hold the line would be replaced by one prepared to use force to save the state. The weight of historical evidence in cases as diverse as the United States, China, Nigeria and Ethiopia demonstrates the tenacity with which states hang on to their unity against threats of secession, almost regardless of the cost. The resort to force is difficult to stop once begun. It might involve rather extensive civil war, and would make the government acutely sensitive to foreign intervention. The location of much of the trouble along the increasingly sensitive boundary between Islam and 'Christendom' would add to the dangers. The willingness of non-Muslim outside powers to intervene in such a situation would be tempered by the still formidable nuclear might of the Soviet Union, and by the inherent difficulty of deciding which side to take. Under civil war conditions, much of the programme of *glasnost* and *perestroika* would disintegrate. As in any civil war, military necessities would dominate politics, and the Soviet Union would become an inherently unstable place. European countries such as Poland, that might be tempted to intervene both for reasons of historical revenge and for possible territorial gain, could do so only at the risk of inviting retaliation. The militarization of domestic politics, when added to the sheer uncertainty of the turmoil, would force the West to keep up its military guard. As several Third World states with imperial domestic structures (Nigeria, Turkey, Pakistan, Iraq, Iran) have demonstrated, the Soviet Union could almost certainly keep itself together by force. Doing so, however, would once again tend to isolate it from the mainstream of the West and cause it to be treated as a potential military threat. Civil war in the Soviet Union would reinforce the hands off policy of 'don't help, don't hinder' that has largely governed Western responses to Gorbachev.

A second, also not unlikely, route to political change in the Soviet Union is through a Slavophile reaction to the consequences of Gorbachev's push for Westernization. This path assumes that the pitfalls of disintegration and civil war sketched above are avoided. The Soviet Union remains intact as a coherent state, and Gorbachev's policy of socialist pluralism, market reforms, and economic and societal opening to the West continues. The trap in this course is that the more it succeeds, the more it will make the Soviet Union appear weak. Gorbachev's policy is to reduce the Soviet Union's one area of conspicuous strength, military power, and to move towards the West in the areas where the Soviet Union is weakest, namely economics and civil society. He needs to cut military spending because maintaining that strength is both an intolerable economic burden and politically counterproductive in the international reactions it engenders. He needs economic and societal contact with the West, in effect riding Eastern Europe's coat-tails into the 'common European house', in order to regenerate the Soviet Union's political economy along more pluralist lines. The gamble appears to be that arms reduction both opens the way for greater contact and releases resources for reconstruction in the Soviet Union. Soviet reconstruction then occurs at such a pace that the country can move towards the West from a position of reasonable strength, or at least not humiliating weakness.

But this is a big gamble. Arms reduction can occur quite quickly, whereas the reconstruction of a political economy is a long and difficult job, often tackled unsuccessfully. The danger is that the more the Soviet Union tries to integrate itself with Europe, the weaker it will appear to be, reverting to its late nineteenth-century status of a relatively underdeveloped periphery, exporting resources and importing capital. Conversely, the more apart it stays, the more it can play to its own strengths, maintaining at least an appearance of power.

It is the attraction of this appearance (and not insubstantial reality) of power that might well trigger an anti-Western, Slavophile reaction against Gorbachev's policies in the Soviet Union. If the Soviet Union appears unable to catch up with the West, and/or is in danger of being too heavily penetrated by Western capital and society, then a policy of withdrawal to a more isolated posture might well capture the political high ground in Moscow. Such a policy would be accompanied by the traditional rhetoric of escape from Western decadence and assertion of Slavic cultural nationalism. The necessity of isolation would justify a return to Russian military traditions of strong land power. One danger in this scenario is that it would intensify ethnic divisions between Slav and non-Slav, and thus drift back towards the prospect of domestic disintegration and/or civil war.

Should communist hardliners remain in power in China, a move of this sort might lead to some form of revival of the Sino-Soviet alliance. By standing back to back, both China and the Soviet Union could more easily pursue their own course of economic nationalism and defensive withdrawal from the West. Although the common ideology of their first alliance would almost certainly no longer exist, both would share a long tradition of reactionary anti-Westernism based on a strong sense of civilizational distinctiveness. As weak great powers within a multipolar international system dominated by a consortium of leading capitalist powers, China and the Soviet Union would have strong incentives to bury their differences in the face of a common cosmopolitanizing threat from the West. Since both have the military security of nuclear weapons, the threat they would face would be more economic, societal and political than military. The challenge from the West would not, as in the past, be the threat of invasion. It would be the challenge of more productive and diversified economies, more dynamic and attractive cultures, and more democratic political systems.

9.3. What Would Be the Character of a New Cold War?

By any of the three routes sketched above, it is clear that Cold War III, if it occurs at all, would be a much narrower, less important, and less tense affair than its predecessors. Its potentially most dangerous version arises from the success of *perestroika* and the renewal of the communist challenge to the West from a revived resource base. But this is in fact almost certainly the least likely possibility. The chances of the numerous conditions for it being met are small, and if they were met, the chance that ideological convergence would largely have eliminated the political divide with the West is high. The other two routes to Cold War through civil war or Slavophile reaction and isolationism point to an introverted Soviet Union, prickly, but not expansionist and on the whole not dangerous if left alone.

While neither the Western- nor the Soviet-triggered routes to Cold War seem very probable taken by themselves, there is a danger that both could come into play simultaneously. Excessive Soviet pressure on Germany over unification could stimulate nationalist reactions. Soviet perceptions of Western, and particularly United States', interference in its domestic troubles could likewise stimulate Slavophile reactions. What might seem like relatively minor events taken individually, have the potential to construct a self-feeding action–reaction spiral of antagonism. This is especially so if these events become domestic political issues. Once fears and hatreds get a grip on domestic political life, it is much more difficult for political leaders to manage their external relations. Leaders who take a too conciliatory line will find themselves under severe pressure from those prepared to respond more vigorously to mass emotion. There is good reason to think that these kinds of national passions no longer operate with significant force in the relations of the Western states with each other. But there is much less reason to think that this restraint operates in Eastern Europe, and some reason to suspect that its new and fragile manifestation between the West and the Soviet Union could break down.

Nevertheless, by any of these routes there will be three major differences between any new Cold War and the one that followed the Second World War. First, and most obvious, is that the Soviet Union no longer controls or occupies Eastern Europe. By mid-1990 events had gone so far in the Eastern European states as to make any reassertion of Soviet control an immensely risky enterprise. Almost everywhere the communist governments and their ruling machinery had crumbled or been swept aside by mass movements. Although the Soviets still had around 400,000 troops in Eastern Europe, they had neither any legitimate basis for intervening to impose their own governments, nor the option of picking off one dissident country at a time. The rapid dismantling of the Iron Curtain also called into question the long-standing inviolability of the politico-military dividing line between East and West in Europe. The sanctity of that line protected the Soviets in their earlier suppressions of Eastern European rebels. But after 1989, it could no longer be taken for granted that the West would not intervene in some way to help resist what would in effect be a full-scale invasion and reoccupation of Eastern Europe. The risks in such an enterprise would make even the most aggressive Soviet generals blanch. Everywhere they would be faced by impassioned mass local resistance, almost certainly supported by the local armies. In East Germany, already half united with the West, a Soviet intervention would create an appalling crisis with West Germany and NATO.

It could be argued that a Soviet reoccupation of Eastern Europe would reconstruct the Cold War along its old lines, with the added tension of a fresh aggression to heighten fear and insecurity all round. If such an event occurred, that would certainly be the result. But by the middle of 1990, the odds against such an event occurring had reached virtually 100 per cent. Every passing month consolidated the freedom of the Eastern European countries in such a way as to lower the attraction, and raise further the costs and risks, to the Soviet Union of taking this path. The longer Gorbachev remains in power, the more likely that Soviet forces in Eastern Europe will be drawn down or withdrawn entirely. The heroic breeching of the Iron Curtain by the Hungarians early in 1989 had by the end of the year moved the political security boundary of the Soviet Union, if not quite yet the military one, back to the Soviet border. Even if Soviet forces continue to be stationed in Eastern Europe for a time, the whole machinery of a hard, narrow boundary of politico-military confrontation has simply disappeared. With it has gone much of the reason for the acute tension of earlier Cold Wars. Cold War III would thus not be about who controlled Eastern Europe, and consequently it would not be about who controlled Western Europe. The liberation of Eastern Europe enormously enhances the security of Western Europe. In so doing it vastly decreases both the incentives for, and the significance of, any return to East–West hostility.

A second difference between any new Cold War and the post-1945 one would be that the Soviet Union would be relatively weaker. The civil war and isolationist routes to Cold War III mean a weaker Soviet Union by definition. Even the route through success and reassertion, unlikely as it is, cannot reconstruct Soviet power to the levels of the 1940s, 1950s and 1960s. As argued above, even the best imaginable Soviet reconstruction could not redress the fundamental shift in the correlation of forces that has occurred as a result of developments in Europe, Japan, China and India. The Soviet Union cannot escape relative decline, the question is simply whether the success or failure of *perestroika* makes that decline less or more precipitous. Although the Soviet Union will remain a formidable power, like the United States it is condemned to a relative decline down to what Paul Kennedy labels its 'natural share' of world power (Kennedy, 1988, p. 690). That natural share will be enough to keep the Soviet Union in the ranks of the great powers in all but the most extreme scenarios of disintegration. But it will not be enough to mount the kind of global challenge to the West that Soviet power made plausible for several decades after 1945. And the Soviet Union will anyway not face just a single opponent as it did after 1945. Instead, it will find itself just one of many major centres of military and economic power in the system. The incentives to mount a Cold War in such a multipolar system are low, since it requires challenging the whole system. If the Soviet Union rejects the path of security through interdependence, then in a multipolar world it will be invited to play a more traditional balance of power strategy for its security.

The third difference between any new Cold War and its predecessors would be the much lower level of ideological challenge and confrontation driving it. If *perestroika* is successful, the probability is high that substantial ideological convergence would have eliminated much of the ground for mutual fear and threat between the Soviet Union and the West. If it is not, the other scenarios lead more towards introverted nationalism than towards any reassertion of Stalinism. Gorbachev has already achieved a substantial deconstruction of Stalinism, and the longer he stays in power, the deeper will *glasnost* have taken root. Even if national emergency or Slavophile reaction drive him from office, there are no strong grounds for expecting a revival of ideologically assertive, globalist Marxism–Leninism. If such ideologues did take control in Moscow, they would no longer possess either the domestic power base or the global network of loyal communist parties that made Cold War I such an intense, dramatic and world-wide event. International communism has fragmented beyond repair. Its globalism has been eaten up by nationalism, its cohesion has decayed into a myriad 'different paths to socialism', and its intellectual credibility has been corroded by its numerous failures when in power to build a political economy that is either efficient or attractive.

The now irreversible political freedom of the Eastern European states means that a substantial buffer has been created between the Soviet Union and NATO. As argued in Chapter 8, this buffer seems likely to be a feature of all the scenarios, and the question is what form it will take for Cold War III. Given a return to tension between East and West, the belt of countries separating the Soviet Union from the European Community would have strong incentives to adopt the strategy of robust, cooperative neutralism pioneered by Sweden, Finland, Yugoslavia and Austria. The first priority for these states would be to preserve their independence, and within that to maximize their freedom of action. A rigorous neutrality combined with a firm policy of non-provocative defence and an active diplomacy designed to create regional linkages would best serve these goals. Neutrality and non-provocative defence would, on the Swedish and Finnish models, reassure both sides in the Cold War. It would create military buffers against surprise attack and political ones against sudden realignments. It would also restrain both East and West from pushing too hard lest they destroy the buffer and precipitate a direct confrontation.

Such a buffer would probably function quite similarly to the Nordic one during Cold War I. Economically, societally and politically it would lean Westward, but militarily and diplomatically it would take an independent line with a strong emphasis on balance, self-reliance and strict territorial defence. Cold War conditions would almost certainly stimulate existing tendencies in these countries to cultivate multinational regional groupings and identities as a way of reinforcing their position. The two conspicuous candidates here would be a Baltic group and a Danubian one. The Baltic group could extend the old Nordic buffer by adding Poland and, if they achieve their independence, the three small Baltic republics, to it. It could also continue to act as a bridge as well as an insulator between East and West. The Danubian group occupies strategically less sensitive territory. Its prime function would be to stay out of trouble, and not offer opportunities (or necessities) for intervention to either side.

One can conclude that there is virtually no prospect for a return to Cold War on anything like the scale or intensity of that which followed the end of the Second World War. The only path back to a full-scale resumption of Cold War leads through Eastern Europe. After the events of 1989 that path is so unattractive and dangerous, and becoming more so almost by the minute, as to be virtually excludable as an option. The condition of a weak Western Europe also looks unlikely, though by no means impossible. Although the EC is not about to become a United States of Europe, the steady growth in the cohesion of its core (the 'British problem' notwithstanding) looks quite firm. Even a collapse of the EC would still leave a formidably strong Germany, effectively restoring the German barrier to Russian power that existed up to 1945, and leading to the fragmentation scenario.

Indeed, use of the term 'Cold War' to describe the likely scenarios of return to a degree of hostility and confrontation between the Soviet Union and the West seems so exaggerated as to be inappropriate. The only real similarity is that the West would face a well-armed and insecure Soviet Union. But the circumstances of that confrontation would be so different from what went before in terms of issues, power balances, geostrategic considerations and scale that comparison is hardly warranted. A Slavophile reaction against *perestroika*, a withdrawal into defensive isolationism and a renewal of the Sino-Soviet alliance, is perhaps the most serious Cold War III possibility. But even this would not pose anything like the levels of mutual threat and fear that East and West inflicted on each other at the height of their global ideological rivalry. Such a situation would call for mutual defensive boundaries, but it would not contain either the means or the purposes that would make each side fear major aggression by the other. It could, indeed, be quite compatible with the scenarios outlined in the next two chapters.

Chapter 10
The Triumph of Integration

In this scenario, the integration of the European Community becomes the dominant political force in Europe, and the Eastern European states increasingly turn towards this new Western centre. The Soviet Union accepts the EC as a new centre in the economic and political spheres, and increasingly, though more slowly, also as one of the actors in the security sphere. The Soviet Union seeks to link itself to the economic centre in the EC, though remaining much more detached than its former satellites in Eastern Europe. The defining conditions for this scenario area; (1) increased cohesion in the EC, and therefore an increase in the power of Europe relative to the United States and the Soviet Union; (2) a relaxed East–West atmosphere, especially in Europe; and (3) a rise in interdependence between Western and Eastern Europe, and Western Europe and the Soviet Union. This scenario could occur in the absence of lowered tension if the EC became much stronger, and the Soviet Union much weaker, than seems likely. A continued reduction in Soviet influence and presence in Eastern Europe is central to it, and results from the changing power balance between Europe and the Soviet Union, and the lowered tension between them.

Under these conditions, the core of the EC will increasingly become the economic and political core of Europe. In the military sphere there will not be a core in the same sense. The United States and Russia will remain military powers whose strength bears on, and perhaps continues to act within, Europe. The major powers of Western Europe (Britain, France and Germany) will act increasingly in the name of the European Community both within and outside NATO. The importance of military issues in defining the location of the European core will anyway decline in salience because of the drop in levels of fear and the formation of an all-European security regime.

The idea of a dominant EC core in political and economic

matters does not require that there be one centre of total power, whether in Brussels, Berlin (or Bonn) or Paris. It means that the EC will form a relatively coherent political entity through which all major political impulses will be processed. One possible configuration for this core is a leading Berlin–Paris–Brussels axis with important secondary spokes to Rome, London and Madrid. Eastern Europe will become more and more a periphery relating primarily to this EC core. The Soviet Union might retain some kind of limited geopolitical last-resort influence in Eastern Europe. More certainly, it will continue to have a say on all-European security issues through the institutions of a European security regime, probably a reformulated CSCE. Political, economic and ideological impulses will, however, travel predominantly from West to East.

This scenario almost certainly contains a version of the buffer zone outlined in Chapter 8. The main questions are whether there will still be significant westward security pressure from the Soviet Union, and whether the primary impulse in Moscow will be to associate with or insulate itself from the EC core. The answers to these questions will determine whether the buffer has to function more as a filter, or more as an insulator. The Eastern European states have almost no choice but to associate themselves with the EC centre, and the EC has almost no choice but to accept responsibility for this periphery. Between the EC and the Soviet Union, however, a much wider range of choices is possible, and the likelihood that either would accept a centre (EC)–periphery (Soviet Union) relationship is small. For Europe it would be too big a responsibility, and for the Soviet Union it would be too big a loss of status.

The next section lays out one basic image for the triumph of integration in Europe in terms of a single centre surrounded by concentric circles. The place of Eastern Europe and the EFTA-countries in relation to the EC core is the main issue, and some of the issues from Chapter 6, particularly the competing French and German visions of Europe, are explored further. The second section adds some important modifications to this unicentric image. It looks at the way in which the new power-political dynamics of Europe, not least the relative strengthening of Germany, might promote the formation of new balances inside the EC that would work against the dominance of a single centre. Pressure to widen the membership of the EC could be a part of such strategies. This development could lead to Europe being a major international actor (a pole in the international system) without having a firm centre. The core cannot be located within the EC, but only as the EC. If integration takes this road, Europe will be organized more as a network than as a hierarchy. This form would be relatively open to linkages with other poles, the United States in particular, but also the Soviet Union. Furthermore, by a curious dialectic, relatively far-reaching integration in the EC contains a possibility of stimulating increased local differentiation. The process of European integration and identity formation interact positively with the formation of sub-regional identities and cooperative patterns. The general weakening of the nation state favours the creation (and often recreation) of sub-regions that either cut across nation-states, or combine nation-states that have been separated for forty years by the rigid socio-economic spheres of the Cold War. Under this logic, not all the circles in Europe will be concentric.

The last section concentrates on the question of the possible international appearance of this new Europe. What determines whether it will be a great power or not? What will the character of this Europe as international unit be, and how will it relate to the other main actors in the international system?

Will European integration create a European great power? Not necessarily. The main feature in this scenario is that Europe is more centred, and has a higher capability for coherent independent action, than in any of the other scenarios. Whether this new political Europe becomes a major global actor, and of what type, is an open question. The EC will certainly be a pole in the international system, increasingly relating to other powers, especially the United States and the Soviet Union (or a post-Soviet Russia), as a single entity. But what constitutes a pole? As explained in Chapters 3, 4 and 8, Europe is 'heavy' enough in capabilities to be a pole, if only it was a coherent political unit. Cohesion is therefore the decisive dimension. Without cohesion Europe will continue to be more a field on which other powers play, than a force in its own right. Traditionally, a pole has always been a state (whereas not all states have been poles, of course). So in order for Europe to become a pole it must take on state-like qualities in some important respects. This does not mean that Europe has to become a state. A European pole does not have to be a United States of Europe. The distinction between state and state-like qualities will be a salient issue for coming debates — and for this chapter. One key to it is the balance between the internal political behaviour of the unit (whether its sub-actors see themselves, and act, more as independent states or more as part of a larger European whole) and the political attitudes of external actors (whether they see Europe, and relate to it more as a single unit or more as a collection of separate state actors).

During the 1980s the EC increasingly came to be seen from the outside as a single actor, as a unit (Allen and Smith, 1990; Ginsberg, 1989). But it remained a hybrid. Other states could relate to the individual European states as well. They would always have the option of going to the constituent states instead of to the EC, and by so doing undercutting the EC as an actor. In principle this strategy can be played against any state: outside actors can play into it by influencing domestic actors. But in the case of a fully sovereign state (excluding those such as Lebanon in which domestic government has collapsed), the central government is much stronger and more authoritative than any actors within the state. Even so, the normal state is not a unitary actor. Regional interests, for example, can play large roles, as they do in Canada, Austria, Czechoslovakia, India and Britain.

Internal power balancing will remain powerful however cohesive the EC becomes. But somewhere there is a critical line beyond which the external balance of power logic (Europe in relation to other major actors) gains the upper hand over the internal balance of power logic (among the European states and nations). When this line is crossed, external necessities start to set the frame inside which different internal constellations are struggling. Until at least the late 1980s, this line had not been crossed. The EC remained less than the sum of its parts, and its internal relations dominated its external ones. But by the early 1990s, under the impact of the 1992 project and the collapse of the Cold War, the dominance of the internal balance of power was for the first time under serious challenge by the external one. Serious proposals for monetary and political union were firmly on the agenda. When the external balance of power dynamic takes over, it is likely that the internal mechanisms and patterns of balancing will go through a qualitative change. One possible consequence of this shift will be that the pattern of state and nation-based EC internal, or 'domestic', politics will decrease in favour of a rise in more transnational, issue-based, interest groups. In other words, as Europe coheres, one might expect its internal politics to shift from being an unusually highly coordinated type of international politics, to being less territorially based, and more like the issue-based domestic politics of an ordinary state.

We stress the external dimension of the integration process in Europe because it is often neglected in the standard interpretations of what is happening by both journalists and integration theorists. It adds a vital element to understanding the recasting of Europe, and one advantage of using Neorealist theory to inform this study is precisely that it focuses on this aspect. The conventional wisdom of integration theory is that spill-over goes from low politics (i.e. economic and social) to high politics (i.e. defence and security), from internal to external relations. In this view integration is incrementally built up from the bottom, and on the inside. Such functional elements of integration have played a central role in the development of the EC, and without them, the foundations for recent developments would not have existed. But now the external dimension is coming more strongly into play, giving a top-down, external impetus to integration. Spill-over goes from high politics to low, and from external to internal, and major strides can replace shuffling incrementalism.

One seemingly paradoxical consequence of this external factor in European integration is to create more room within Europe for a measure of decentralization. This chapter investigates the pole scenario, and is thus about the triumph of integration. The elements of decentralization discussed here are therefore by definition not about disintegration of the pole, which would spell fragmentation. Instead, they concern political rearrangements inside the limits set by the cohesion necessary for the EC to function as an international actor. This line of reasoning takes us back again to the transformational possibilities that arise when the EC crosses the line that makes it more rather than less than the sum of its parts. Then an important dialectic is likely to unfold. Historically, in state formation as well as in the development of the EC so far, many elements of heavy-handed centralization have been necessary in order to reach the take-off phase in the creation of a new larger international actor. But once the EC gains full recognition as an international actor, it will to a very considerable extent be kept in place by the international political dynamics that will operate on it. In other words, integration will be supported externally as well as internally. This additional support means that various kinds of decentralization and maybe also expansion of the EC will be possible, and even desirable, that were previously seen as dangers threatening to unravel the integrated whole.

10.1 The EC as the Core of a Europe of Concentric Circles

The essence of concentric circles is a hierarchy of rings. Power, influence and activity increase as one moves towards the centre circle. The different circles are organizationally distinct, but the inner one has the decisive dynamism and thereby sets the terms which the next circle has to adapt to. The inner two set the terms for the third, and so forth. In this way a group of countries larger than any organization obtain direction, shared policies and industrial standards in areas where they could not have agreed had they all been sitting around one table in one large organization. In the model of concentric circles the different spheres of Europe do not form opposing coalitions. This logic makes the metaphor of concentric circles attractive to French as well as German policy makers (cf. Chapter 6). It includes a wider Europe and thus makes for an open EC, but at the same time it draws a firm line between EC members and non-members, thus forming a closed core.

In concrete terms, one can see this pattern as four rings, two inside the EC and two outside. The core circle comprises the countries most committed to integration: the original six plus Spain. Next is a circle encompassing the remaining members whose commitment to the EC contains reservations about the pace and extent of further integration: Britain, Denmark, Greece, Ireland and Portugal. The first external circle takes in the EFTA countries, which together with the EC form a so-called 'European economic space'. Beyond that is a wider Europe including the reform countries in Eastern Europe, but not the Soviet Union. (A possible fifth, outermost, and loosest circle would comprise the rest of CSCE Europe, basically the United States, the Soviet Union, Canada and Turkey, which is independent from the core, but relates to it for certain purposes.) What makes these circles concentric is that neither EFTA nor Eastern Europe is a real counterweight or equal partner to the EC. These two outer circles have the same centre as the EC in that they adapt to policies emanating from the inner circle. The policy of the inner circle is decided amongst a limited number of states, but operates effectively on behalf of a larger number. It will be discussed in section 10.2 how the distinction between the first two circles is likely to be undermined. The outer circles and their relationship to the core look somewhat more durable.

EFTA is crucial in this scenario. After years of tense, competitive relations, EFTA and the EC were, after 1984, increasingly drawn into a relationship of coordination and consultation. The previous EC attitude of only talking to the EFTA countries individually was replaced by a degree of recognition of EFTA as a group. The EFTA countries were frightened by the prospect that international trade was being grouped into blocs centred around the United States, Japan and the EC, and that they would be excluded from this system. The 1992 project amplified this dilemma, pushing the individual EFTA members to adapt to EC standards as much as possible in order to retain access to the single integrated market (Jamar and Wallace, 1988). This process of adaptation lent a certain reality to the idea of a common economic space covering all of Western Europe. It illustrates clearly the idea of concentric circles. The role played by fear of losing out to a world dominated by regional economic blocs also reinforces the case that external pressures are beginning to play a key role in European integration.

Difficulties for EFTA came mainly from two sources. First, its structures are so weak that it is difficult for it to enter mutual commitments with the EC. Secondly, individual countries kept open the option of leaving EFTA for direct membership of EC, as Britain, Denmark and Ireland did in 1972, and as Austria wants to do now. Despite these problems, EFTA gained a more crucial position in the European architecture when more and more commentators started to suggest that it would be the ideal half-way house for countries such as Hungary, whose desire to join the EC is not realistic at present. This idea strengthened the image of concentric circles since in this perspective EFTA would take on a bridge-builder role between the EC core and the newly independent states of Eastern Europe.

In the longer run the development of a concentric circles Europe creates an extremely difficult situation for EFTA countries who stay outside the EC, whether of their own free will, or because they are not allowed inside. The prospect is of a two-level Europe: the EC is first class, and then there will be a second class of 'in-between Europe' consisting of EFTA and Eastern Europe, with Sweden, Austria and Finland as therapists for broken post-planned economies. Under such conditions, EC policy might well go in the direction of treating the two outer circles more and more as one zone. For political reasons, Eastern Europe will have a higher profile than EFTA, and thus tend to determine the terms for EC policy towards the whole outer European zone.

Especially in Austria there is a growing fear that they could become the victims of Western European *Ostpolitik*. A recent article in *European Affairs* (Schmiedling, 1989) was summarized as saying:

The inclusion of East European states in EFTA makes better economic and political sense than maintaining separate COMECON, EFTA and EC trading blocs. Membership applications to the EC by Austria and other current EFTA states would be counterproductive. EFTA is seen as a bridge between East and West Europe with tangible benefits for Hungary, Poland, Bulgaria and Yugoslavia, as well as for the EC countries.

But what about the EFTA states themselves? The big dramatic issues of late twentieth-century Europe are the 1992 project and the East European reform and democratization project. EFTA is easily reduced to being a useful instrument located between these two projects, but not part of either. In this perspective, the pursuit of self-interested policies by EFTA countries is labelled counter-productive in relation to wider European aims, whether of the EC or Eastern Europe.

It could be that the EFTA countries would benefit from a bridge position. The Finnish case has shown the value of extensive engagement in Eastern markets. The EFTA countries might get the best of both worlds without being presented with the EC bill. But there is reason to be sceptical about this perspective. As the 1992 project enters into the more sensitive areas of harmonization, it will be increasingly difficult for non-EC countries to carry through the necessary decisions. In the EC countries this will only be domestically possible because Community membership makes it obligatory. In the end the major role of 1992 might be to carry decisions through in national parliaments that were actually not supported by a majority. Here the EFTA countries will be blocked by particularistic interests preventing their adoption of the common standards and thereby limiting their competitiveness and access. The prospect is, therefore, possibly one of quite deep institutional differences getting locked into place between EC members and the countries in the outer two circles.

The bridge role may also be unacceptable in itself. The idea of Austria as ideological buffer between East and West is often sharply rejected by Austrians with counter-arguments like: 'Nobody lives on a bridge. You build it from solid foundations. Austria is in a sociopolitical and economic sense part of Western Europe and can adequately fulfil its role *vis-à-vis* the East only as long as it is firmly anchored in the internal market of the EC' (a civil servant in the Austrian Foreign Ministry, quoted by Luif, 1989).

Within the EC core, the idea of concentric circles gained increasing support in the late 1980s as it seemed to be a meeting point for French and German thinking about Europe. The Germans tended to emphasize openness towards the East, and the French insisted on a clear line or demarcation, on borders, on an identity, on defence, in other words on an EC with state-like qualities (cf. Holm *et al.*, 1989; Waever forthcoming). Concentric circles is a compromise in the sense that it includes Eastern Europe in Europe, but it retains a major difference between the EC as a core actor and those who are led and helped by it.

Why not enlarge the EC then? First, because enlargement is not wanted by all non-EC members. In Eastern Europe recently recovered national independence is likely to prove incompatible with the EC's integration project. Second, because not all EC members will support it, for reasons examined below. Third, enlargement probably *will* come, but only to the extent and at the speed that a first priority to deepening allows for. Thus some elements of concentric circles' logic seem unavoidable if the dynamism of the European project is to be sustained and if Europe is to become a pole. An element of concentric circles is necessary for the relationship between the EC and the former socialist states, and for some time probably also in relation to the neutrals in EFTA. That said, however, it may well be that the two inner circles within the EC will not continue to operate smoothly. Especially not with the arrival of German unity. As argued above, the progress of integration in the EC points towards a reconstruction of its internal relations. In the longer run, there could be a contradiction between inner and outer concentricity.

10.2 The Internal Relations of a European Pole

A key element in the formation of a European pole is the movement of the EC towards a single market, an economic and monetary union and political union, referred to as the EC Union. A spectrum of possibilities exists as to what the centre of gravity for, and the driving forces for, this EC Union, will be. At the extremes of this spectrum are on the one hand a decentralized and complex network EC, and on the other hand a monocentric Europe with Germany as hegemon.

A network EC

So far the French-German tandem has been the main driving force for the EC project. However, the position of the two has not been static. In spite of the Southern enlargements of the EC, the balance has in the last decade slowly shifted towards a growing influence for West Germany through both its increasing economic power, and the increasing acceptability of West German political influence. As memory of the Second World War has faded away, it has become more difficult to argue that the political power of the Federal Republic should not match its economic power. The strategic goal of France has been to give itself a new strong position in international affairs by making Europe a pole in the international system, while at the same time controlling West Germany by weaving it into the EC. The aim of making Europe a pole is at present within reach. The EC integration has achieved a momentum of its own. In this respect the partnership between France and West Germany has been a success.

The aim of integrating West Germany into a European network has also been achieved. But for France, this second success has spawned a dilemma: because of the increasing strength of the Federal Republic, a continued Franco-German leadership of the EC project will give Germany an ever greater role, reducing France to playing second fiddle. A strong, unified Germany combined with the successful revolutions in Eastern Europe look set to trigger a qualitative jump in the dimensions of this dilemma.

If the revolutions attempted in Eastern Europe and the Soviet Union are successful, this will be advantageous for Germany. West Germany's tradition of *Ostpolitik* plus East Germany's good contacts with Eastern Europe and the Soviet Union mean that a united Germany will be in a very favourable position to take advantage of new economic opportunities in the east. Furthermore, Austrian membership of the EC after 1993 now seems to be generally accepted among the EC members (*Information*, May 8, p. 2). Because of the close economic, historical and cultural links between Germany and Austria, it is possible that some members will fear that Austrian membership will also enhance the strength of Germany within the EC. France is in danger of finding itself as the small wheel on a penny-farthing rather than as one of two equals on a tandem.

Under the balance-of-power mechanism outlined in Chapter 1, the emergence of a strong power is likely to trigger closer cooperation among other states in order to match the power of the strong. Today, Germany is such an emerging strong power. The question is whether there are any political forces in Europe (and outside Europe), that are capable of acting as balancers? To answer this question, it is necessary to scan the European horizon in order to identify potential candidates or mechanisms, for the role of balancers. These might be found at the level of states in the short run, as traditionally. But in the longer run balancing seems likely to shift towards the all-Union level of the EC.

At the level of states, the logic of the balance-of-power points to France, which should be looking for new partners in order to help match Germany. A major element in the French strategy of recent years has been the tandem with Germany driving EC integration further, and defining a crucial role for France in the EC. This strategy would seem to endanger French aims in the EC project as a whole. Fortunately for France the German-French partnership is not the only possibility for achieving the goal of a European pole. Indeed, as the internally and externally driven process of European integration acquires an independent momentum, the need for the tight core circle of the Franco-German axis diminishes.

France could achieve its second strategic goal for restraining German power by building the EC project on close relationships with several EC states, including Germany. Candidates for this partnership must have sufficient economic and political weight to function as balancers, which limits the possibilities to Britain, Italy and perhaps Spain. Because of the political weakness of Italy, and the relative lightness of Spain, Britain is probably crucial to this scenario, at least in the immediate future. Its window of opportunity may not last long if the other actors find the role attractive and rise to it. It does not seem impossible that Britain take an active, positive role in the European project, though it cannot do so until Mrs Thatcher relinquishes power. The bona fides of the Labour Party's new-found enthusiasm towards Europe are still in doubt. A balancer role in the European core group would in some ways fit the centuries old British tradition of always acting to balance the strongest power on the continent.

There are also balancing possibilities for France in enlarging the EC by recruiting politically solid smaller states. The Nordic countries could be attractive members for France and Britain, especially when it becomes impossible to prevent Austrian membership. Austria might be seen as an expansion of Germany in the Community, and this could open the way for further entrants to compensate. If Norway, Iceland and Sweden, and later Finland, were accepted into the EC, along with Denmark they could help constitute a counterweight to Germany. This could explain why in the Spring of 1990 the Danish minister of foreign affairs began to urge the other Nordic countries to join the EC. He predicted that they would have become members by the year 2010 (*Information*, 13 March 1990, p. 8), a development that would certainly serve Danish balancing interests within the Community. An enlargement of the EC was also outlined in an interview with the EC Commissioner, Henning Christophersen. He predicted that after 1993 the EC would be enlarged by the accession of Austria, Norway, Sweden and Iceland and 'by the end of the 90s also with Czechoslovakia and Hungary' (*Information*, 17–18 February 1990, p. 1).

There are, however, limits to the possibilities for balancing by adding new members. First, there have to be willing candidates and, as argued above, not all of those in the outer circles, and especially not the newly liberated states of East-Central Europe, are necessarily keen to join the EC. Second, potential balancers must be economically and politically robust, and it is not clear that the fourth circle states in Eastern Europe will measure up by either criteria. Enlargement is therefore probably neither the most important nor the most likely mechanism for balancing. For France enlargement threatens its preference for deepening the existing institutions within firm boundaries, and raises the threat that pursuit of an expanded balancing strategy might weaken the overall framework that binds Germany.

The most likely method of balancing is deepening the EC integration in the form of major jumps towards economic and monetary, as well as political, union. This implies bringing more issues under the authority of the EC, as well as extending its institutions. Balancing is achieved in this process by counterposing weighty actors and strong institutions. In the EC model that has existed so far, the heads of state were the decisive political element. This gave a great say to states with strong economies, notably West Germany. To the extent that more democratic procedures are instituted in the EC, even a unified Germany will constitute a minority.

The 1992 project as a pure market integration scheme has been overtaken by events. Changes in Eastern Europe and Germany have rearranged the political landscape in which 1992 was originally assumed to be implemented. Furthermore, the effects of the 1992 project itself had already before 1989 started to push the EC project in a different direction. Without a social charter and minimum environmental standards, the EC Union would create a major reshuffling of societies and socio-political balances in Europe, as capital moved to low cost areas (Däubler *et al.*, 1990; Rentmeister, 1989).

Consequently, support for a more far-reaching EC integration has been building up. Density has been rising within Europe, and especially in the EC. Multiplying economic, political, cultural, scientific and personal links have resulted in public support for European cooperation either growing or remaining stable at a high level in the different countries (*Eurobarometer*, No. 32, 1990, vol. 1, pp. 6–12). New and still more urgent problems, like pollution, are calling for multinational cooperation. Even in former strongholds of anti-EC sentiment, such as Britain and the Nordic countries, attitudes towards the EC are becoming more positive. This is also true among left social democrats in West Germany, who were previously concerned about the balance between deepening and widening/opening. They now tend to stress, along with President Mitterrand and Jacques Delors, head of the EC Commission, that it is also in the interest of the East Europeans that the integration process of the EC is pushed ahead, because only a closely integrated EC can shoulder the titanic task of assisting the transformation of Eastern Europe. Underlying this shift is the sense that only a strong EC can secure the political stability in a post-Cold War Europe that will prevent a slide into national rivalries (Glotz, 1990).

Part of the process of deepening cooperation will be a more democratic EC. So far, the EC public have not had much chance to have direct political influence at the EC level. But as the revolutionary processes in Eastern Europe show, it is vital for the success of political projects today that they enjoy public support. If Europe is not to disintegrate into fragmentation, the EC must develop into a real political union. Such a union requires that the EC parliament develops into a politically integrative body, where policy-making ties together inputs from the state level, the sub-regional level and the all-Union level. This function is crucial to a network EC, which would generate complex interactions of interests that would be impossible to steer only with the mechanism of top-level contacts. The main mechanisms for balancing through institutionalization are a strengthening of binding rules and decision-making processes. In the EC the main issues have been: (1) a more effective decision making system, (2) more democracy, and (3) greater coordination in external relations. The EC has, with the Single Act of 1986, strengthened its internal decision-making system, introducing majority voting in a number of areas. One of the main goals in the present effort in further political integration is to strengthen this even more.

Speculations about, and preparations for, these issues developed rapidly on the European agenda from the end of 1989. Many of the classical issues relating to a federal Europe suddenly seemed more relevant than ever, and it became clear that the issue of an institutional framework for the EC would be high on the agenda for the coming years. Should there be a democratically elected first chamber, with an upper house representing the states on the American model? Or should state-level representation continue in the form of the European Council (the heads of state meeting), where the representatives are responsible to national parliaments? How should, nationalities be represented, where, as in many places, they do not line up with states?

Pursuit of these constitutional questions points to a process where the balancing mechanism itself transcends, and in a sense overlays, the balance of power issue in Europe. The strategy of balancing by deepening might thus eventually eliminate the problem it is designed to contain. In the effort to tie Germany, the EC might quite quickly take integration beyond the point where the main patterns of EC internal politics followed national lines. The best way to limit the effects of German surpluses in balance of payment is to erase them by proceeding beyond internal balances of payment to the point where there is only a balance EC–external world, and member-to-member balances cannot be meaningfully counted any more.

Given these considerations, it may seem paradoxical that it was West Germany and France that took the major joint initiative towards an EC Union with the Kohl–Mitterrand letter of April 1990. The reasons for this are outlined in Chapters 6 and 7. Many Germans also support the binding of Germany into the EC as a way of addressing their fear that German unification will destabilize Europe. This is a major component in the overall grand bargain between German, French and Russian Europes. For German unity to proceed in a relatively harmonious way it is necessary to compensate the French through a qualitative jump in the deepening of the EC. The concept outlined here of a network

Europe is basically a project for dealing with many of the complex problems of the whole of Europe.

This discussion of power balancing at the core of the core might give the impression that an EC-Europe would be strongly centralized, with all processes following a pattern of transmission from the core to the outer concentric circles. But there are reasons to expect that integration in Europe will allow other patterns to re-emerge. It is therefore worth looking at the potential sub-regional dynamics which might well come to play a significant part in the internal politics of the EC.

In an EC Union, the sub-regional level is likely to gain increasing importance alongside the state level and the all-Union level. The 1980s have already witnessed a growing interest in a number of sub-regional communities in Europe. Other kinds of differentiation are likely to be less and less suppressed as the EC project gains a steady inner dynamic. In earlier periods true Euro-bureaucrats promulgated heavy handed attempts at standardization (Galtung, 1989, pp. 22–36). These attempts were motivated by an old fashioned idea of identity-building as necessarily following the pattern set by the nineteenth century formation of nation-states (cf. section 4.2). They also assumed that integration was a matter of bottom-up, internally driven, incremental steps. But once the critical line has been crossed where external pressures outweigh internal ones as drivers of integration, there is likely to be less emphasis on the use of Euro-symbols like a common flag, anthem and President, and more room for sub-national identities to express themselves. If, however, the balance-of-power mechanism is not triggered, then another possibility for the internal politics of the EC is hegemonic leadership by Germany.

A monocentric EC: Germany as hegemon?

An alternative way to organize the political economy of Europe is to let the strongest power play the role of leader. The only possible candidate for this role is Germany. There is a well-understood body of theory, usually referred to as hegemony theory (or 'hegemonic stability theory'), that deals with this idea (Kindleberger, 1981; Buzan, 1984b; Keohane, 1980, 1984; Gilpin, 1987; Gill and Law, 1988; Kennedy, 1988). This literature focuses on the problem of leadership in the global political economy, and deals mostly with the period of British hegemony during the nineteenth century, American hegemony since 1945, and the problems that arise when hegemons decline, as in the inter-war years and the 1980s. What is puzzling is that despite all of the concern about a revival of German power, there has been no attempt to set it into the relatively benign framework of hegemony theory. The EC, like the global political economy, needs leadership in order to sustain the efficiencies of a multinational economic system. In the case of the EC, unlike the global political economy, this might be done by collective institutions. But if institutions cannot be made strong enough in relation to states, then hegemonic leadership is the best, and probably the only, alternative.

According to Kindleberger, the functions of a hegemon are: 'to provide a market for distress goods, a steady if not countercyclical flow of capital, and a rediscount mechanism for providing liquidity', as well as to 'manage, in some degree, the structure of foreign exchange rates, and provide a degree of coordination of domestic monetary policies' (Kindleberger, 1981, p. 247). Germany already plays some of these roles through its central position in the European Monetary System (EMS). There is also a security function in which the hegemon supplies political order and military security as the underpinning for a multinational economy. This has been important on the global level, and the strain of carrying disproportionate military burdens has been one major explanation why hegemonic powers such as Britain and the United States tend to decline (Kennedy, 1988). Given the nervousness about Germany as a military power (including in Germany), this requirement might be seen as excluding Germany as a hegemon for Europe. But given also the relatively benign international environment in which Europe finds itself in the post-Cold War era, and the more restricted scope of regional security, this military function seems likely to be of secondary importance, not requiring strong central provision. Europe might well be able to function under a political and economic hegemon while keeping more evenly-distributed arrangements for defence.

To the extent that a German hegemon offers an efficient and available means to achieve a deepening of European integration, this course should be attractive to proponents of European integration. While a hegemon does reap some benefits from leadership, the theory suggests that it also diffuses capital, technology and organizational skills into the other centres of strength within its sphere (Skidelsky, 1976, pp. 163–4). Those concerned about anything that might enhance German power can also take comfort from the theory's prediction that the function of hegemon tends to wear down the hegemonic power, leading to its eventual decline. There are several mechanisms that contribute to this effect. An excess of military spending is unlikely to affect a German hegemon for the reasons given above, but two other mechanisms would operate. One is the diffusion of capital, technology and organization mentioned above, which tends to export the comparative advantage of the hegemon to its competitors, so closing the gap between them. The current position of the United States in relation to Japan and the EC illustrates this effect over the last four decades. The other is a decline in the competitiveness of the hegemon as a result of its own success. Success breeds increasing wage and time demands from its own population, and these cumulatively tend to make the hegemon less efficient than its rivals (Olson, 1982).

If hegemonic leadership can both support European integration and in the longer run constrain German power, there is much to be said for it as a transition mechanism towards a deeper and wider EC. The much touted problem of the crisis of management and/or succession that arises when a reigning hegemon declines would not arise for the EC. By the time a German hegemon declined, the institutional structure of the Community would be strong enough to take over the leadership role.

Despite its attractions two problems probably block this option: one practical and one political. The practical problem is whether Germany is powerful enough to act as hegemon for the EC. West Germany alone has a GNP of approximately 25 per cent of the EC. With East Germany added the result would be around 30 per cent. With expected growth rates this would proceed towards a third of the EC, but only slowly.

The political problem has to do with the history and geography of Europe, both of which contribute to resistance to explicit acknowledgement of German leadership. On the historical side, there is an understandable and probably ineradicable opposition to giving to Germany what it so blatantly tried to take in two bloody world wars. Although it is entirely within the realm of the politically possible that Germany is accepted as a normal and equal state in Europe, it will be a long time yet before its history ceases to influence European political relations. Reinforcing this is the geographical issue. Germany is in the heart of Europe. Nine countries share land borders with it. Living so close to a hegemon is, as Canadians know, less easy than living with one that is located at some remove.

For both of these reasons the internal politics of Europe are more likely to follow the balance of power and institutionalizing paths discussed above, than they are to follow the hegemonic route. Perhaps the main impediment to balance of power and institutionalization is the curious British policy of opposing the EC as a whole. If sustained, this might conceivably block both paths, thus opening the way to German hegemony (and Britain's marginalization) by default. But assuming that the British problem is somehow solved, the avoidance of German hegemony might be seen as a lost opportunity for Europe, the wasting of an asset. Perhaps most likely is that elements of hegemonism, particularly on monetary matters, will *de facto* be allowed, though dressed up in EC institutional frameworks.

Summary: Hegemony, Balancing and Concentric Circles

The scenario of Europe as a pole thus contains a spectrum of possibilities ranging from a monocentric one (probably with a German hegemon) to a network Europe. These are laid out in Figure 10.1. The key questions are: (1) whether or not the EC expands to cover most of Poland-to-Portugal Europe, or whether it becomes the core of a concentric circles arrangement; and (2) whether the political structure of Europe is more monocentric or more network in character. There cannot be an anti-German EC based on a constant coalition against Germany because this would erode the EC and lead to the fragmentation scenario. Either Germany leads according to hegemonic stability theory or the internal balance-of-power (together with the external one) pushes towards a lead into deepening.

Figure 10.1 Political Arrangements in a European Pole

	EC internal structure	
Structure of Europe		
	Mono-centric	Network
Expanded EC 'One Europe'	2	4
EC/EFTA/EE concentric circles	1	3

Until the late 1980s the situation was clearly 1. Development 2 is the vision/nightmare of a great power Europe with one centre (German or Franco-German). As argued in this section it is more relevant to speculate about 1, 3 and 4. Option 1 is likely to evolve towards 3 under the pressure from the increasing all-European role of EC. It remains an open question whether and at what speed this will lead to widening of the EC and thus model 4. It seems more likely to lead to a deepening: transforming the EC into a coherent political actor, but one without a constant centre, and perhaps increasingly more like a true pluralist community with shifting coalitions across the old state lines. Thus, the EC would be the core of Europe, but there would be no core of the core. Some combination of 3 and 4 seems the most likely outcome for the medium term: in other words a network EC, perhaps slightly expanded, as the core of a concentric circles Europe, but where these circles are blurred by an array of sub-regional linkages.

10.3 Sub-Regions: Differentiation Within the Pole

Section 10.2. might give the impression that an EC-Europe would be strongly centralized, with all processes following a pattern of transmission from the core to the outer concentric circles — and with either Germany or a strong Brussels at the centre of the centre. But there are reasons to expect that integration in Europe will allow other patterns to re-emerge alongside the new centralization. It is therefore worth looking at the potential sub-regional dynamics which might well come to play a significant part in the internal politics of the EC. These emergent sub-regions are probably not strong enough at present to be important players in the balancing game discussed above, but they could easily be the most important side-effects of an EC deepening. In an EC Union, the sub-regional level is likely to gain increasing importance alongside the state level and the all-Union level. The 1980s have already witnessed a growing interest in a number of sub-regional communities in Europe.

The main reason for this interest is probably the loosening of the state framework in Europe as a result of the steady opening up of a European political space. Partly, this European space has been created by the transfer of authority to the EC and partly (especially in Eastern Europe) it came with the surge of independence following the withdrawal of Soviet control. As argued above, the EC may in some fields be a proto-state, but it is much less threatening for minority identities than nation-states. There is no one EC language, and no attempt to create a unified school system. The homogenizing enthusiasm of the nation-state is not likely to be repeated at the European level. Europeanization therefore tends to go hand in hand with strengthening of political and cultural sub-state projects. Some of these exist as formal organizations of a more or less consolidated character, for example: Alpe-Adriatic, Alpe-Arg, Donau, and German-French-Swiss cooperation. Others exist mainly as a literature about the identity of the sub-region, notably: Central Europe (and Mitteleuropa), Mediterranean, Barcelona-to-Milan, Baltic/Hanseatic, Norden, Balkans and the Scandinavian High North. These projects are mostly not anti-state or orientated towards overthrowing the existing order. They try to benefit from an additional identity.

In the 1970s there was in politics as well as much social science a strong belief in a tendency away from the nation-state towards a simultaneous strengthening of sub- and supranational identities. At that time, however, the movements below the existing states were all more or less ethnic projects aimed at strengthening smaller nations like Scotland, Wales, Brittany, Corsica, the Basque country and the Lapp people. These were classical movements of secession, though sometimes softened as claims for increased autonomy for a specific people. This rising of the micro-nations has been visible since the end of the First World War, which set the principle of national self-determination firmly on the road. 'Then the small nationalities started to move . . . Why were their national traits less important than those founding the existing nation states?' (Knudsen, 1989, p. 7).

The sub-regional projects of the 1980s and 1990s are quite different. They are not constructed around an ethnic core or an idea of a possible nation. Instead, they stress cross-national affinities among peoples who remain different from one another, and also distinct from other parts of the nation-state to which they belong. Their cross-national affinities stem from historical links, and shared interests in economy and ecology. These sub-regional identities are therefore not in opposition to either the state or the European level. Compared to the earlier sub-national movements of the 1970s, they are much more compatible with simultaneous political identities at other levels. They can be seen as attempts by local power elites to gain more power relative to the national power centre. Therefore, as with most nation-building projects of the nineteenth and twentieth centuries, they emanate not from the broad masses, but from the cultural and political elites. Nevertheless, when presented widely they are often popular, since all kinds of local identities are still alive all over Europe.

Developments of this kind are elements in the more general multiplication of identities (Knudsen, 1989) that is often assumed to have taken place in Europe in the 1980s (call it post-modernity or whatever). Social identities are seen as less fixed, less to be reduced to one foundational entity, and more as a question of creating for oneself as many identity-setting relationships as possible. The creation of 'European' as an identity should therefore be understood in its intricate relationship to processes of identity formation (and identity differentiation) on many levels (cf. Chapter 4).

That the multiplication of identities can have a stabilizing function in relation to political conflict is well understood. The Scots and the Welsh can add a 'British' layer to their identities far more easily than they could ever be persuaded to think of themselves as English. This understanding probably explains the October 1989 proposal of Gorbachev for closer links between the Nordic council and the Baltic republics. Whereas many politicians in the Nordic countries had feared that links to the Baltic republics could be destabilizing, or upset Moscow, the strategy of Gorbachev seemed to rely on an effect along the lines of multiple identities. If the Estonians become partly Nordic (for cultural and to some extent political and economic purposes), it might be easier for them to remain 'Soviet' for some economic and formal legal purposes, while also becoming more Estonian and more Central European. This is a more manageable conflict than one only in terms of Estonia versus the Soviet Union. If the Nordic links were thought to risk accelerating the conflict in the Soviet Union, then the 1989 proposal would not have been made.

Thus several trans-, sub- and supranational communities can interact in ways that create new political options. This tendency will be reinforced and its geographical scope widened, to the extent that the Soviet Union lives up to its federalist constitution and evolves towards a loser framework compatible with multiple identities.

These sub-regional movements are often Europeanist in their orientation, as were some of the traditional secessionists. Support for European integration is assumed to be a way to weaken the grip of the nation-state and so create more room for parallel identities. Sovereignty transferred to Brussels is less threatening than the local state power. Nevertheless, local powers already possessing high levels of autonomy, such as Bavaria, rightly fear that Brussels might sometimes go further than their home state. Therefore, Bavaria did not ratify the European Single Act in 1987, as they did not ratify the West German Basic Law (constitution) in 1949! And Bavaria with other *Länder* has a voice in a special committee in relation to the second chamber where they have to be heard on all EC matters which influence the *Länder*.

In West Germany one often hears talk about a Europe in which the *Länder* will be more important. There will be less need for a 'Federal Republic of *Germany*' in a 'Federal Republic of Europe' where the member states should allegedly be the *Länder*, not 'Germany'. In relation to the recreation of the 'states' (*Länder*) in East Germany, there has been some speculation about reorganizing the West German *Länder* by reducing their number and making them all economically realistic. One major argument was the perspective of a more truly federal Europe where the member states would be of something like equal economic size (*FAZ*, 19 April 1990). A key problem in this vision is France: one and indivisible.

A recent example of a similar logic was a statement from Slovak leaders that it was acceptable to continue with a   Czechoslovak federation for the time being, but when a United States of Europe was created the member state would be Slovakia, with no necessity for any intermediate Czechoslovak federation.

Linking to up to these emerging patterns of sub-regional and sub-state political identity and territorial politics could be crucial to the future of Eastern Europe. The revival of independence and 'identity' in post-bloc Eastern Europe could easily take the classical track of building up overly strong national identities which would make it difficult for Eastern Europe to benefit maximally from the changes in Western Europe. A possible alternative could be a strengthening of multiple identities, local, regional and national. This would both make it easier for Eastern Europe to link up to EC developments, and give Eastern Europe a chance to escape the perennial dilemmas of national conflicts and insecurities within and between states.

The sub-regions are sometimes built around geography as an organizing structure. This is most evident in the case of environmental concern leading to cooperation around seas and rivers. Thus, the Baltic ('Hanseatic') area is rediscovered as a possible community. Historical and cultural links also play an important role in the recreation of sub-regions. Sometimes this is presented as a rediscovery of 'natural' older arrangements in contrast to 'false' newer ones. This has been the case in parts of the discourse on Central Europe (cf. Chapter 4). However, the builders of the sub-regional projects are well aware that other historical patterns have existed at other times and other cultural flows have been important too. Thus, the projects are often conscious of their participation in the creation of a complex pattern of overlapping identities. Many of these sub-regional formations were submerged by the Cold War overlay, which aspired to arrange all relations in correspondence with the overarching bipolar order. Thus as Europe reappears, several smaller patterns emerge with it. They are not security complexes, in fact they often have very little to do with security. But they are made possible by the removal of overlay. The new European order is likely to make all the smaller European sub-regional identities easier to (re-) develop.

Paradoxically, the triumph of integration scenario is likely to prove the most hospitable for these sub-regions. In the East-Central European buffer zone (see Chapter 8), security could remain rather closely linked to cultural and socio-political orientations within the West–East grey area. A Central European identity would probably flourish in this scenario, since it will be more or less identical with the grey-zone developing out of the former Soviet satellites. The Cold War III scenario obviously hinders the re-emergence of sub-regions. Fragmentation precludes the establishment of the network of overlapping formations, since it will re-establish the European security complex and force states to seek alliances and thereby exclusive groups instead of multiple overlapping networks of cooperation. With pressure in the direction of exclusivity, each country will have to relate to its own allies, its group. It would not be easy for example, for a Croat to be also Yugoslav, Alpe-Adriatic, Balkan and Central European at the same time under renewed Cold War conditions. The present scenario of one relatively soft centre is more likely to open a certain space below the security order and below the issue of major powers competing. Of course these sub-regions are not unpolitical. They are constructed as identity projects mainly by historians and writers as the nation-states were. And they influence power relations and economic flows. But they are detached from the security sphere, at the same time as their chances are enhanced by the relative weakening of the nation-state.

The re-creation of sub-regions is thus to some extent the other side of the coin in a process of Europeanization. Fragmentation as well as Cold War III imply that strong lines continue to be drawn across Europe, thereby promoting exclusive identities. The scenario of Europe as a pole will entail, at least in the short and medium run, a clear differentiation between those who are most European (EC) and those who are 'European, too' (EFTA/Eastern Europe): a hierarchical Europe. But the rise of sub-regions points towards the long-range perspective of a more differentiated Europe without any one major line across the continent. The most 'centralized' of our scenarios, the European pole, could well be the one that in cultural terms allows the largest degree of differentiation.

10.4. The International Character of Europe as a Pole

Will Europe as a pole in the international system acquire the same features as the two (ex) superpowers? Will it become 'Fortress Europe' or will it be open to the outside world? Will it become a military power and seek to acquire a sphere of influence? These are hard questions to answer. The past history of the EC offers little guidance. Not only will the EC Union be a rather different type of actor than it has been, but also the international environment within which it will have to operate will be very different from the Cold War. The interplay between these two sets of changes is likely to unleash quite new relationships across a quite different agenda of issues. Nevertheless, some trends pointing towards the future status of a European pole in the international system can be discerned.

Strength and weaknesses

It is a defining characteristic of this scenario that Europe has become a pole in the international system. At present this seems to be the main trend of development. But because of its historical background and geographical position, there are some features that make Europe's position as a pole vulnerable. These features influence the strength that Europe can wield in the international system.

Unlike other poles in the international system, such as the United States and Japan, Europe is not an actor with a high degree of socio-political cohesion. For Europe, there are many cohesion-building years ahead. The EC core, made up of states with long centuries of independence, many spent in mutual hostility, has still to prove its ability to function as a political and economic unit. The main question determining the character of a European pole is about the choice between deepening and/or widening: concentric circles or equal EC membership for all European states? There will be pressures in two opposite directions regarding the issue of enlargement. On the one hand, the process of deepening (quasi-state formation), for external as well as Germany-binding purposes, points to a continuation of concentric circles in relation to Eastern Europe rather than to complete enlargement. On the other hand, the internal balancing mechanism requires as many counter-balancers as possible against the prospect of domination by Germany. France is aware not only of the need for deepening the EC but also of the potentialities of additional balancers: the Paris–Moscow axis, and the revitalization of the inter-war 'Little Entente'.

In the outer ring of the concentric circles are states undergoing a revolutionary transformation, the success of which is still hanging in the balance. Deepening the EC integration while at the same time helping the transformation of the former Soviet satellites will demand enormous resources and a fine balancing of the two processes. If Europe is to stay a pole there is no escape from this dual task. If it succeeds, Eastern Europe will add to the strength and security of Europe as a whole. If both deepening and helping Eastern Europe fail, Europe might well end up in the fragmentation scenario. If deepening succeeds, but the East stagnates into chronic instability, then the EC will be saddled with a version of the difficult relationship that the United States has with Latin America.

Geographical proximity and historically close ties to potential trouble spots will influence the strength of Europe regardless of the outcome in Eastern Europe. This goes for the Soviet Union, whose present attempt at a revolution of Westernization is still very undecided. It goes for the Middle East and Africa, where local conflicts, rapid increases in the population and erosion of the arable land threaten to trigger large-scale migrations. Derived consequences could be increasing racism and political extremism in Europe, with possible downstream effects on both the direction of political development in EC, and on the ability to handle tensions among the European nations.

External relations

The political issues outlined above will force an EC Union to be relatively open to the outside world. This will also be the case with economic factors and especially for the purpose of future technological development. There is a relatively widespread consensus that in the long-run 'policies of protection and economic nationalism will tend to be counterproductive' (Malmgren, 1987, p. 32). Even a superpower such as the United States needs close links to the outside world for everything from selling surplus grain to international cooperation in the production of cars and weapons. This will also be the case for an EC Union. Within a network Europe, close links to other poles in the international system would be part of the internal balancing, making it possible for 'outsiders' to be 'European' in specific issue areas. The functionally defined network structure makes exclusiveness less likely. Also the perspective of Germany as hegemon will favour an open Europe. The German strategy for power and wealth is one of decreasing divisiveness of borders. The post-war German experience is one of marked benefits from free trade, probably more so than the French one. The collective memory of what inter-war protectionism led to, makes Germany the least likely candidate for creating a fortress Europe. A Europe along German lines is likely to be an open one. Furthermore, Germany is likely to continue keeping a low profile militarily. The experience of Japan and Germany winning the post-war peace economically by not building up the traditional power basis is likely to be a lasting one both for a united Germany or a Germany-led Europe.

A military power?

One would expect acquisition of military power to be part of a process of state building, as military power in some sense is the essence of sovereignty. The question is whether this will be the case for an EC Union that assumes more and more state-like features? At present quite a few things suggest that this will not be the case, at least not for quite some time. The prospect of an early backlash in the Soviet Union can certainly not be excluded. Given the present military might of the Soviet Union, to build an alternative to NATO that can match the Soviet threat will take many years. The attraction of having to face all over again the many daunting obstacles that have been overcome in order to get real cooperation and integration in NATO is distinctly small. Consequently, NATO is not likely to be given up easily. Doing so would simply necessitate repeating the same hard construction work within an EC framework.

Nuclear weapons pose a major difficulty. Unlike conventional military power, they cannot be transferred gradually. Nuclear sovereignty is an all or nothing question (Boserup, 1990). NATO provides a very convenient vehicle for avoiding the difficult question of a European nuclear force. Since the nuclear deterrence needs of a post-Cold War Europe will be much less pressing than previously, a continued American nuclear umbrella, held more at arms length, is yet another reason for keeping NATO in being. Furthermore, the French (and Russians and most others) seem interested in keeping the Americans in as part of the 'balancing Germany' game. It has been said that if NATO did not exist today, the French would have to invent it. In a similar direction, Kissinger argued (*International Herald Tribune*, 7 May 1990, p. 7) that de Gaulle would today have been an advocate of NATO.

The present alliance arrangement has the advantage of being able to accommodate a wide range of viewpoints on national security among the states within the EC: from neutrals to those who want to strengthen the 'European pillar' within NATO. There are several forums within which this diversity can be managed: the French-German and the French-British defence cooperation; the West European Union, trying to formulate a West European stand in security matters; the Independent European Programme Group, which includes West European states who want to rationalize military procurement; the Eurogroup, which consists of West European NATO members who try to promote a European stand in transatlantic defence. Sticking to the present framework will make it possible for non-members of the EC to join the EC, even if they are neutrals, such as Sweden and Austria.

For all these reasons it seems more attractive to the Western European countries to keep the existing cooperation in NATO and to combine it will an all-European (CSCE) framework. The overall European pattern in this scenario is therefore a balance of imbalances: the political and economic field is dominated by the EC; here the Soviet Union becomes the periphery of the periphery. The military field is organized around a much more institutionalized CSCE pulling NATO in as a less confrontational alliance. For quite some time the Soviet Union will, with some 30 per cent of military forces between the Urals and the Atlantic (the CFE-ceiling for individual states) be the single strongest power and the one putting most effort into the all-European organization. The continued existence of NATO and the Soviet aspirations for CSCE have some complementarity. But there are problems to be solved within NATO over what justifies it. In this scenario it is unacceptable for NATO to be conspicuously aimed at either the Soviet Union or Germany. In addition, the Soviet Union may find it hard to live with NATO if the alliance comes to symbolize a continued Soviet exclusion, or marginalization, from the Western club. This durability of NATO is likely to lead not to a fusion of CSCE and EC, but to a development where the EC is pushed away from the military sphere but gains hegemony in the politico-economic sphere (Wæver, forthcoming).

It seems, therefore, that for the short to medium term, the main pattern in the military area will be an increasing all-Europeanization, with an important place for the Soviet Union and a place for NATO/USA. The EC will speak more loudly inside these forums, but military organization will not happen within it unless something drastic changes. In the long term, much will depend on whether the process of Westernization of the Soviet Union continues or not. If it breaks down, does the then existing Soviet Union or Great Russia constitute a major military threat? Maybe. Will the United States still be willing to commit military forces for the defence of Europe? Probably. Will Europe want to rely on these? Probably not. Then we would see pressure for the construction of a full military power in Europe, at least as a coherent second pillar. This, however, demands a specific time sequence: the EC pole forms, and then later the Eastern dimension breaks down. If tension increases very soon and the grand bargain fails, it is more likely that the large-scale EC project will fail too. Then events move towards one of the two other scenarios.

In Europe's relations with the South, Third World countries have often signalled a hope that Europe will conduct a more fruitful policy than the superpowers, for whom the military component has been central (Széntes, 1988; Brock, 1988). Several European countries, especially the smaller ones, have given less weight to ideological or geopolitical considerations, more sensitivity to local needs and sometimes even less to their own industrial and export policy (but not always). It is a question of whether this aspect is threatened by Europe becoming a major actor at the highest international level. In the long term it is likely that threats from developing countries will come more on the agenda. The race between the West and the East in the 1960s and 1970s has left many developing countries with a growing military capability. It is hardly to be expected that the United States will continue to play the role of global policeman on Europe's behalf. This regional management role could well cause a certain pressure for European military organization. Since this will be difficult to sell to all EC members, and some will still find it difficult to imagine German EC soldiers in the Middle East, it is likely that this will be dealt with mainly by cooperation among the former colonial powers. Perhaps the Western European Union will finally find its role in fulfilling this 'out of area' function.

Chapter 11
The Triumph of Anarchy: Europe Fragmented

The fragmentation scenario is based on the re-emergence of the European security complex as the primary framework for the regional international relations of the continent. It presupposes that overlay continues to break up, and that there is no return to superpower hegemony and Cold War. It also presupposes that the grand package-deal of German reunification, plus security guarantees for the Soviet Union (a CSCE-based security regime and a 'common European house'), plus security guarantees for France (a deeper EC), plus a continued role for Britain and the United States in NATO, breaks down. This breakdown is more likely to be partial than complete, but the scenario assumes that breakdown will be sufficient to ensure that the anarchic structure of sovereign states prevails decisively over that of integration. This could occur either because Germany becomes too big a problem to handle, or because the strain of trying to make so many large adjustments simultaneously causes the political process to break down in the face of fast-moving events. Its consequence would be the collapse of the project to build a European pole sufficiently integrated to play an independent role in the international system.

The main variable in the necessary conditions for this scenario is fear. It requires a decline in fear between the United States and the Soviet Union sufficiently large to allow both of them to disengage substantially, though not completely, their national security concerns from Europe. The big two would continue to have an interest in Europe's stability, and an engagement in European alignments, but neither they nor their rivalry would dominate European security. The scenario also requires a significant reduction in the degree of fear between Europe and the Soviet Union. If fear on this axis remains high, then both the disengagement of the United States and the breakup of Europe become hard to envisage. A Western Europe frightened by the Soviet Union would not be likely to provide for the disengagement of the United States, neither would it dare to abandon its security and other organizational structures to the level of fragmentation. Since the Soviet Union would now find it difficult to intervene directly in the affairs of its former satellites under almost any circumstances, the degree of fear between the Soviet Union and the peoples of East-Central Europe has already become less significant. These lowered levels of fear outside Europe provide the opportunity for levels of fear *within* Europe to rise. Germany would almost certainly be at the centre of such fears, and it would most likely be concern about German domination that would drive the reconstruction of the security complex as the new framework for European security.

In power terms, the fragmentation scenario requires a weak Europe and a weak Soviet Union. Europe would be weak because it was fragmented, though it would contain several quite powerful states. Given the failure of the pole project, fragmentation would almost certainly unleash a degree of rivalry. The key security question in such a Europe would be, as it was before 1939, how the European powers related to each other. The exact role of the United States and the Soviet Union in Europe would depend on the answer, though there can be little doubt that both would continue to play a role in the European complex as they did before 1939.

A weak Soviet Union is necessary because without it a restoration of the indigenous balance of power relations of the security complex would not be possible. How weak the Soviet Union becomes will determine how it relates to a reactivated European security complex. The breakup of the outer Soviet empire and the increasingly likely decomposition of the Soviet Union itself, taking place simultaneously with German unification, constitute a political double act the significance of which is weighted with historic burdens. As in the Cold War III scenario, the first step of a decomposition of the Soviet Union is likely be the success of national liberation movements in the Baltic and the Caucasian republics.

A Soviet Union consisting mainly of the Russian republic and a few others not yet ready to leave, could be quite a weak power. Although still militarily formidable, it might well be politically adrift and either unable or unwilling to play an active international role. If it is striving against the efforts of the liberation movements, the Soviet Union is most likely to become introverted and preoccupied with domestic troubles. If it was not for its military technology, its geographical size and its legacy as one of the world's superpowers, it would hardly play a role in the international arena of any greater significance than the one played by China. Yet, even weakened and frustrated, Great Russia will remain a factor on the international stage. A Soviet Union made nervous because of weakness in economic and political terms might be a troublesome neighbour in the new European house, especially if its military power remains sufficiently potent in technical terms to threaten invasion of Europe and nuclear bombardment of the United States.

The fragmentation scenario opens two options for the Soviet Union. One has already been sketched in the Cold War scenario: the Soviet Union becomes introverted, obsessed with holding the inner empire together, militarized, nationalistic and highly sensitive to any outside attempts to interfere in its domestic turbulence. Such a Soviet Union would try to hold its distinctive world position. Like the United States, it would not be part of the European security complex, though it would of course have influence on it as part of the global interplay of the great powers. The other option presupposes that the disintegration of the Soviet Union proceeds peacefully and that most of the successor states look to Europe for both economic and cultural links, and political models. Along this track, Great Russia might downgrade much of its global role and become clearly part of the European complex as it was before 1914. Its role could then become a counterpoint to that of France, using nuclear strength to offset its historic fears of economic, industrial and organizational inferiority to Germany.

In the fragmentation scenario, interdependence between Europe and the United States would probably remain high, though the precise outcome would depend on how badly reactions to the failure of the package-deal damaged the EC, and how protectionist the European states consequently became. Within Europe, interdependence would drop from its high levels, though perhaps not much. It is very hard to imagine anything close to 1930s style protectionism in Europe under the economic conditions of the 1990s. Between Europe and the Soviet Union it would rise from the Cold War low, how much depending on the degree of Soviet openness, but possibly to quite significant levels in the benign decomposition option.

A re-emergence of the European security complex could take two forms: (1) a reconstruction of traditional balance of power behaviour and rivalry under contemporary conditions; or (2) a failed version of the pole scenario in which the CSCE becomes the framework for a loose European security regime. Before exploring these options one has to ask first how likely it is that the breakup of overlay will release the old logic of the European security complex? To answer that question one needs to examine the events that could trigger a collapse of the pole option.

11.1. The Triggers of Fragmentation

A breakdown of the current trend towards the pole scenario could occur either because German unification creates unresolvable problems, or because the strain of trying to deal with it in such a short space of time causes the political process to break down.

The German trigger

For the first trigger of fragmentation the issue at stake is not whether the two German states will unify or not, but how this process takes place and particularly what issues it raises. As argued in the previous chapter, German unification can be handled within the pole scenario because deepened EC structures can be used to make it acceptable to other states. But if the two German states seemed to ignore the concerns of their respective allies and neighbours by uniting very quickly and without constructing a consensus with either the superpowers or the rest of Europe, then Germany could still trigger fragmentation. At worst, this could take Germany out of the structures of the EC, NATO and CSCE, in the process wrecking both the existing and some possible future security structures. Whether the one-sided unification happened because of arrogance on the part of political leaders in Germany, or because they were driven by a self-concerned and impatient German public, or because they found themselves forced to ignore the rest of Europe by the East Germans voting with their feet, might make little difference.

In this first trigger the key issue resulting from unification that could wreck the pole scenario is the raising of territorial demands by Germany outside the present borders of the East and West German states. The most likely target of such demands is Poland, because it was there that the post-war restructuring of Germany removed large swaths of the country's 1937 territory. The sensitivity of this question, both internationally and for German electoral politics, was already apparent early in 1990 as Poland and subsequently most of the CSCE countries demanded, and Kohl for a time refused (until after unification), guarantees of its present boundaries. The process of German unification is already so far developed that such demands could only gain a serious place on the policy agenda after the unification process had *de facto* created a new German state. In order for territorial revisionism to rise to the top of the German agenda, major changes would have to occur within the German polity. These changes would have to override the well-established current patterns in both German domestic politics and foreign policy. Such a process would take some time even in the present exceptionally fluid political environment. The internal and external constraints against Germany taking this route are enormous, and we do not see this eventuality as at all probable. But because the political character of a united Germany is an unknown quantity, the possibility exists. Since this particular possibility embodies such strong historical fears, it is worth examining in some detail if only to see why it is so unlikely.

The demand for a reunified Germany within the 1937 borders is most likely to happen if the right-wing Republican Party or other similar political forces gain strength far beyond what is the case at the beginning of the 1990s. As of mid-1990, there were very few, if any, signs of such a resurgence. In local elections held early in 1990 the Republicans lost ground, even in Bavaria. The most fertile ground for the far right is a crisis-ridden economy coupled with the existence of minority groups, such as immigrants, especially coloured immigrants, that can be made scape-goats for the economic misery, while white (here German) superiority can be praised. The West German economy shows little sign of becoming crisis-ridden even with the strain of unification. Nevertheless, immigrants have been made a central issue in discussions of housing and other community problems. These problems are not likely to diminish as the stream of migrants from East Germany and other ex-socialist countries are added to those from Turkey and the smaller numbers of coloured immigrants coming into Germany via France and Italy.

In fact, however, this set of issues has not worked to favour right-wing extremism. The refugees are mostly Germans. It is difficult to mobilize a German national mood against newcomers when the newcomers are actually Germans, and their inflow is related to the coming together of the German nation. It is therefore difficult to link up fear and social envy, on the one hand, and nationalist tenets, on the other. The SPD candidate for Chancellor, Oscar Lafontaine, has captured most of the social qualms. The nationalist right has found it difficult to mobilize feelings against coloured immigrants. Only in East Germany does the anti-foreign mood seems to be growing (*Die Zeit*, 4 May, 1990, p. 93).

If, despite these trends, economic and racial problems do come to dominate the German political agenda, they could lead to a demand for a greater *Lebensraum*. The Republican party's natio-nalist policy has attracted many of those with aspirations to regain what they consider to be historical German territories. The merger with East Germany might strengthen this trend in West German politics, similar to the way in which the flow of immigrants from Eastern Europe reinforced the ultraconservative demand for more land in Israel during the 1980s. In the emerging new all-German political landscape, this tendency would have to be weighed against the anti-militarism that is strong in both Germanies because of their front-line role in the Cold War over the past four decades. Nevertheless, it is not impossible that the far right might be considerably strengthened by a combination of domestic issues and reactions against overly vigorous foreign expressions of concern about the rise of German power. This latter mechanism opens the possibility of a self-fulfilling prophecy on the part of those outside Germany who condemn unification as automatically giving rise to a malign power.

A hint of this pattern emerged in December 1989–January 1990, when German public opinion was very disappointed by the wavering attitude of Britain and France towards unification. France especially was seen as violating the expectations stemming from the close Bonn–Paris axis, and President Mitterrand's diplomatic adventures in East Germany and Kiev were interpreted as anti-German. But as the Soviet and French policies became more positive during February, followed a bit later by the British, this potential vicious circle of external fear and internal resentment appeared less and less threatening. Symbolic gestures, like the Kohl–Mitterrand letter of April and the Dublin EC summit in May, had a very positive effect on German public opinion in relation to the feeling of support versus betrayal.

On this basis, the right-wing finger for a German trigger does not look likely to arise from current trends. Two possible future events might revive it. First would be a general renationalization of Europe which followed from a breakdown of the '2 + 4' negotiations. This takes us into the process breakdown trigger discussed below. Second would be domestic political changes in Germany caused by the effects of unification. The economic and social effects are utterly unpredictable. Most, but definitely not all, German experts expect the overall economic effect of unification to be positive. They also expect that for many years a marked difference between living standards in the western parts of Germany and those in the former East Germany will remain. The possible effects of this differential could be that the migration wave will increase again, that resentments will grow in one or the other half of Germany, and/or that the ex-communists in the Party of Democratic Socialism (PDS) will be able to become a real political force in the Northern part of former East Germany (and in particular in Berlin). Whether the PDS will become an all-German political force, whether it will mainly be able to organize strong protests in East Germany about continuing differentials, and whether this would increase polarization within political life in a united Germany to the advantage of the right are open questions.

If the rise of the German right produced a massive verbal attack on the present Polish borders, it would be a provocation not only to Poland, but also to the four powers that delineated Europe's frontiers in 1945. Among those four, the Soviet Union and France would be the ones to feel their position most immediately threatened, though the rest of Europe would have good reason for feeling frightened and for re-awakening their threat-image of Germany. The reactions to such developments on the part of the CSCE states are likely to be very strong. The historical memory of Hitler's campaign to reclaim German land would shine with renewed brightness, feeding fear all through Europe. By making such claims the new Germany could easily tear apart the CSCE structures. All of a sudden it would turn from being an EC and NATO partner to being a potential danger for Poland, Austria, Czechoslovakia and France, not to mention Germany's small neighbours like Denmark and the Benelux countries.

Their reaction, as well as that of all the other CSCE states, would almost certainly be aimed at deterring the new German state from making similar demands on other states' possessions. The EC structures would suffer irreparable damage. NATO, on the other hand, would probably be asked not only by West European but also by the East European states, Poland in particular, to perform a controlling and restricting role in relation to Germany. This would bring the United States firmly into the picture. It would threaten the cooperation between Washington and Bonn/Berlin and open the question of whether containing Germany was to become the principal purpose of NATO. The effect of a German territorial claim on Poland, especially if promoted in a demanding manner, is likely to be the isolation of Germany from more or less all the European states. They would not necessarily unite against Germany, but the strain on the fabric of interdependence would be immense in all directions. Tension would arise between the desire to keep clear of alliances or deals with Germany, except for the most necessary, and the pressure of the day-to-day economic agenda. If Poland resists the claim, it is hard to see how Germany could win the territories. A military assault is out of the question. Even a hint of a military option would indicate that Europe had learned nothing from its experience since 1914 and was incapable of managing its own security affairs.

A German diplomatic offensive, seeking the blessing of all CSCE states for a major readjustment to the Polish–German border, does not look any more promising, especially not if conducted by a government dominated, or even conspicuously influenced by, the far right. Such an offensive could be argued on the grounds of reason and history, within the appropriate international structures such as the UN and the CSCE, and in bilateral contacts with Poland. The thrust of such a campaign would be to reduce the element of fear of the German threat in the international community. If Germany's claim could be made to look legitimate, perhaps buttressed by plebiscites, Poland might find it more difficult to find allies for defending its borders. But even a peaceful process leading to the inclusion of the Upper Silesian region of Poland as another *Länd* in the new German republic, is still likely to create profound unease throughout Europe. It too could not escape comparison with Hitler's strategy. In the unlikely event of international agreement to a territorial transfer, Poland is most likely to feel betrayed, and Poles and others would be reminded of the Western powers selling out Czechoslovakia in 1938.

By either route, a German claim to territory outside the existing two states is thus most likely to lead to paralysis, succeeding only in poisoning the European political atmosphere. Even a peaceful expansion would stimulate fierce opposition. The larger Germany that would result could not avoid triggering balance of power reactions to itself. This would be true even if relative power were the only consideration in play. But since the ethnic and historical principles that validated German claims to Poland could be extended to France, Austria, Czechoslovakia, and possibly Russia, Switzerland and even Italy (German Tyrol), these reactions would be even stronger. Germany can be at peace within Europe, but if it attempts to reconstruct a comprehensive German state, it cannot help but threaten all of Europe.

Given these problems, it is hard to see why almost any German government would embark down this road. The certainty of fierce international reaction is a major deterrent, and historical memory works as powerfully within Germany as outside it. Reintegrating East and West Germany is a big job that will preoccupy the country for many years. The appeal of taking on territories that are now much less German in population, and in an even worse economic and environmental condition than East Germany, must be rather small. The Germans, even more than most other Europeans, have learned that under modern economic conditions wealth and power do not require control of a large territory. To the extent that the EC becomes the economic and political core of Europe, all of the advantages of economies of scale are available by much easier, more attractive and better established routes. The only reason to make the former eastern territories an issue is a kind of emotional atavism, and it seems rather unlikely that this will ever seize the imagination of more than an extremist fringe.

Any German 'expansion' into Silesia is likely to take transnational rather than territorial forms. As argued in Chapter 7, German thinking about Europe and the nation has moved increasingly towards a policy of decreasing the dividing effects of borders. In relation to the 'lost' territories in the East the goal is not to recreate the nation-state in its 1937 borders, but to reconstruct a certain cultural and economic space in Central Europe, and thus to reconnect the nation. This goal is expressed most clearly in the slogan of the Silesian leader Jan Kroll: 'We want to live in a Europe without borders' (*Die Zeit*, 4 May 1990, p. 92) Countries with large parts of their population living outside the state, such as Germany and Hungary, are naturally putting much effort into the creation of internationally guaranteed minority rights, a policy that might also come to appeal to a post-imperial Russia. Indeed, as argued in Chapter 10, the rise of Sub-state groups, including minorities, could well be a feature of European politics in the the 1990s. More porous borders, for example the weakening of control over Silesia by Warsaw, would create more room for links between minorities and their home states, in this case to Bonn and Berlin, without raising territorial questions. The picture is one of acceptance of state borders, but with intensified linkage between regions and peoples. At this point it is impossible to say whether this will come to be seen as an expression of the European peace policy of the 1990s, or as nineteenth century nationalist policy continued 'by other means' (Tromer and Wæver, forthcoming). What is clear is that these transnationalizing forces will be able to work much more smoothly under conditions of European integration than under the more competitive and territorially divided conditions of fragmentation.

The process breakdown trigger

The second possible trigger of fragmentation is linked not to the inner drives of one nation but to the nature of the larger European regional process, to the grand package deal. A possible grand bargain is visible as outlined in Chapters 5 and 6 (Germany gets unity and economic expansion in East-Central Europe, France gets a tight and deepened EC with a high international profile, the Russians get a system of collective security in Europe, and the Anglo-Saxon powers get the survival of NATO). Numerous contradictions can be pointed out in this arrangement, but by mid-1990 the attempts at mutual adjustment towards it were already significant. There seemed to be a high degree of consensus among the main actors that this package was the best way of responding to the changes in Europe

The key threat to this solution is that *too much has to be negotiated and reconstructed in a very short time*. To keep up the balance between German developments and European ones, it is necessary to create a deepened EC and an all-European security system as fast as the reality of a united Germany, and maybe a German *Mitteleuropa*, is coming into being. The deeper EC that is being created is not so very different from the one anticipated in existing blue prints, but it has to arrive five times faster than planned. An all-European system of collective security has also been mooted by experts from time to time, but very few had expected to see it on the real agenda in this century. If the package is to survive, there has to be a certain balance among these elements as they unfold. The project is extremely ambitious. International diplomacy has moved slowly and carefully for forty years, and suddenly it is expected to work at almost supersonic speed. As most notably in the deepening of the EC, many of the developments required are not just symbolic, but processes involving hundreds of concrete decisions affecting many aspects of socio-economic life for millions of people. There is no guarantee that such things can actually happen quickly enough, and much in the past record (even of the relatively booming 1992 project) to suggest that they will not. German unity, however, is unfolding apace. If Europeanization lags too much behind, the balance is lost and diplomatic breakdown becomes a possibility. The key forums here are the inter-German negotiations, the '2+4' talks, the negotiations about EC monetary and political union, and the range of East–West arms control and arms reduction talks (START, CFE). The key question is whether German unification will outrun other developments to such an extent as to shift attitudes in several decisive countries away from the package-deal.

Loss of balance among German, EC and all-European developments is a serious problem primarily because German unification is a potential threat to the status of France and Russia. They have to be compensated. This is partly a question of reassurance in relation to Germany but it is more than that. (Wæver, forthcoming). The overall process has to offer to these two a positive new perspective on their role in the recasting of the European security order. Any sense of defeat or humiliation for them in the current events would strengthen nationalist forces in their domestic politics and thereby feed the process of breakdown and fragmentation. Process breakdown could lead to the German trigger by generating a strong right-wing reaction in Germany over the lack of trust in its good behaviour (and therefore in its national character) expressed by other powers. It is, however, more likely that the grand bargain will be broken by one of the others.

Germany gets what it wants: unity and economic expansion in Eastern Europe. The main risk in the short run is that one of the two main losers, France or Russia, will react against the whole process. This could be caused by other powers resisting the mechanisms of compensation. Britain's opposition to the deepening of the EC could be read in this way, and it is by no means impossible that some Western countries would not want to give the Russians a sufficient role in a properly developed all-European system of security. The Germans are most likely to favour these compensations since they have most to gain by the bargain working out. But whether they can, or will, slow their unification process that threatens it is an open question. It is important therefore not to focus only on Germany: for the coming years Europe is as likely to have a French or a Russian problem, as a German one.

French domestic debates could start in 1990 to show concern that the present policy is radically wrong, and that it is time for a change away from the very EC-orientated policy (Adolphsen, 1990; and Manfrass-Sirjaques, 1990, pp. 116–121). The major argument has been that the policy of strengthening the EC, as a pole of attraction for Eastern Europe and as means of containing the Germans, was doomed to failure because the developments in Germany took place much faster than those in the EC. Some wanted to focus instead on bilateral relations with Germany (the director of *Le Monde*, cf. Adolphsen, 1990), but most of the reactions along this line took a more radical turn. A majority of the political elite still supports the Mitterrand line (EC and European confederation) and, according to polls, a majority of the people are positive towards German unity. But two important minority groups have pointed towards a possible new course.

In the Gaullist party (RPR) the right wing has mobilized around the idea that EC cooperation died with the events in Eastern Europe and Germany. At the party conference in February former minister of the interior, Charles Pasqua, argued for a return to a 'Europe of the fatherlands'. In the Socialist Party (PS), a nationalist wing is headed by the minister of defence, Jean-Pierre Chevènement, who argues in the same manner that Delors's (and implicitly Mitterrand's) plans for strengthened integration in the EC are 'the wrong answer to the right question' (Adolphsen, 1990). In his vision Mitterrand's European confederation should not be (as probably intended by Mitterrand) an extension of the EC vision, but a way to avoid a political union in the EC context.

These neo-nationalist voices from relatively influential circles are still no more than interesting straws in the wind. As argued in Chapter 7, the EC programme has an essential role in the political thinking of the political class in Paris and will not be lightly dismissed (see also Holm *et al.*, forthcoming 1990). A general feeling of insecurity and lack of control in relation to European developments do, however, indicate the possibility of more panicky reactions. Such reactions would most likely pick up on the arguments of people like Pasqua or Chevènement. Their main argument is that Germany will be too strong to be bound by the EC deepening, so France had therefore better avoid giving away more sovereignty and instead keep its independence at a maximum.

Developments in the Soviet Union are even more troubling. For many reasons the present leadership operates on the basis of unstable domestic balances. German-European developments could be the straw that break the camel's back. There were some early indications from Gorbachev that German unity could be the final reason for his fall. Mitterrand quoted him as saying: 'On the day when Germany is unified a Marshal will be sitting in my chair'. (*Le Quotidian de Paris*, 22 November 1989). The emotional importance to Russia of the presence in, and control over, East Germany has been presented in Chapter 6. The memory of the Second World War has been assiduously maintained in a campaign of devotion that dwarfs even British excesses in this regard. Although public opinion is not opposed to German unity, the re-emergence of a unified Germany at the same time as the Soviet Union is weak, and has lost its glacis in Eastern Europe, is likely to be an issue that can be used for political mobilization against Gorbachev. The leaders in Moscow cannot afford to be seen as giving in to developments without winning any concessions. Because of its role as one of the four occupying powers, the Soviet Union is involved in the German unification process through the '2 + 4' talks. It has a kind of veto power which means that it will either have to sanction events or denounce them and take some action to try to block them. It is therefore decisive for the Soviet government whether or not a symbolic compensation materializes.

Given the massive economic problems of the Soviet Union, large scale economic compensation would seem to make most sense, including better access to Western economic clubs such as GATT. But although this might be part of the bargain, it cannot be all. For one thing, the Soviet economic problem is too big to be transformed by outside support. For another, this type of compensation is not political enough: the Soviet Union needs to be given a new status in Europe. Therefore a new European political order or, more likely, a new security system for Europe, is probably the necessary solution. The main question is whether the West will be willing to deliver this traditional Russian object of desire at a time when the Soviet Union is too weak to be able to force it through.

The German foreign ministries are very much aware of this problem and are working actively to secure compensation for the Soviet Union. As Genscher said in an interview (*The European*, 11–13 May 1990, p. 9):

'We do not want to push the Soviet Union to the edge of Europe. She should rather continue to be incorporated in Europe as a whole, and that includes the political dimension of Europe.... We do not want anyone to feel themselves the loser because of German unification. . . . The CSCE provides a guarantee for the Soviet Union that it can play a full role in Europe. The Soviet Union has opened its doors and in such a situation we must go through the door, not let someone slam it shut from this side

One senses a manifest fear that Germany's Western allies will not be willing to deliver enough to the Soviets. Moscow's policy towards claims for national independence by some of its republics could easily lead to opposition in the West, and the United States in particular, to granting the Soviets a strong position in a new European system. This could trigger Soviet attempts to block the '2 + 4' negotiations and thereby the process of German unity (or if inner and outer aspects of unification are delinked, at least preventing Germany regaining full sovereignty). Moscow might for instance upgrade its demands for special limits on German forces and its opposition to German NATO membership. This in turn could feed into German domestic politics, pushing events towards a German trigger for the breakdown of the grand package-deal.

Similar vicious circles were visible in Franco-German relations in late 1989–early 1990, when both of the foreign ministries tried to soothe the other party over unification tensions. Since the general mood at the time was frustration about being let down by the closest ally, the processes of frustration and concessions seemed to be mutually reinforcing. The more clear the danger of breakdown, the more necessary for responsible politicians on both sides to give further concessions across the Rhine. As a result, discontent grew at home: critics on both sides complained that the Franco-German relationship constantly forced their governments to abstain from the optimal policy for Europe and for the nation (Holm *et al.*, 1990a, pp. 235f.). This spiral of deepening and undermining was interpreted by many as the demise of the Bonn–Paris axis, but at the EC Dublin meeting of May 1990 it became clear that this tense phase had, at least in the first round, led to a jump forward. Nevertheless, resentments remain widespread, and in a new crisis it would be easy to mobilize negative feelings.

During the first half of 1990, the problem of coordinating the grand bargain seemed to focus on the question of NATO membership for Germany. This is actually a question about the European order, a question to be solved by manipulating two variables: what kind of all-European security system can grow out of the CSCE, and what kind of new profile can NATO assume when linked to this all-European system? Without change in alliances and European institutions there can be no meaningful compromise on Germany's position in Europe. But these changes cannot be of the 'either NATO or CSCE' variety without wrecking the package deal. Options start to appear if the meaning of NATO membership changes and the choice between transcending the alliances in a European peace order and being member of NATO becomes less and less absolute. Discussions of a more political, less military, NATO clearly point towards this solution.

All components of the grand bargain are interdependent, and many of the components are highly sensitive in domestic politics. Because this is so, the package deal is vulnerable to cascading reactions should any part of it break down. Even though the whole project of reorganizing Europe in two years has been triggered and kept going at high speed by events in Germany, the stumbling block could arise outside Germany. Domestic politics in one country, for example the United States or Britain, could turn against an element of the bargain which is decisive to another actor, for example an all-European security order to the Russians, or EC deepening to the French. The loser therefore stops playing along and begins to oppose elements necessary to other actors. Under these circumstances, German unification still takes place, even though some 400,000 men of the Red Army still stand in East Germany. But it happens without general consent, in a mood of confrontation and unilateralism, and almost certainly with only some elements of the other bargains in place. As the potential major losers, the French and the Russians are likely to support each other in such a situation. The result will be much more fear of Germany, many fewer international structures in Europe, and more 'self-help' security policies. In this eventuality, German policy will not be based on a continuation of the Adenauer–Brandt foreign policy line of gradually rebuilding confidence in West and East, and gradually regaining sovereignty through self-limitation. Instead it will rest on a unilateral founding act in which German power underpins unification, and sovereignty is asserted despite the lack of confidence and/or consent from some other members of the CSCE.

Such a course of events would inaugurate a quite different Europe from the one that would result from completion of the grand bargain.

11.2. The Dynamics of a Revived European Security Complex

The re-emergence of a powerful German state in the heart of Europe will exercise a potent political and psychological pressure on its neighbours. In theory there are two responses to an uneven distribution of power among the states in the international system. The first is called 'bandwagoning', in reference to jumping on the bandwagon. It captures the idea that one response to unequal power is for weaker states to align themselves with the stronger power. The second response is called 'balance of power', in which the weaker states group together against the dominant power in an attempt to offset its strength. The pole scenario represents an unusual fusion of these two policies. There is bandwagoning, in the sense of clustering around a strong core, but there is also balance of power in the use of the EC institutions to enmesh Germany into a dense network of checks and balances.

The revival of the European security complex would result from the failure of this integrative attempt, which would throw individual states back on their own resources in dealing with an uneven distribution of power. As the strongest power in Europe and one whose position is much affected by living memory of recent wars, Germany cannot avoid being at the centre of this logic. Although Germany is the biggest power, it is by no means overwhelmingly dominant. Using the figures from *The Military Balance 1989-90* (IISS, 1989) one can calculate that a united Germany will account for only 29 per cent of the GNP and 23 per cent of the population of the EC. France, Britain and Italy provide substantial counterweights. France alone accounts for 16 per cent of the GNP and 21 per cent of the population of the EC. France, Italy and Britain together account for 54 per cent of the GNP and 50 per cent of the population of the EC. So in no sense is there a lopsided hegemonic situation like that of the United States in relation to Latin America and NATO, or as the Soviet Union used to have in relation to COMECON and the Warsaw Pact. But perception of German power is unavoidably amplified by memory of its formidable military efficiency and its present superior economic performance. In addition there is what almost nobody has expected since the early days of Adenauer's vision of the end of the Cold War, that German reunification would take place alongside Soviet collapse. In the pole scenario, the decline of the Soviet Union empowers the EC as the core of a new European power centre. But if that project fails, then the waning of the Soviet Union empowers Germany. The combination of a strong Germany and a weak Soviet Union could reintroduce the fear factor into intra-European security relations, so triggering balance of power responses.

The political and power configuration that results from the breakup of overlay and the failure of the pole project bear some resemblance to the conditions of the period 1917–45. The biggest political difference is the absence of 1930s-style extreme ideological divisions among the major powers. The 1990s look set to be dominated by a broad consensus on the political economy of the social market. Fascism is largely relegated to the political fringe, and communism has eliminated itself by conspicuous competitive failure. Even if fascism, or 'social nationalism' to use Jahn's term (Jahn, 1989) reasserts itself in Eastern Europe or the Soviet Union, ideological differences will still play a much smaller role in European security than they did during the inter-war period. The biggest military difference is the paralysis of the war option in relations among the great powers. This is a consequence partly of the possession of nuclear weapons by Britain, France and the Soviet Union and partly of the widespread, and deeply rooted, anti-war attitudes amongst the populations.

The general power configuration, however, will be rather similar to 1917–45, and it would not be surprising if similar alignments emerged. Germany will be seen as the central problem needing to be 'balanced'. Britain and France will club together as the core of a counterweight to Germany. They will be open to the possibility of using extra-European powers such as the United States and the Soviet Union as allies against Germany. Groups of smaller states might well form in an effort either to avoid entanglements or to give themselves better resistance to leverage from larger powers. The leading contenders here reflect the same sub-regional forces discussed within the pole scenario, and include a Danubian grouping, reconstructing the ambit of the old Austro-Hungarian Empire, and a Baltic grouping, extending the current Nordic community into the Baltic states and Poland. As after 1917, Russia will sit on the periphery, perhaps once again in a state of post-revolutionary introversion. It will be strong enough to play a role in the European balance of power, but not so strong as to threaten domination. Germany's obvious strategy would be to use its economic weight to encourage bandwagoning, especially among the smaller and weaker states of East-Central Europe. This is yet another reason for it to avoid making territorial demands on Poland.

Given the relative lack of ideological divisions, the continuing restraint imposed by nuclear weapons in the hands of several states and the likely anti-militarism of Germany, the security dynamic of this complex will be very much less driven by military fears than during the inter-war years. Historical memory of the vast destruction wreaked by the last round of warfare will reinforce this tendency, as will current knowledge of the unwinnability of any major war in Europe. In the absence of an acceptably homogenizing and even-handed European Community, the driving concern of the European security complex will be to prevent the economic and political domination of Europe by Germany. Because of the centrality of Germany, its policy will play a key role in shaping the character of relations in the revitalized European security complex. If the problem is merely that Germany is a relatively big power, then a security regime is possible. If Germany is both big and domineering, then a somewhat more tense balance of power dynamic could emerge.

The relatively benign security regime outcome is most likely to follow from the process breakdown trigger, and at least initially there would be no reason to expect high tension. The balance of power response is most likely to result from the German trigger. For the reasons already given, the malign variant is unlikely in the short run because there are no strong signs of the necessary German policy to trigger it. But in the longer run, as we have argued, the process breakdown trigger could also pull the German one, and so move Europe towards balance of power behaviour.

Malign fragmentation: a return to power balancing

The most likely, though not probable, key to this scenario is a Germany politically dominated by the hard right, and pursuing domineering, if not militarily aggressive, policies. Indeed, the scenario as a whole depends on a broad dominance of right-wing nationalism in many countries. Given the lowering of East–West tensions and the collapse of Soviet power, a return to a Europe of nations is a real alternative to the integrative project of the EC. It has a constituency ranging from the anti-EC little-Englandism of Mrs Thatcher, through national nuclear-socialists in France, to the newly surfaced nationalisms in the decolonized parts of the ex-Soviet empire.

The likely effect of a domineering Germany in both the EC and the CSCE is to discourage Germany's co-members from using these organizations for any substantial economic and political issues. The weakening or even withering away of these institutional frameworks means that balance of power will constitute the basis for cooperation and group-formation. The weakening or breakdown of the EC and the CSCE structures would lead to an economic and political set-back for Europe. If the structures for international economic cooperation disappeared altogether it would be difficult for Europe to escape an intense economic crisis involving loss of confidence, drastic organizational readjustment and competitive protectionism. These penalties are so high that it is hard to imagine even a hard-right government in Germany bringing them about. In the political economy of the 1930s, there was still the possibility for a coalition between fascists and national capital in support of economic nationalism and aggressive foreign policy. But in the political economy of the 1990s, capital is much more internationalized and would not lend its weight to such narrowly-based political projects. Because of this constraint, there is almost no possibility that the EC would disappear altogether, though the political integration side of the project would almost certainly be a victim of these developments.

The relationship of Germany to NATO would be central in this scenario. One purpose of NATO has been 'to keep the Germans down', and it is therefore not impossible that a headstrong nationalist government in Germany would leave the organization. An excuse for this could be found in the need for Germany to reassure the Soviet Union, which as of May 1990 was still rejecting the idea of a reunified Germany within NATO. This excuse would only serve provided that the Russians had not yet woken up to the fact that in the emergent European security complex it would be considerably to their advantage to have an institutionalized, United States-backed, constraint on Germany. Moscow is probably playing a slightly desperate game here, using the NATO issue as a bargaining chip to obtain all-European security structures, while also appearing to respond to Russian domestic concerns about Germany. If Germany did leave NATO it would be almost impossible for the alliance to avoid drifting into a *de facto* anti-German posture. The United States would have to deploy its forces in France and Britain, so raising again the configurations of 1917–19 and 1941–5. Germany outside NATO would be too big and too centrally located to be in any meaningful sense neutral. It could not avoid being a power. The logic of a free-floating Germany would be either to bring Russia into closer alignment with the rump of NATO (the 1941–5 model), or to pull Russia and Germany towards each other (the Rapallo Treaty of 1922 and the 1939–41 models), thus completing the analogy with the pre-1945 period.

It is hard to imagine why Britain and France should support anything that increases the likelihood of this scenario, and it is not clear that the Thatcher government has thought through the consequences of its stance. Its promotion of a Europe of nations vision seems primarily to be motivated by the Prime Minister's dislike of the European political project. Life in the fragmentation scenario would certainly enhance the role of national identity and sovereignty that lie behind much of the anti-EC sentiment. She seems willing to risk the fragmentation scenario as a tactic in her long campaign to block the development of the EC. How this is preferable to dealing with the German problem within the EC framework is not clear. Balancing Germany with the whole of the EC looks much easier than trying to construct a countervailing coalition outside it, especially given the unreliability of Russian power for the foreseeable future. Perhaps it is simply that Mrs Thatcher would prefer the continuation of even a rump NATO, with its familiar and comfortable Anglo-American role for Britain, to the unknowns of life inside a European pole, where NATO was strongly enmeshed within the CSCE and EC frameworks. As indicated above there is also a French version of Thatcherism ready if the EC project fails: on the left wing of the PS, Chevène-ment, on the right wing of the Gaullists, Pasqua.

In the Soviet Union, the disintegration of monolithic commu-nist power is unleashing a whole spectrum of political forces. Prominent among these is a Russian nationalist movement with strong anti-Semitic tendencies and a distinctly right-wing man-ner. Comparisons of the post-communist Soviet Union with Weimar Germany are common. In the turbulent 1990s political environment of Soviet life, large numbers of individuals may well shift their political loyalties from the totalitarian left to the totalitarian right. Sharp and extreme realignments of this kind are not unknown: think, for example, of the many socialists, including Oswald Mosely, who switched from left to right during the 1930s. If this tendency became dominant in Russia, its most likely outcome would be an attempt to hang on to those parts of the empire that had not already broken away irredeemably. Down this path lies the introverted, turbulent, militarized and hyper-sensitive Russia sketched in the Cold War scenario. Perception of a strong, unleashed Germany would almost certainly strengthen the position of nationalist forces in Russia.

In this scenario the desire of the East-Central European states to find their own national roots blends easily into a Europe of nations. From the Caucasus to Czechoslovakia, protests are aimed at the Communists' efforts to create 'soviet-type societies' and 'homo sovieticus'. The new states are therefore rather likely to try to achieve a kind of diverse individuality. Their outlook may resemble the experience of many Third World countries after their own decolonization: a desire to carve their own identities, and a jealous protection of newly-won sovereignty. After forty-five years of a very dense overlay by one of the superpowers the newly liberated states might react against the 'political finality' of the EC, and be not unhappy to see it reduced to a weaker economic role. Despite the fact that the new East European governments are well aware of the need for economic coope-ration, fear of enforced homogenization within the not-yet-finally-shaped political and social systems is likely to be lurking in

East-Central Europe no less than in Britain. This despite the fact that participation in the EC is also seen as a guarantee for the new democracies, as it was a decade or two ago for Spain, Portugal and Greece. The East-Central European states might well prefer to work within the looser CSCE framework. As indicated by the Havel plan and other Czech documents (for example the 'Memorandum on the European Security Commission', 6 April 1990), their main interest seems to be: (1) an all-European security organization which serves both to reassure the Russians (and get them out of the ex-satellite countries!), and possibly to offer an eventual Western security guarantee to those nations squeezed between Germany and Russia; and (b) developing an all-European framework for economic and cultural Europeanization.

These states may well look to the European community for practical solutions to some, mainly economic, problems. But like Mrs Thatcher, they are likely to react against the Community's efforts to produce a homogenized and integrated Europe. As expressed by Adam Michnik: 'Europe's chance lies in the pluralism of national cultures, and in the mosaic of the diverse traditions' (Michnik, 1990). Mrs Thatcher is the most popular Western politician in Poland and Armenia alike and will be more than pleased to support such sentiments, so putting another spoke into the wheels of what she considers an expansionist EC. Whether the nationalism of the East-Central European countries could be used to weaken the EC by bringing them inside it, or whether the EC would already have been politically weakened by reactions against Germany, were considered in Chapter 10.

Within the balance of power dynamics of the European security complex, the obvious role for these countries is as buffers between the great powers. Here again, some version of the Nordic security model (outlined in Chapter 8) may come into play. Probably without exception, these countries will want to maintain the low level of fear between the Soviet Union and Europe, particularly Germany. They will be keen to cultivate good relations with both sides. They need economic assistance from Germany, and they understand that their security depends on reassuring the Soviet Union that they pose no threat to it. Their strong nationalism will fit nicely with neutralist defence and foreign policies. In this scenario, the sub-regional groupings around the Baltic and the Danube, which will almost certainly exist also in the pole scenario, could take on a specific security dimension. If Germany is expansionist towards Poland, then these groupings might well become alliances, perhaps linked to both the rump NATO and the Soviet Union. If the situation is less tense, the structure and function of these groupings might well resemble the Nordic model during the Cold War: mutually supportive neutralism or qualified alliance, firm non-provocative defence, sub-regional security community, strong social interchange, and some coordination of economic and political activity. The existence of these two groupings between Russia and Germany could provide a useful moderator to the balance of power. By asserting their own activity and independence between Russia and Germany, they could both reassure the two powers against each other, and in so doing reinforce their own freedom from being locked in the middle of a great power confrontation.

The malign scenario poses the danger of a Europe that is less than the sum of its parts. Economically it would be less efficient: European products would have a weaker position on the world market, and European industry would have a lower technological profile and all that follows from that. In security-political terms, it raises the historic danger that the internal dynamics of European power balancing usually ends in wars. Some restraints against this outcome would remain high, most notably nuclear deterrence and fear of war, but this scenario by definition means that the major political-institutional contraint against war, the EC, is decisively weakened. Politically Europe would be less present in the world, becoming a field for, rather than a force in, great power relations. For East-Central Europe it is further problematic since there will be no organized Western policy for assisting the post-totalitarian systems. Their prospects in the international political economy will be as an underdeveloped region vulnerable to exploitation by Germany.

Benign fragmentation: a European security regime

If fragmentation occurs because of process breakdown, and if the German problem is more one of relative bigness than nationalist domineering, then this scenario takes on a possibly more benign aspect. The power structure and dynamics of the security complex remain broadly the same, but there is less tension, less rivalry, less destruction of existing institutions, and more possibility for a security regime.

A fragmented Europe does not necessarily mean one Balkanized, vulnerable to penetration and making little impact on the global stage. We have argued that for Europe, political cohesion is the decisive source of strength as regards the emergence of a European pole of power in the international system, and this remains true. Under fragmentation, the key source of weakness, or rather the lack of source of strength, is the lack of structured cooperation within organizations entitled to represent the region as a whole. But if the Soviet Union is no longer overwhelmingly strong, and is either politically introverted or dependent, then fragmentation does not mean that Europe is vulnerable. With the Cold War gone, the United States more at arms length and the Soviet Union withdrawn, a fragmented Europe would not necessarily be an area of conspicuous weakness or insecurity. So long as it could keep its own house in order, it might well continue to be relatively prosperous, stable and influential. It is not without significance that the period of Europe's greatest global influence during the nineteenth century was when its security complex was operating in a relatively benign mode (the Concert of Europe). Europe's historical influence arose in good part because it was fragmented. It was not a European empire that colonized the world, but the European security complex. Although this comparison cannot be pushed too far under the more high density and interdependent conditions of the late twentieth century, neither is it without significance. A fragmented Europe, stable and at peace with itself and its neighbours, could conceivably make a global impact not far short of a European pole turned in on itself, preoccupied with the complexities of its own political processes, and trying to deal with a host of poorly developed countries on its borders.

The necessary condition for this benign view is the existence of a security regime. The essence of a security regime, according to Robert Jervis, is a belief among the major powers in reciprocal behaviour without the dominance of short-term effects. This means that the powers within it are supporters of the status quo, that they believe in each other's commitment to restraint (i.e. that none will seek a short-term advantage), and that all have a desire to avoid war (Jervis, 1982, pp. 357–62). It is possible that these conditions could be met after a breakdown of the pole project. The organizational framework for such a regime would be the EC, CSCE and NATO. The EC would continue to exist, though shorn of its political aspirations. As a common market, it would, however, sustain the restraining effect of interdependence on national military rivalry. NATO would continue to exist with Germany inside it, at least as a political member on the lines set by France since 1966. The continuity of NATO would keep the United States attached to Europe as a kind of arms-length holder of the ring for the European powers. A continued formal link with the United States would reassure France, Russia and Britain, as well as many of the smaller states, by acting as a check against any German hegemonic tendencies.

CSCE would continue as a grand forum for European security, possibly growing in the range of its functions and importance, and in the formality of its institutions. The CSCE might well become the forum for the security regime and could develop a range of coordinating functions on issues of common concern such as environmental management and illegal immigration. CSCE would also give the Soviet Union a position in Europe, and it would reflect the nationalist desire to use the breakup of overlay to maintain and restore national cultures and traditions within a framework of cooperating sovereign states.

The existence of the CSCE might be particularly important for Russia if the breakup of the Soviet Union spawns a variety of mostly small successor states around its western and southwestern borders. Achievement of national independence on the part of the Baltic and Caucasian republics will lead to creation of new states identifying themselves as European. Should the Ukraine also become independent it would make a large addition to this group (and also considerably shrink the power of Russia). In the first phase of their existence these states will be relatively weak in economic terms. One possible short-term source of political strength will be, as in the case of the East European states, their fight against suppression and the West's moral obligation to support the fight and the people leading it. The three Baltic states will have no problem being accepted as European and will find a welcoming and ready-made local community as the Nordic group expands into a Baltic one (in spite of the fact that Lithuania is definitely not a Nordic country and Latvia speaks a rather foreign language, too). CSCE might well provide a helpful framework for these states to find a new position between Russia and Western Europe.

But the southern republics, Georgia and Armenia, might in this scenario find themselves in a tragic position. The liberation movements' argument for getting away from the Soviet Union is based on a European self-understanding contrasted to the anti-European (nearly Asian) Russia. Once free they may find themselves at odds with Russia, sitting on the increasingly politicized boundary between Christendom and Islam, and yet looked down on by Europe, and perhaps not accepted as part of it. Like the South African whites and the Israelis, they are too far away geographically and culturally to be easily accepted as part of Europe. True, that for a Dane or a Briton Armenia is not so much further away than Sicily; however, the vast Russian land between 'us' and Armenia will create a psychological distance too big for the Europeans to consider the Caucasian people as their fellows. For this reason they may stay within, or closely associated to, the Russian state. If the three central Asian republics break away, they will simply become part of the Third World. They will be poor, landlocked, economically dependent on Russia, and vulnerable to Iranian and Afghan propaganda and infiltration.

A loose, CSCE-based European security regime could develop

quite far as long as no major crisis occurred. There is even a possibility that it might evolve back into the pole scenario, acting as a temporary way-station for a less than terminal process breakdown. But its long-term stability is doubtful. It would carry within itself the tensions created by the failed package-deal: Germany would be unified without other powers having received adequate compensation. The cooperative mechanisms would be weak in relation to the security management task in Europe, and as observed above, fragmented Europe would be a field rather than a force in global great power relations. The characteristic behaviour of fragmented regional security complexes is to draw outside powers into their internal disputes, as for example, those in South Asia, the Middle East and Southeast Asia have done. There is no reason to think that a fragmented Europe would escape this fate.

If a crisis blew up, there is also no reason to think that the loose structure of the CSCE regime could cope. All experiences with the League of Nations and United Nations seem bleak. A conference diplomacy with some loose organizational structure is not worth much in a major crisis. There is no comparison between a situation in which the CSCE is the sole key security organization and one in which it works together with the EC as a relatively coherent international actor with its core in the West. In a fragmented Europe, CSCE would be better than nothing, and for some period free of major crisis it could cultivate interesting ways of cooperation. One could hope that this would prove able to transform the climate and gradually the nature of relations, but the prospects are not promising. The danger is that process breakdown would lead to the German trigger, and thus to power balancing, rather than to an evolutionary European security regime.

Epilogue

This epilogue was written on 20 July 1990, some two months after the completion of the first eleven chapters. It is impossible to draw definitive conclusions about a historical process that is still in full flood, but our theoretical framework has enabled us both to expose the fundamental forces at work, and to narrow down the alternative outcomes. At the centre of the recasting of the European security order lies the European security complex. The key question is how this complex emerges from the breakup of the Cold War overlay? Does it resume its traditional form of rivalry and balance of power among the major European states? Or is it transcended by the construction of a European pole centred on the EC? The context in which this question will be answered is a transformation of the global power structure. From an international system dominated by two superpowers, and in which military strength was the prime factor, we are moving rapidly towards an arrangement of several great powers, and a pattern of relations in which economic, societal and environmental factors are as important as military ones. This dual transformation makes the outcome in Europe part of a wider global change. But it also means that the global changes play a major role in shaping European options.

The central theme in this book has been that European security is being recast by dramatic shifts in both the distribution of power and the pattern of fear among the United States, Europe, and the Soviet Union. The bipolar distribution of power that sustained the Cold War has collapsed. Although the United States remains strong, the Soviet Union has suffered a drop in power so sharp that even its survival as a state is in question. At the same time, the European Community seems to be on the brink of achieving sufficient political coherence to emerge as a pole of power on the international scene. The success or failure of this enterprise stands out as the central remaining uncertainty in the recasting of the European security order.

Part of the change in the Soviet Union has been a massive ideological U-turn forced by the cumulative economic, societal, environmental and political failures of communism. The first security fruit of this reversal was to enable Gorbachev to redefine the threat perceptions of the Soviet Union in such a way as to abruptly downgrade the fear of military attack or political subversion from the West. From these changes stemmed the liberation of Eastern Europe from Soviet control, and the broad relaxation of tensions across almost the whole spectrum of East-West relations. A revolution of Westernization unfolded across the whole Soviet empire as civil society asserted itself against the crumbling power and legitimacy of the communist–ruled states. These developments have now progressed so far that it is impossible to envisage how a return to the Cold War conditions of the postwar era could come about, though the dismantling of communism, and the accompanying political, societal and economic reconstructions, may well result in prolonged instability, and in some places considerable violence.

We are nevertheless witnessing the greatest *peaceful* political change ever to occur in the international system. In the past, a transformation of the international power hierarchy on this scale has always been accompanied by a major power war. At the core of this change is a great double act. On the one side, an overcentralized, anachronistic Russian empire is struggling to find a balance between decentralization and disintegration, and one can only watch in fascination the extraordinary manoeuvring of Gorbachev as he balances between the decaying structures of the communist state, and the still weak forces of a civil society stunted by seventy years of totalitarian rule. On the other side, a traditionally over-fragmented Europe is struggling to reconcile its deeply-rooted national identities with the need and the desire to create a more integrated European political economy. At the centre of this process lies a rapidly unifying Germany, and the unease of many at the prospect of German power once again dominating Europe.

Although both sides of this double act are primarily driven by forces within themselves, there is an increasingly massive interplay between them. The growing attraction of the EC core, combined with the loosening grip of Soviet military and political power, have transformed the politics of East-Central Europe from Estonia to Albania. Most dramatically, these twinned developments have opened up political space for the rapid unification of the two Germanies. This unification might have triggered an older pattern of fear in Europe centred on German power. So far, however, this pattern shows no sign of becoming dominant, though there have been politically significant rumblings in Britain, Poland and the Soviet Union. Germany is willingly tied into an increasingly robust EC framework. Unless there are major collapses in the institutional framework binding Germany into Europe, the decline of the Russian problem in European security does not look set merely to be the curtain-raiser to a revival of the German problem.

Europe as a whole seems to be moving towards the creation of a regional security regime, though uncertainties about this increase as one moves further east, especially southeast. In both Eastern and Southeastern Europe there are major unresolved questions about the relationship between states and nations. The Soviet Union and Yugoslavia may not survive in their current form, and throughout the region state boundaries are under pressure from national groups divided by them. Eastern Europe is undergoing a kind of decolonization, and the outcome may have some Third World-type characteristics in the form of weak states, disputed boundaries, and ethnically dominated politics. It is not difficult to imagine the emergence of a turbulent Balkan security sub-complex, though much harder to think that it will ever regain the significance it once had for the European security complex as a whole when the European powers were themselves engaged in intense military rivalry.

In the background to this peaceful upheaval stands the United States. The Soviet bid for equal status having failed, the United States is now the last superpower. As such, it is still the anchor of international order, playing a vital role in stabilizing the international system. The United States has been a dominant force in all of the major power struggles of the twentieth century. In the First World War, it was decisive in tipping the balance against Germany. During the interwar years, its isolationism was central to the mounting international economic and political disorder. In the Second World War, the United States, in marked contrast to the Soviet Union, proved its ability to fight two great power wars simultaneously, and in the aftermath played a historic role in bringing the renegade great powers Germany and Japan firmly into the Western community. In the post-war era, it took on the communist challenge unleashed by the successful war against fascism. It organized the West, and stood off the Soviet Union so successfully that much of the Soviet leadership now wants to follow Germany and Japan into the camp of what was once its most bitter enemy.

On this record, the United States provides a crucial political ballast for the current process of change. It does not threaten other major powers with invasion, and its military power and presence stand as a massive deterrent to any thought of military aggression by other great powers. Its liberal ideology puts it in harmony with the change towards pluralism, and constrains any return to isolationism. It has close and well-institutionalized relations with the other major centres of capitalist power. The presence of the United States is thus a major factor in the recasting of the European security order even though in global terms it is on the periphery of the major centres of change, and is waning from superpower status to being merely the greatest of the great powers. The very fact that the United States is not changing dramatically when almost all the other major powers in the system are, is its principal contribution to international security at the end of the American century.

As argued in the preceding chapters, the main direction of events is towards the formation of a European pole in the international system. Central to this is the construction of a grand package deal to make the huge shifts in power and status politically, and especially domestically, acceptable to all of the major states involved, particularly the major potential 'losers' of the 1989–90 events, France and Russia. The question is how successfully this package deal is unfolding. Are the pace and difficulty of international negotiations, or the massive domestic problems of adaptation to change in Germany and the Soviet Union, pushing events towards process breakdown? On this outcome depends the entire shape of the power structure that will set the European security agenda in the coming decades.

As argued in Chapter 11, process breakdown is still a possibility. The pace of German unification drives forward with relentless speed, putting pressure on all the other parts of the slower-moving package. Agreement within Germany on the quick route to unification via article 23 (accession of individual Länder to the Federal Republic) has nearly been reached, and all-German elections are in the offing by December 1990. Britain is still fighting a rearguard action against the deepening of the EC, and in so doing threatens the French need for a stronger EC to make German unification acceptable. During the spring of 1990, the issue of the Baltic Republics imposed a strain on relations between the United States and the Soviet Union, and opened possibilities for domestic backlash on both sides. Soviet fears of outside intervention are increased by the fact that several Western powers never recognized the legitimacy of the Soviet annexations during the Second World War. The Baltic issue threatened to restrict Soviet access to the Western economy, and so reinforce Cold War behaviour on both sides, slowing down the accommodation of Russia into the new arrangements. More broadly, there is the question of whether the Soviet Union will remain a coherent actor in the package deal process. There are questions about its ability to sustain government. For any Soviet government there are other serious security questions such as how to deal with the advantages that the decline of Soviet power gives to the Asian powers China and Japan.

For a time, arms control issues also seemed to threaten process breakdown. The CFE talks faced problems because of the rapid collapse of the East-West framework within which they were originally designed to operate. The breakup of the Warsaw Pact and the swift decline in fear that occurred during 1989–90 undercut the objectives of CFE, which was to negotiate conventional force reductions between NATO and the Warsaw Pact. As the Cold War came abruptly and unexpectedly to an end, the original reduction targets looked increasingly as if they belonged to another era. In addition, the CFE talks became entangled with Soviet manoeuvering over the future of Germany. Soviet stalling at CFE became a tactic for putting pressure on the German question, and the Soviet Union resisted the incorporation of East Germany into the existing NATO arrangements of West Germany. Soviet demands for unilateral restrictions on German forces were met by Western responses on the need to avoid sowing dragon's teeth by singularizing Germany, and so recreating the instabilities of the 1919 Treaty. The desire to solve the German issue within a collective framework gave the CFE a potentially central role in the military side of the package deal as a device by which force levels for Germany could be set within a general agreement on force levels in Europe.

Although enough signs of process breakdown existed to give cause for concern, much else supported the view that the package deal was in fact taking shape, and that it would emerge triumphant. German diplomacy remained exceptionally active and creative, moving to create maximum reassurance all round. Soviet desires for face-saving transitional arrangements in East Germany were met half way, and German rhetoric strongly supported upgrading the CSCE as an all-European security framework. Germany was attentive to Soviet economic concerns arising from the trade and financial disruptions caused by unification. By mid-July, Germany's reassurance diplomacy, especially its willingness to accept limits on its military strength, and its prominent leadership in finding economic assistance for the Soviet Union, won a rapid series of major prizes: Gorbachev's agreement that united Germany could remain within NATO, the early phasing out of four-power control in Berlin, arrangements for the phased withdrawal of Soviet forces from East Germany, and settlement of the border issue with Poland. In relation to its European partners and the United States, Germany was firm in its commitment to both NATO and the EC. Germany and France acted together to help cool the Baltic crisis. A further advance in Europeanization came on 19 June with the Schengen accord. This promised to scrap border controls among Germany, France and the Benelux countries. It overcame earlier reservations about the effects of German unification, and Italy and Spain indicated their desire to join the accord.

Although the CFE talks fell behind the general pace of change, that did not mean that the military balance was itself immobile. On the Soviet side, the major unilateral reductions promised by Gorbachev in his 1988 UN speech continued, as did the effects of the withdrawal agreements negotiated with Hungary and Czechoslovakia. Within the Soviet Union, there were substantial attempts to convert factories from military to civilian production (IISS, 1990, p. 24). On the Western side, there was a very visible slowdown in the pace of arms acquisition, and a continued lowering of the nuclear profile in Central Europe. Military budgets were cut, and major debates opened on how to re-formulate NATO's strategy and deployment to meet the lower level of threat. In response to the unification of Germany, the Alliance effectively abandoned forward defence, though keeping the nuclear ambiguity of flexible response. Moves began towards lighter and less forward deployments, more integrated command structures, and a posture stressing mobilization rather than preparedness for instant response.

The British challenge was visibly losing steam as the govern-ment was forced by its own high inflation rate towards joining the European Exchange Rate Mechanism. Although Mrs. Thatcher remained hostile to economic and political union in Europe, Britain's weak economic position left her increasingly margi-nalized, less able to veto events, and forced to follow for fear of being left behind. In the Soviet Union, the awkward Baltic crisis seemed to peak, and then move towards a longer-term process of negotiation. Boris Yeltsin's initial moves as the new President of the Russian Republic opened up a last chance for the survival of the Soviet Union on a confederal basis. By putting Russie itself on the side of decentralization, he weakened the contradiction between Russian interests and the autonomy desires of the smaller inner empire Republics. A pattern emerged in which virtually all of the republics were seeking greater autonomy from the weakening Soviet centre, and in which the political institu-tions of the Soviet Union were being reshaped to reflect this new reality. American policy remained firm in a minimalist fashion: not exploiting the difficulties of the Soviet Union, and allowing European developments to unfold in their own way. The United States supported German unification, and affirmed the continuity of its commitment to stability in Europe and to participation in NATO, albeit in a way adjusted to take account of the much reduced military security problem. There was general agreement to give more weight and substance to the CSCE by expanding its roles and strengthening its institutions, though disagreement on how much, and what the relative importance of NATO and CSCE should be in the new European security regime.

It was widely observed that NATO would have to become less military and 'more political' in order to adjust to the changes in Europe, but the matter is not so straightforward as that. In the past, NATO has been important as both the political voice and the military organization of a North Atlantic alliance confronting Soviet power. In the post-Cold War era, both of these functions will decline in importance. The end of the confrontation with the Soviet Union lowers the profile of military security and lessens the need for Europe's security to be served by an Atlantic voice. In relation to these old Cold War functions, NATO will become what the International Institute for Strategic Studies aptly terms 'an insurance policy'. (IISS, 1990, p.11). Its political role will also be reduced by the consolidation of the CSCE as the security forum for what were previously classified as East-West relations.

In the post-Cold War era, Europe will increasingly find its own political voice in the European Community, and this development cannot but reduce the political weight of NATO in world politics. Furthermore, as the relative importance of military security issues declines, the political security role of the EC will rise. This shift from military – to politically–based security will ease the transition of the EC into the previously sensitive security area. A major part of Europe's security problem has always been its political fragmentation. In the confrontation with the Soviet Union, Europe's dividedness cost it dear. Both Western Europe and China faced similar threats from the Soviet Union. Europe was better armed, better organized militarily, and wealthier than China, and it had a powerful ally that China lacked. Yet while the credibility of China's deterrent against the Soviet Union was almost never questioned, that of Europe was the subject of ceaseless doubt. The difference was made by China's political cohesion and Europe's lack of it. As Europe becomes a pole in the international system it will reap great security benefits from its own integration. This by itself will reduce its military needs. Political cohesion or the lack of it, is, as any Lebanese will confirm, the absolute foundation of security for any society.

In several ways therefore NATO's military and political roles will both decline, but this does not mean that the Alliance will become unimportant. In the military sphere its principal tasks will be to maintain the Atlantic insurance policy and to provide continuity in military coordination within Europe. NATO already provides a level of Western European military integration which exceeds that in foreign policy. It would be wasteful to undo the laboriously created machinery for military cooperation only to have to reconstruct it all over again from scratch. Creating a European Army will anyway be a low priority int he relatively unthreatening military environment of the post–Cold War era. What will almost certainly happen is that adjustment will take place within NATO. There will be a smaller United States presence both in the field and in the command structures. A larger European role can be accommodated comfortably within an over-all Alliance deployment that is both much smaller than in the past, and probably somewhat more integrated (possibly by having army corps composed of divisions from several countries).

On the political side, NATO seems likely to increase in import-ance as the forum for coordinating United States–EC relations. It will keep the United States 'in' in European politics, and cement its role in the CSCE. Like the EC, it might also come to be seen as part of the Germany-binding institutions that make German unification acceptable. Just as the EC serves to balance German hegemony, so NATO might provide a generalizing framework for what might otherwise become either too much a German–American alliance, or, in the fragmentation scenario, too much an alliance against Germany. This arrangement will reassure both those who fear Germany and those who still fear Russia. It will also reassure the United States that it will not be squeezed out of Europe.

On the trend of developments as of mid–1990, it looked increasingly safe to say that the post–Cold War European security order would be shaped much more by the integration scenario than by the fragmentation one. Should these trends hold, and a European pole emerge as an international actor, then not only Europe's, but also the world's, security order will have been recast.

References

Adolphsen, Gynther (1990) 'Svaret på Stortyskland er et stærkt Frankrig' (The answer to Germany is a strong France), *Information*, 15 February.

Allen, David and Michael Smith (1990) 'Western Europe's Presence in the Contemporary International Arena', *Review of International Studies*, 16:1, pp. 19–39.

Ananjev, Andrej (1989) 'Aral, et døende hav' (Aral, a dying Sea), *Fakta om Sovjet*, no. 4, April, pp. 31–35.

Anderson, Benedict (1983) *Imagined Communities: Reflections on the Origin and Spread of Nationalism*, London: Verso.

Andorka, Rudolf and Tamàs Kolosi (eds) (1984) 'Stratification and Inequality', *Hungarian Sociological Studies*, no.4, April, pp. 17–25.

Andreyev, Y.V. (1988) East–West Economic Cooperation and the Demise of Détente, in Björn Hettne (ed.), *Europe: Dimensions of Peace*, London and New Jersey: Zed Books Ltd.

Aron, Raymond (1966) *Peace and War: A Theory of International Politics*, New York: Doubleday

—— (1970) *Main Currents in Sociological Thought 2: Durkheim, Pareto, Weber*, London: Pelican.

Arutyunyan, Ju. W. and Ju. W. Bromlei (1986) *Sotial'no-kulturnyii Oblik Sovetskikh Natsii* (The Social-cultural Character of the Soviet Nations), Moscow: Nauka.

Ash, Timothy G. (1985) *The Polish Revolution: Solidarity*, London: Hodder and Stoughton.

—— (1989a) 'Revolution in Hungary and Poland, *New York Review of Books*, vol. 36, 17 August.

—— (1989b) 'The German Revolution', *New York Review of Books*, vol. 36, 21 December.

—— (1989c) *The Uses of Adversity*, Cambridge: Granta Books.

—— (1990a) 'The Magic Lantern', *New York Review of Books*, vol. 37, 18 January.

—— (1990b) 'Eastern Europe: The Year of Truth', *New York Review of Books*, vol. 37, 15 February.

—— (1990c) 'The East German Surprise', *New York Review of Books*, 37:7, 26 April.

Bahr, Egon (1988) *Zum Europäischen Frieden*, Berlin: Corso bei Siedler.

Baker, James (1989) 'Speech to the Berlin Press Club', 14 December, *Survival*, 32:1, pp. 88–9.

Bender, Peter (1986–7) 'The Superpower Squeeze', *Foreign Policy*, 65, pp. 98–113.

Bialer, Seweryn (1989) 'The Yeltsin Affair: The Dilemma of the Left in Gorbachev's Revolution', in S. Bialer (ed.), *Politics, Society and Nationality Inside Gorbachev's Russia*, Boulder and London: Westview Press, pp. 91–120.

Bihari, Mihály (1989) 'The Budapest Model', Paper presented at the International Conference on The Challenge of Reforms in East-Central Europe', Bonn, 29–31 May.

Bjøl, Erling (1983) Nordic Security, *Adelphi Papers* no. 181, London: IISS.

Blumenwitz, Dieter (1988) 'Minderheitenregelungen einst und jetzt', in H. Duchhardt (ed.), *In Europas Mitte : Deutschland und seine Nachbahn*, Bonn: Europa Union Verlag, pp. 173–8.

Boserup, Anders (1990) 'Military Structures in Future Europe', presentation for the Copenhagen Study Group on Germany, February.

Bossu-Sygma, Regis (1990) 'The New Superpower', *Newsweek*, 26 February.

Bozeman, Adda (1984) 'The International Order in a Multicultural World', in Bull and Watson, 1984, pp. 387–406.

Brandt, Willy (1978) *People and Politics: The Years 1960–1975*, London: Collins.

Bredow, Wilfred von and Rudolph Horst Brocke (1986) *Das Deutschlandpolitische Konzept per SPD*, Erlangen: Deutsche Gesellschaft für seitgeschichtliche Fragen.

Brock, Lothar (1988) East-West, North-South Conflict, in Bjørn Hettne (ed.), *Europe: Dimensions of Peace*, London and New Jersey: Zed Books Ltd.

Brocke, Horst (1985) *Deutschlande Politische Positionen der Bundestagsparteien — Synopse*, Erlangen:Deutsche Gesellschaft für zeitgeschichtliche Fragen.

Brown, Archie (1989) 'Ideology and Political Culture', in S. Bialer (ed.), *Politics, Society and Nationality Inside Gorbachev's Russia*, Boulder & London: Westview Press, pp. 1–40.

Brown, Chris (1988) 'The Modern Requirement? Reflections on Normative International Theory in a Post-Western World', *Millennium*, 17:2, pp. 339–49.

Brückner, Peter (1979) *Versuch, uns und anderen die Bunderepublik zu erklären*, Berlin: Klaus Wagenbach.

Brus, Wlodzimierz (1973) *The Economics and Politics of Socialism*, London: Routledge.

Brzezinski, Zbigniew (1984–5) 'The Future of Yalta,' *Foreign Affairs*, 63:2, pp. 279–302.

Bull, Hedley (1977) *The Anarchical Society*, London: Macmillan.

—— (1983) 'European Self-Reliance and the Reform of NATO', *Foreign Affairs*, 61:4, pp. 874–92.

—— and Adam Watson (eds) (1984) *The Expansion of International Society*, Oxford: Oxford University Press.

Bunce, Valerie (1983) The Political Economy of the Brezhnev Era: The Rise and Fall of Corporatism', *British Journal of Political Science*, 13:1, pp. 129–58.

Buzan, Barry (1973) 'The British Peace Movement 1919–39', London University, Ph.D thesis.

—— (1984a) 'Peace, Power and Security: Contending Concepts in the Study of International Relations', *Journal of Peace Research*, 21:2, pp. 109–25.

—— (1984b) 'Economic Structure and International Security: the limits of the liberal case', *International Organization*, 38:4, pp. 597–624.

—— (1986) 'A Framework for Regional Security Analysis', in Buzan and Rizvi, *et al.*, *South Asian Insecurity and the Great Powers*, ch. 1.

—— (1987) 'Common Security, Non-provocative Defence, and the Future of Western Europe,' *Review of International Studies*, 13:4, pp. 265–79.

—— (1987b) *An Introduction to Strategic Studies: Military Technology and International Relations*, London: Macmillan.

—— (1988) 'The Southeast Asian Security Complex', *Contemporary Southeast Asia*, 10:1, pp. 1–16.

—— (1991a) *People, States and Fear: An Agenda for International Security Studies in the post-Cold War Era*, 2nd edn. forthcoming, Hemel Hempstead: Wheatsheaf (1st edn, 1983).

—— (1991b) 'Rethinking Structure', in Barry Buzan, Charles Jones and Richard Little, *The Logic of Anarchy*, forthcoming. An earlier version was presented as 'Systems, structures and units: reconstructing Waltz's theory of international politics', BISA/ISA Conference, London, April 1989.

Byrnes, Robert F. (ed.) (1983) *After Brezhnev: Sources of Soviet Conduct in the 1980s*, London: Frances Pinter.

Calleo, David (1987) *Beyond American Hegemony: The Future of the Western Alliance*, New York: Basic Books.

Carlsnaes, Walter (1986) *Ideology and Foreign Policy: Problems of Comparative Conceptualizaton*, Oxford: Basil Blackwell.

CIA Report (1990) *Eastern Europe: Long Road Ahead to Economic Well-being*, Report prepared for the Joint Economic Committee of Congress and released at a committee hearing 16 May.

Cohen, Eliot A. (1982–3) 'The Long-Term Crisis of the Alliance', *Foreign Affairs*, 61:2, pp. 325–43.

Cooper, Julian (1989) 'Nuclear Milking Machines and Perestroika', *Détente*, no. 14, pp. 11–14.

Craig, Gordon (1984) *The Germans*, Harmondsworth: Penguin.

—— and Alexander George (1983) *Force and Statecraft: Diplomatic Problems of Our Time*, Oxford: Oxford University Press.

Csaba, László (1989) 'Some Lessons from Two Decades of Economic Reform in Hungary', *Communist Economies*, 1:1, pp. 17–29.

Dashichev, Vyacheslav (1990) 'On the Threshold of a European Home', *Moscow News Weekly*, No. 5, p. 12.

Dau, Mary (1989) 'Foreign Policy in an Open World', in Barfoed, Bredsdorff, Christensen and Nathan (eds) *The Challenge of an Open World*, Copenhagen: Munksgaard, pp. 64–7.

Däbler, Wolfgang with contributions by G.Fles, M.Hilf, W.Weidenfeld and U.Weinstock (1990) *Sozialstaat EG? Die andere Dimension des Binnenmarktes*, Gütersloh: Verlag Bertelsmann Stiftung.

Davies, Norman (1981) *God's Playground: A History of Poland, vol.II*, Oxford: Clarendon Press.

Dietrich, Stefan (1990) 'Polens Finanzminister Hütet den Zloty wie seinen Augapfel', *Frankfurter Allgemeine Zeitung*, 2 April.

Dyson, Kenneth H. F. (1980) *The State Tradition in Western Europe: A Study of an Idea and Institution*, Oxford: Martin Robertson.

Economist Intelligence Unit (1990a) *Czechoslovakia*, Country Report: Analysis of Economic and Political Trends Every Quarter, no. 1 and 2.

—— (1990b) *Hungary*, Country Report: Analysis of Economic and Political Trends Every Quarter, no.1.

Eckstein, Harry (1982) 'The Idea of Political Development: From Dignity to Efficiency', *World Politics*, 34:4, pp. 451–86.

Elias, Norbert (1982) *The History of Manners: The Civilizing Process; vol.1*, New York: Pantheon Books.

—— (1982) *Power and Civility: The Civilizing Process; vol.2.* New York: Pantheon Books.

—— (1983) *The Court Society*, New York: Pantheon Books.

—— (1989) *Studien über die Deutschen: Machtkämpfe und Habitusenwicklung im 19. und 20. Jahrhundert*, Frankfurt: Suhrkamp.

Eppler, Erhard (1989) 'Speech for the Bundestag in commemoration of the rising in Berlin and GDR 17 June 1953', *Bulletin; Presse-und Informationsamt der Bundesregierung*, no.64, pp. 566–71.

Estrup, Jørgen (General Rapporteur) (1990) 'Draft General Report on Economics of East-West Rapprochement', *The North Atlantic Assembly*, May.

European Strategy Group (1988) *The Gorbachev Challenge and European Security*, Baden-Baden: Nomos Verlagsgesellschaft.

Finkelstein, Janet (1989) 'The Pledge of Allegiance and the Test of Alliance', in Wæver, Lemaitre and Tromer (eds) *European Polyphony*, London: Macmillan, pp. 85–98.

Finkielkraut, Alain (1987) *La Défaite de la Pensée*, Paris: Éditions Gallimard.

Finnish Commission of Military History (1985) 'Aspects of Security: The Case of Independent Finland', *International Review of Military History*, no.62.

Fontanel, Jacques (1986) 'An Undeveloped Peace Movement: The Case of France', *Journal of Peace Research*, 23:2, pp. 175–82.

Foucault, Michel (1979) 'Governmentality', *Ideology and Consciousness*, vol.6, pp. 5–21.

Fülöp, Mihály (1989) Minderheitsvertragsentwurf', *Külpolitika* (Hungarian Journal of Foreign Policy), special issue.

Furdson, Edward (1979) *The European Defence Community*, London: Macmillan.

Galtung, Johan (1989) *Europe in the Making*, New York: Crane Russak.

Gammelgaard, Karen (1990) *Aktuelle tendenser i Tjekkoslovakiet: politik, økonomi, kultur.* (eng overs.) Lecture at the Centre for Peace and Conflict Research, Copenhagen, 19 January.

Garstin, L. H. (1954) *Each Age Is A Dream: A Study In Ideologies*, New York: Bouregy and Curl.

Genscher, Hans-Dietrich (1989) Interview in *Der Spiegel*, no. 39.

Gerner, Kristian (1988) 'Commentary: International Consequences of the Reform Process with Emphasis on Demographic and Ethnic Relations', *NUPI-rapport*, Oslo, no. 115, May.

—— (1989) *Svårt att vara Ryss* (Hard to be Russian), Lund: Signum.

Gill, Stephen, and David Law (1988) *The Global Political Economy: Perspectives, Problems and Policies*, Brighton: Harvester-Wheatsheaf.

Gilpin, Robert (1987) *The Political Economy of International Relations*, Princeton: Princeton University Press.

Ginsberg, Roy H. (1989) *Foreign Policy Actions of the European Community*, Boulder: Lynne Rienner Publishers.

Glotz, Peter (1990) 'Gesamteuropa – Skizze für einen schwierigen Weg', *Europa Archiv*, 45:2, pp. 41–50.

Goble, Paul A. (1990) 'Three Realities in Search of a Theory: Nationalities and the Soviet Future', Paper for a Conference in Copenhagen: Minority Rights – Policies and Practice in South-East Europe.

Goldman, Stuart D. (1988) 'Soviet Nationalities Problems', *Congressional Research Service*, no.88–668 F, Washington, 13 October.

Graebner, Norman (1986) 'Introduction: The Sources of Postwar Insecurity,' in Graebner (ed.), *The National Security: Its Theory and Practice 1945–1960*, New York: Oxford University Press, pp. 7–27.

Grosser, Alfred (1980) *The Western Alliance: European–American Relations since 1945*, London: Macmillan.

—— (1987) 'Frankreich, die Bundesrepublik und das Problem der Nation in Europa', in M. Funke, H-A. Jacobsen and H-P. Schwarz (eds) *Demokratie end Diktatur: Geist und Gestalt politischer Herrschaft in Deutschland und Europa* (Festschrift für Karl Dietrich Bracher), Düsseldorf: Droste Verlag, pp. 417–23.

—— (1988) *Das Deutschland im Westen*, Munich: Deutscher Taschenbuch Verlag, 2nd edn.

Gruner, Wolf D. (1985) *Die Deutsche Frage. Ein Problem der Europäischen Geschichte seit 1800*, Munich: C. H. Beck.

Gurr, Ted Robert (1971) *Why Men Rebel*, Princeton: Princeton University Press.

Habermas, Jürgen (1987) *Eine Art Schadensabwicklung*, Frankfurt: Suhrkamp Verlag.

—— (1990) 'Der DM-Nationalismus', *Die Zeit*, no. 14, 30 March, pp. 62f.

Hacke, Christian (1988) *Weltmacht wider Willen: die Aussenpolitik der Bundesrepublik Deutschland*, Stuttgart: Klett-Cotta.

Haftendorn, Helga (1985) *Security and Detente*, New York: Praeger.

Halicz, Emanuel (1982) *Polish National Liberation Struggles and the Genesis of the Modern Nation*, Odense: Odense University Press.

Hankiss, Elemér (1989) 'Reforms and the Conversion of Power', Paper presented at the International Conference on 'The Challenge of Reforms in East-Central Europe', Bonn.

—— (1989) 'Privileges and Rights: Is it possible to transform a system of privileges into a system of rights?', Paper prepared for the Conference on 'Human Rights as a Security Issue in East–West Relations' in Leiden and Wassenaar.

—— (1990) 'In Search of a Paradigm', in 'Eastern Europe . . . Central Europe . . . Europe', *Dædalus*, 119:1, pp. 183–214.

Hanrieder, Wolfram (1981) *Fragmente der Macht*, Munich: R. Piper.

Hassner, Pierre (1968a) 'Change and Security in Europe. Part I: The Background', *Adelphi Papers*, no.45, February.

—— (1968b) 'Change and Security in Europe. Part II: In Search of a System', *Adelphi Papers*, no.49, July.

—— (1989) 'Can the Division of Europe be Ended?' unpublished, manuscript (July).

—— (1990) 'Modelling while Rome burns? Another impressionistic paper about architecture and revolution or about obstacles to TF II', unpublished paper 1990.

Herz, John H. (1957) 'Rise and Demise of the Territorial State', *World Politics*, 11:2, pp. 157–80.

—— (1981) 'Political Realism Revisited', *International Studies Quarterly*, 25:2, pp. 182–97, 201–3.

Hoffmann, Stanley (1978) *Primacy or World Order: American Foreign Policy since the Cold War*, New York: McGraw-Hill.

—— (1979) Fragments Floating in the Here and Now: Is There a Europe, Was There a Past, and Will There Be a Future? or: The lament of a transplanted European', in *Dædalus*, 108:1, pp. 1–26.

—— (1983) *Dead Ends. American Foreign Policy in the New Cold War*, Cambridge: Ballinger.

Holloway, David (1984) *The Soviet Union and the Arms Race*, New Haven and London: Yale University Press.

Holm, Ulla (forthcoming) *French Thinking on Security in 1990*.

——, Henrik Larsen and Ole Wæver (1989) 'East–West Relations Between Bonn and Paris: Conceptions of State, Nation and Europe as Sources of Contention and Cooperation', presented at the 11th Nordic Peace Research Conference, Elsinore, August 1989, *Working Paper 4*, CPCR, Copenhagen.

——, —— and —— (1990) 'Forestillingen om Europa: en studie i fransk og tysk tænkning efter revolutionerne i Østeuropa', *Vandkunsten*, no.2, March, pp. 212–37.

——, —— and —— (forthcoming) *'Europe' in French and German: Concepts of State, Nation, Security and Politics*.

Holzgrefe, J. L. (1989) 'The Origins of Modern International Relations Theory', *Review of International Studies*, 15:1, pp. 11–27.

Howard, Michael (1983) 'Deterrence, Consensus and Reassurance in the Defence of Europe,' in *Defence and Consensus: The Domestic Aspect of Western Security, Part III, Adelphi Paper* No. 184, London: IISS, pp. 17–26.

Howorth, Jolyon (1986–7) 'The Third Way,' *Foreign Policy*, no.65, pp. 114–34.

Hyde-Price, Adrian (1989) 'Europe Beyond the Berlin Wall: Five Scenarios of the European Security System in 2010', presented at the BISA Conference, University of Kent, December.

IISS (1987) *Strategic Survey 1986–87*, London.

—— (1989) *The Military Balance 1988–89*, London.

—— (1990) *Strategic Survey 1989–1990*, London.

Jahn, Egbert (1981) 'The Tactical and Peace-Political Concept of Détente', *Bulletin of Peace Proposals*, 12:1, pp. 33–43.

——, Pierre Lemaitre, and Ole Wæver (1987) *European Security: Problems of*

Research on Non-military Aspects, Copenhagen Papers no. 1, Copenhagen: CPCR.

——, —— and —— (1988) Understanding the European Security Configuration Through Concepts of Security', in C. Alger & M. Stohl (ed.), *A Just Peace Through Transformation: Cultural, Economic, and Political Foundations for Change*, Boulder and London: Westview Press, pp. 573–91.

—— (1989) *Europe, Eastern Europe, and Central Europe*, Peace Research Institute Frankfurt, Research Report no. 1.

—— (forthcoming) 'Mitteleuropa: The Emergence of a New Continent', in *Current Research on Peace and Violence*.

Jamar, Jimmy and Helen Wallace (eds) (1988) *EEC-EFTA: More Than Just Good Friends?*, Bruges: Catherine Press for College of Europe.

James, Patrick and Michael Brecher (1988) 'Stability and Polarity: New Paths for Enquiry', *Journal of Peace Research*, 25:1, pp. 31–42.

Jervis, Robert (1982) 'Security Regimes', *International Organisation* 36:2, pp. 357–78.

Joenniemi, Pertti (1986) 'Norden and the Development of Strategic Doctrines: From a Buffer Zone to a Grey Area?', *Current Research on Peace and Violence*, 9:1–2, pp. 54–73.

—— (1990) 'Norden Bortom det Kalla Kriget', forthcoming in Karin Lindgren and Nikolaj Petersen (eds) *Trysel eller tillid? Nordens omverdensbilleder under forandring* Stockholm: Nordsam.

John Paul II, Pope (1989) 'Message Concerning Minorities', in *Regional Contact*, no. 1.

Jones, Christopher D. (1984) 'National Armies and National Sovereignty', in David Holloway and Jane M. Sharp (eds), *The Warsaw Pact: Alliance in Transition?*, London: Macmillan, ch. 4.

Jopp, Mathias, Berthold Meyer, Norbert Ropers and Peter Schlotter (1985) *Zehn Jahre KSZE-Prozess*, Report no. 7/1985, Peace Research Institute, Frankfurt

Kaiser, Karl *et al.* (1983) *Die EG vor der Entscheidung. Fortschritt oder Verfall*, Bonn: Union Verlag.

Kaldor, Mary (1978) *The Disintegrating West*, Harmondsworth: Penguin.

Katz, Mark N. (1990) 'The Decline of Soviet Power', *Survival*, 32:1, pp.15–28.

Keane, John (ed.) (1988a) *Civil Society and the State: New European Perspectives*, London: Verso.

—— (1988b) *Democracy and Civil Society*, London: Verso.

Kelstrup, Morten (1988) 'SPD's Europapolitik' (The Europe Policy of the SPD), in Jens-Jørgen Jensen, *Europa i Opbrud*, Esbjerg: Sydjysk Universitetsforlag, pp. 170–189.

—— (1990a) 'The Process of Europeanization: On the theoretical interpretation of present changes in the European regional political system', *Cooperation and Conflict*, 25:1, pp. 21–40.

—— (1990b) 'Den tyske enhedsproces og dens politiske konsekvenser' (The Process of German Unification and its Political Consequences), *Økonomi og Politik*, no. 1 (forthcoming).

—— (1990c) 'Politologisk Integrationsteori og den ny dynamik i Vest- og Østeuropa' (Theories of Political Integration and the Dynamism in

Western and 'Eastern Europe, *Institute of Political Studies, Copenhagen*, Research Report, no. 3.

Kennedy; Paul (1982) 'A Historian of Imperial Decline Looks at America', *International Herald Tribune*, 3 November.

—— (1988) *The Rise and Fall of the Great Powers: Economic Change and Military Conflict 1500–2000*, London: Fontana Press.

Keohane, Robert (1980) 'The Theory of Hegemonic Stability and Changes in International Economic Regimes 1967–1977', in Ole Holsti, R. Siverson and A.L. George (eds), *Change in the International System*, Boulder: Westview Press.

—— (1984) *After Hegemony: Cooperation and Discord in the World Political Economy*, Princeton: Princeton University Press.

Kersten, Krystyna (1985) *Narodziny Systemu Wladzy: Polska 1943–1948* (The Rise of the System of Power: 1943–1948), Paris: Libella.

—— (1989) *Jalta: W Polskiej Perspektyvie* (Yalta: A Polish Perspective), London: Aneks Publishers.

Kincade, William and T. Keith Thomson (1990) 'Economic Conversion in the USSR: Its Role in Perestroyka', *Problems of Communism*, January–February, 39:1, pp. 83–93.

Kindleberger, C. P. (1981) 'Dominance and Leadership in the International Economy', *International Studies Quarterly*, 25:2–3, pp. 242–54.

Kis, János (1988) 'Why Be Afraid?', *East European Reporter*, 3:3, pp. 51–5.

—— (1989) *Politics in Hungary: For a Democratic Alternative*, Boulder: Social Science Monographs.

Kissinger, Henry (1957) *A World Restored: Castlereagh, Metternich and the Restoration of Peace 1812–1822*, Boston: Houghton Mifflin.

—— (1966) 'Domestic Structure and Foreign Policy' in 'Conditions of World Order', *Dædalus*, 95:2, pp. 503–30.

—— (1968) 'The White Revolutionary: Reflections on Bismarck', in 'Philosophers and Kings: Studies in Leadership', *Dædalus*, 97:3, pp. 888–924.

Klausen, Susanne (1990) Den Anden Revolution: Ungarns vej fra dobbeltsamfund til pluralisme', (The Second Revolution: Hungary's Way from Dual-Society to Pluralism), *Vandkunsten*, no. 2, March, pp. 141–56.

Knudsen, Anne (1989) *Identiteter i Europa* (Identities in Europe), Copenhagen: Chr. Ejlers.

—— (forthcoming) 'From Political Culture to Culture as Politics', *Current Research on Peace and Violence*, forthcoming.

Koenen, Gerd (1990) ' "Pamjat" und die russische "Neue Rechte" ', *Osteuropa*, 40:3, pp. 203–9.

Komarek, Walter (1989) 'Towards Prognoses of the Further Development of Civilization', Paper for the 2nd Niels Bohr Symposium, May, Copenhagen.

Komarov, Boris (1980) *The Destruction of Nature in the Soviet Union*, New York: White Plains.

Kornai, János (1985) *Contradictions and Dilemmas*, Budapest: Corvina.

—— (1980) *Economics of Shortage*, Amsterdam: North-Holland Publishing Company.

—— (1986) 'The Hungarian Reform Process: Visions, Hopes and Reality, *Journal of Economic Literature*, 24:4, December, pp. 1687–737.

Korte, Karl-Rudolph (1988) 'Deutschlandbilder — Akzentverlagerungen der deutschen Frage seit den siebziger Jahren' in *Aus Politik und Zeitgeschichte*, B3, pp. 45–53.

Köves, András (1985) *The CMEA Countries in the World Economy: Turning Inwards or Turning Outwards*, Budapest: Akadémiai Kiadó.

Krag, Helen (1989) 'Sovjets mange nationer' (The Many Nations of the Soviet Union), in Per Jacobsen (ed.) *Opbrud i Øst*, Copenhagen: Reitzel, pp. 72–89.

Kvistad, Gregg O. (1989) 'Radicals and the State: The Political Demands on West German Civil Servants', in James A. Caporaso (ed.), *The Elusive State: International and Comparative Perspectives*, Newbury Park: Sage, pp. 97–128.

KVM (Környezetvédelmi És Vízgazzdalkodási Minisztéium) (1989) *State of the Environment in Hungary*, Budapest.

Lane, David (1985) *Soviet Economy and Society*, Oxford: Basil Blackwell.

Lapidus, Gail W. (1989) 'State and Society: Toward the Emergence of Civil Society in the Soviet Union', in S. Bialer (ed.), *Politics, Society, and Nationality Inside Gorbachev's Russia*, Boulder & London: Westview Press, pp. 121–48.

Larrabee, F. Stephen (ed.) (1989) *The Two German States and European Security*, London: Macmillan.

Lemaitre, Pierre (1989a) 'Eastern Reform Processes and the Policy of the West', *Journal of Peace Research*, 26:4, pp. 337–41.

—— (1989b) *Crisis and Revolution of Soviet-Type Systems: Implications for European Security*, Working paper, no. 16, Centre for Peace and Conflict Research, Copenhagen.

Lengyel, László (1990) 'Europe through Hungarian Eyes', *International Affairs*, 66:2, pp. 291–8.

Lider, Julian (1986) *Correlation of Forces: an analysis of Marxist-Leninist concepts*, Aldershot: Gower.

Link, Werner (1987) Aussen-und Deutschlandpolitik in der Ära Schmidt 1974–1982' in Wolfgang Jäger and Werner Link, *Republik im Wandel 1974–1982: Die Ära Schmidt*, Geschichte der Bundesrepublik Deutschland in 5 bd, 5:1; DVA/Brockhaus, Stuttgart/Mannheim, pp. 275–432

Luif, Paul (1988) *Neutrale in die EG? Die westeuropäische Integration und die neutralen Staaten*, IWP 11, Wilhelm Braumüller, December.

—— (1989) 'Austria between European Integration and Mitteleuropa', Paper presented at the Conference on 'the Inner Fringes of Europe', Lysebu Conference Centre near Oslo, November 1989.

McNeill, William H. (1963) *The Rise of the West: A History of the Human Community*, Chicago: University of Chicago Press.

—— (1986) *Polyethnicity and National Unity in World History*, Toronto: University of Toronto Press.

May, Brian (1984) *Russia, America, the Bomb and the Fall of Western Europe*, London: Routledge and Kegan Paul.

Magris, Claudio (1989) *Danube*, New York: Farrar, Straus and Giroux.

Malmgren, Harald B. (1987) 'Technological Challenges to National Economic Policies of the West', *Washington Quarterly*, 10:2, pp. 21–33.

Manfrass-Sirjacques, Françoise (1990) Die französische Europapolitik und die Deutsche Frage', in *Die Neue Gesellschaft Frankfurter Hefte*, no.2, pp. 116–121.

Mastny, Vojtech (1989) 'Eastern Europe and the West in the Perspective of Time', in Griffith (ed.), *Central and Eastern Europe: the Opening Curtain?*, Boulder: Westview Press, pp. 12–36.

Meissner, Boris (1990) 'Gorbachev in a Dilemma: Pressure for Reform and the Constellation of Power', in *Aussenpolitik*, 41:2, pp. 118–35.

Memorandum on the European Security Commission, from the Embassy of the Federal Republic of Czechoslovakia, Prague, 6 April 1990.

Meyer, Berthold (1989) 'Common Security Versus Western Security Cooperation? The Debate on European Security in the Federal Republic of Germany', in Wæver, Lemaitre and Tromer (eds), *European Polyphony*, London: Macmillan, pp. 168–85.

Michnik, Adam (1990) editorial in *Gazeta Wyborcza* 29 January.

Moïsi, Dominique (1989) 'French Policy Toward Central and Eastern Europe', in W. E. Griffith (ed.), *Central and Eastern Europe: The Opening Curtain?*, Boulder, San Francisco and London: Westview Press, pp. 353–66.

Morell, Renate, 'Bedeutungsdimensionen der gegenwärtigen Mitteleuropa-Diskussion', Nürnberg July 1985, unpublished.

Morgenthau, Hans J. (1978) *Politics Among Nations: The Struggle for Power and Peace*, 5th edn. rev., New York: Alfred A. Knopf.

Mrela, K. and J. Zielonka (1987) *The Crisis Problems in Poland II*, Research Project: Crisis in Soviet-type Systems, Directed by Zdenek Mlynar, Study no. 13a, Vienna.

Møller, Bjørn (1990) 'A Common Security System for Europe? "Worst Case" and "Best Case" Scenarios for Europe of the Nineties and Beyond', paper for a seminar on 'Non-offensive defence' in Moscow, April 1990; reprinted as *Working Paper 1990/6* of the Centre for Peace and Conflict Research at the University of Copenhagen.

—— (1991) *Resolving the Security Dilemma in Europe: the German Debate on Non-offensive Defence*, London: Brassey's.

Narojek, Winicjusz (1986) *Perspektywy pluralizmu w Upanstwowieonym spoleczenstwie* (Perspectives for pluralism in a state-society), London: Aneks Publishers.

Neuman, Stephanie (1984) 'International Stratification and Third World Military Industries', *International Organization*, 38:1, pp. 167–97.

Nielsen, Peter Michael (1988) 'CSCE-processen i Regimeteoretisk Perspectiv' (The SSCE Process in the Perspective of Regime Theory), unpublished MA thesis, Institute of Political Studies, University of Copenhagen.

Nipperdey, Thomas (1986) *Nachdenken über die Deutsche Geschichte. Essays*, Munich: Beck'sche Verlagsbuchhandlung.

NOAH (1986) *Som Vinden Blæ ser: miljø problemer i Polen, DDR and Tjekkoslovakiet* (As the wind blows: ecological problems in Poland, GDR and Czechoslovakia), København: NOAHs Forlag.

Nolte, Ernst (1974) *Deutschland und der Kalte Krieg*, Munich: Piper Verlag.

Nye, Joseph (1988) 'Neorealism and Neoliberalism', *World Politics*, 40:2, pp. 235-51.

—— and Keohane, Robert (1977) *Power and Interdependence*, Boston: Little, Brown.

Olson, Mancur (1982) *The Rise and Decline of Nations: Economic Growth, Stagflation, and Social Rigidities*, New Haven: Yale University Press.

Pacewicz, Piotr (1990) 'Uda Sie, ale nie na Pewno' (We will succeed, but not for sure), *Gazeta Wyborcza*, 21. March.

Pedersen, Jesper Karup (1990) 'Fri prisdannelse i Sovjetunionen' (Free price formation in the Soviet Union), *Information*, May 16, p.3.

Petersen, Philip A. (1990) 'The Emerging Soviet Vision of European Security', unpublished paper.

Picht, Robert (1989) 'How Western is the Federal Republic?', lecture at the University of Copenhagen, November.

Polanyi, Karl (1944) *The Great Transformation*, Boston: Beacon.

Prybyla, Jan, special editor (1990) 'Privatizing and Marketizing Socialism', *The Annals*, vol. 507.

Ravenal, Earl C. (1973) 'The Case for Strategic Disengagement,' *Foreign Affairs*, 51:3, pp. 505-21.

Rengger, N. J. (1989) 'Incommensurability, International Theory and the Fragmentation of Western Political Culture', in John R. Gibbins (ed.), *Contemporary Political Culture*, London: Sage, pp. 237-50.

Rentmeister, Heinrich (1989) 'Die "soziale Dimension" des Binnenmachtes. Probleme und Defizite des europä ischen Einigungs- prozesses', *Europa Archiv*, 44:20, pp. 627-34.

Rode, Reinhard and Hanns-D. Jacobsen (eds) (1985) *Economic Warfare or Détente*, Boulder and London: Westview Press.

Rosenau, James N. (1984) 'A Pre-Theory Revisited: World Politics in an Era of Cascading Interdependence', *International Studies Quarterly*, 28:3, pp. 245-306.

Rosenfeldt, Niels Erik (1978) *Knowledge and Power: The Role of Stalin's Secret Chancellery in the Soviet system of Government*, Copenhagen University, Institute of Slavonic Studies. Copenhagen: Rosenkilde and Bagger.

—— (1980) *Stalinstyrets Nervecenter* (The Stalin Regime's Nerve Centre), Copenhagen University, Institute of Slavonic Studies, no. 2.

Rutanen, Pasi (1990) 'Finlandization: The Myth of a Model for the East', *International Herald Tribune*, 23 February.

Rywkin, Michael (1982) *Moscow's Muslim Challenge*, New York: Armonk.

Sampson, Steven (1989) 'Nationens frelse; Rumænien: Fra stalinisme til antikommunisme' (The Rescue of the Nation; From Stalinism to Anti- Communism), *Vandkunsten*, no.2, March, pp. 197-211.

Saslawskaja, Tatjana (1990) 'Soziale Aspekte der Perestroika in der UdSSR', *Aus Politik und Zeitgeschichte - Beilage zur Wochenzeitung Das Parlament*, B 19-20/90, May, pp. 16-21. (See also: Zaslavskaya, Tatyana)

Schmeljow, Nikolai (1990) 'Wirtschafts- und Finansreform im Zechen der Perestroika', *Aus Politik und Zeitgeschichte — Beilage zur Wochenzeitung Das Parlament*, B 19-20/90, May, pp. 22-9.

Schmiedling, Holger, (1989) 'A Concept for a Pan-European Economic Integration', *European Affairs*, 3:3, pp. 33-8.

Schöpflin, George (1988) 'The Stalinist Experience in Eastern Europe', *Survey*, 30:3, October, pp. 124–48.

—— (1990) 'Why Communism Collapsed', *International Affairs*, 66:1, pp. 3–16.

Schwartz, Hans-Peter (1966) *Vom Reich zur Bundesrepublik: Deutschland im Wiederstreit der Aussenpolitische Konzeptionen der Besatzungherrschaft 1945–49* , Neuwied.

Schweigler, Gebhard (1989) 'Normalität in Deutschland', *Europa Archiv*, 44:6, pp. 173–83.

Seiffert, Wolfgang (1989) *Gorbatschow und die Deutschen*, Erlangen: Straube.

Senghaas, Dieter (1986) *Die Zukunft Europas*, Frankfurt: Suhrkamp Verlag.

Seton-Watson, Hugh (1977) *Nations and States*, London: Methuen.

Shelton, Judy (1989) *The Coming Soviet Crash*, New York: The Free Press.

Shenfield, Stephen (1989) 'Between Moscow and Brussels: The Future of Eastern Europe', *Détente*, 1989:15, pp. 7–8.

Simon, Gerhard (1990) 'Der Umbruch des Politischen Systems in der Sowjetunion', *Aus Politik und Zeitgeschichte — Beilage zur Wochenzeitung Das Parlament*, B 19–20/90, May, pp. 3–15.

Skidelsky, Robert (1976) 'Retreat from Leadership: the Evolution of British Economic Foreign Policy 1870–1939', in Benjamin Rowland (ed.), *Balance of Power or Hegemony: The Interwar Monetary System*, New York: New York University Press.

Skubiszewski, Krzysztof (1990) 'Die vîlkerrechtliche und staatlich Einheit des deutschen Volkes und die Entwicklung in Europa', *Europa Archiv*, 45:6, pp. 195–203.

Smolar, Aleksander (1978) 'La Planification comme processus dapprentissage. Le cas sovitique', *Revue d'Etudes Est–Ouest*, 9:3, September, pp. 88ff.

Snyder, Glenn (1984) 'The Security Dilemma in Allance Politics', *World Politics*, 38:4, pp. 461–95.

Stalin, J. V. (1954–55) *Works*, vol.1–13, Moscow: Foreign Languages Publishing House.

Staniszkis, Jadwiga (1984) *Poland's Self-Limiting Revolution*, Princeton: Princeton University Press.

—— (1989a) 'Fragment Wiekszej Calosci'(A fragment of a bigger entity), interview in *Tygodnik Solidarnosc*, 27 October, pp. 1 and 8.

—— (1989b) The Dynamics of a Breakthrough in the Socialist System: an Outline of Problems', *Soviet Studies*, 41:4, pp. 560–73.

Sternberger, Dolf (1990) *Verfassungspatriotismus*, Schriften vol. 10, Frankfurt: Insel.

Strange, Susan (1990) 'Helping Eastern Europe: A Piecemeal Approach Won't Work', and 'Helping Eastern Europe: The Marshall Plan Had Clever Ideas', *International Herald Tribune*, 24 November, p. 4 and 25 January, p. 4.

Szczypiorski, Andrzej (1986) *Den smukke fru Seidenman* (The beautiful Mrs Seidenman), Copenhagen: Hekla.

Széntes, Tamàs (1988) 'Europe and Centre–Periphery Conflicts: Lessons from the Global Crisis' in Björn Hettne (ed.) *Europe: Dimensions of Peace*, London and New Jersey: Zed Books, pp. 85–126.

Süzcs, Jeno (1988) 'Three Historical Regions of Europe', in John Keane (ed) *Civil Society and the State*, London: Verso, pp. 291–332.

Sørensen, Søren Ø. (1990) 'Minearbejdere vil bevare kulminer men Lenin skal skrottes i Mecsek' (The miners want to keep the coalmines but Lenin is to be scrapped in Mecsek), *Information*, 8 January, p. 3.

Thompson, E. P. (1982) 'Beyond the Cold War' (1981), in his *Beyond the Cold War*, London: Merlin Press.

Thomsen, Helle Dalgaard (1990) 'Dialog på scenen: Bulgariens vanskelige vej mod pluralismen' (Dialogue on the stage: Bulgaria's difficult way towards pluralism), *Vandkunsten*, no.2, March, pp.173–85.

Thomson, Janice E. (1989) 'Sovereignty in Historical Perspective: The Evolution of State Control Over Extraterritorial Violence', in James A. Caporaso (ed), *The Elusive State: International and Comparative Perspectives*, Newbury Park: Sage Publications, pp. 227–55.

Thygesen, Niels (1989) 'The Delors Report and European Economic and Monetary Union', *International Affairs*, 65:4.

Tiedtke, Jutta (1985) *Abrüstung in der Sowjetunion*, Frankfurt & New York: Campus Verlag.

Tomaszewski, Jerzy (1989) *The Socialist Regimes of East Central Europe: Their Establishment and Consolidation 1944–67*, London & New York: Routledge.

Toynbee, Arnold J. (1957) *A Study of History*, abridged by D.C. Somervell, New York: Dell.

Tromer, Elzbieta (1989) 'Theories of Crisis in the Soviet Type Systems. An Attempt at Explanation by Economical Sociology by Winicjusz Narojek', *Working Paper*, no. 20 from Centre for Peace and Conflict Research at the University of Copenhagen.

—— (1989a) 'Political Obstacles to Economic Reforms in Poland; the Reforms in 1956 and 1973', *Working Paper*, Centre for Peace and Conflict Research at the University of Copenhagen.

—— (1989b) 'Vi havde fin kontakt med Honecker — dengang. . . .' (We had a good contact with Honecker — at that time. . . .), *Information*, 23 November.

—— and Ole Wæver (forthcoming) *The German–Polish Triangle*.

United States Information Service (1990) 'East European Reformers Hardship', CIA Report, 17 May.

Vajda, Mihàly (1988) 'East-Central European Perspectives', in John Keane (ed) *Civil Society and the State*, London: Verso, pp. 333–61.

van Eekelen, Willem F. (1989) *Future European Defence Cooperation: The Role of the WEU*, Paris: ESG Occasional Paper, September.

Väyrynen, Raimo (1987) 'Neutrality, Dealignment and Political Order in Europe,' in Mary Kaldor and Richard Falk (eds), *Dealignment: A New Foreign Policy Perspective*, Oxford: Blackwell, pp. 178–9.

Vaxberg, Arkady I. (1989) 'Civil Rights in the Soviet Union', *The Annals*, vol. 502, pp. 109–14.

Völgyes, Ivan (1987) 'Political Culture', in Klaus-Detlev Grothusen, *Ungarn*, Göttingen: Vandenhoeck & Ruprecht, pp. 191–212.

von Laue, Theodore (1987) *The World Revolution of Westernization: The Twentieth Century in Global Perspective*, Oxford: Oxford University Press.

von Staden, Berndt (1990) 'Nothing less than the whole of Europe will do . . .', *Aussenpolitik* (English language edition), 41:1, pp. 24–37.

Walker, Robert B. J. (1989) 'Ethics, Modernity and the Theory of International Relations', unpublished paper.

Wallace, Helen, and Wolfgang Wessels (1989) 'Towards a new partnership: The EC and EFTA in the wider Western Europe', *EFTA Occasional paper*, no.28, March.

Wallace, William (1990) *The Transformation of Western Europe*, London: Pinter/Royal Institute of International Affairs.

Waltz, Kenneth N. (1979) *Theory of International Politics*, Reading Mass.: Addison-Wesley.

Watson, Adam (1984) 'Russia and the European States System' in Hedley Bull and Adam Watson (eds), *The Expansion of International Society*, Oxford: Oxford University Press, ch.4, pp. 61–74.

Weber, Eugen (1976) *Peasants into Frenchmen: the Modernization of Rural France*, London: Chatto and Windus.

Weidenfeld, Werner (ed.) (1983) *Die Identität der Deutschen*, Munich & Vienna: Carl Hanser Verlag.

Westwood, J. N. (1981) *Endurance and Endeavour: Russian History 1812–1980*, Oxford: Oxford University Press.

Wettig, Gerhard (1990) 'The Political Implications of Change in Eastern Europe', *Aussenpolitik*, 41:2, pp. 107–18.

Stephen White, John Gardner and George Schöpflin(1987) *Communist Political Systems: An Introduction*, London: Macmillan.

Wight, Martin (1977) *System of States*, Leicester: Leicester University Press.

—— (1986) *Power Politics*, Harmondsworth: Penquin Books (First published in Pelican Books 1979).

Wilkinson, Christopher (1988) 'Les Depenses Militaires Soviétiques. Tendances et Perspectives', *Le Courrier des Pays de L'Est*, no.332, pp. 38–46.

Wilsford, David (1989) 'Tactical Advantages versus Adminstrative Heterogeneity: The Strengths and the Limits of the French State', in James A. Caporaso (ed), *The Elusive State: International and Comparative Perspectives*, Newbury Park: Sage Publications, pp.128–73.

Winiecki, Jan (1988) *The Distorted World of Soviet-Type Economies*, London: Routledge.

Wojna, Ryszard (1990) 'Problem Niemiecki 1989–1990', *Stowarzyszenie Pax*, Warszawa.

Wæver, Ole (1989a) 'Conflicts of Vision — Visions of Conflict' in Wæver, Lemaitre and Tromer (eds) *European Polyphony*, pp. 283–325.

—— (1989b) *Hele Europa. Projekter. Kontraster*, Copenhagen: SNU.

—— (1989c) 'Ideologies of Stabilization — Stabilization of Ideologies: Reading German Social Democrats', in V. Harle and P. Sivonen (eds) *Europe in Transition: Politics and Nuclear Strategy*, London: Pinter Publishers, pp. 110–39.

—— (1990) 'European Identities — An Introduction', *Current Research on Peace and Violence*.

—— (1990, forthcoming) '3 Competing Europes', *International Affairs*, 66:3.

——, Pietre Lemaitre and Elzbieta Tromer (eds) (1989) *European Polyphony: Perspectives Beyond East–West Confrontations*, London: Macmillan.

Z (1990) 'To the Stalin Mausoleum', in 'Eastern Europe...Central Europe', *Dædalus*, 119:1, pp. 295–344.

Zaslavskaya, Tatyana (1988) 'O Strategii Sotsial'nogo Upravleniya Perestroikoi' (On the strategy of the social administration of Perestroika), in Yurii Afanas'ev (ed) *Perestroika: Glasnost' Demokratiya. Socializm. Inogo Ne Dano* (Perestroika: Glasnost. Democracy. Socialism. There is no Alternative), Moscow: Progress. (See also: Saslawskaja, Tatjana)

Ziegler, Charles E. (1987) *Environmental Policy in the USSR*, London: Frances Pinter.

Økonomiske Råd, Det (1989) *Dansk Økonomi 1989'* (Danish Economy 1989), Copenhagen.

Østergaard, Uffe (1988a) ' "Deutschland über Alles"? Temaer, begreber, historie', *Den Jyske Historiker*, no.43–4, pp.5–29.

—— (1988b) Hvad er en Nationstat? (What is a Nation-State?), Centre for Kulturforskning, Aarhus University, *Working Paper*, no. 12.

Åslund, Anders (1989) *Gorbachev's Struggle for Economic Reform*, London: Pinter Publishers.

Index